TOLERABLE ENTERTAINMENT

TOLERABLE ENTERTAINMENT

Herman Melville and Professionalism in Antebellum New York

⇒ JOHN EVELEV

University of Massachusetts Press

Amherst and Boston

LC 2005018490
ISBN 1-55849-516-9

Designed by Sally Nichols
Set in Monotype Bell
Printed and bound by The Maple-Vail Book Manufacturing Group

Library of Congress Cataloging-in-Publication Data

Evelev, John, 1965–
Tolerable entertainment : Herman Melville and professionalism in antebellum
New York / John Evelev.
p.   cm.
Includes bibliographical references and index.
ISBN 1-55849-516-9 (cloth : alk. paper)
1. Melville, Herman, 1819–1891—Homes and haunts—New York (State)—
New York. 2. Authors, American—Homes and haunts—New York (State)—New
York. 3. Authorship—Social aspects—New York (State)—New York.
4. Professions—New York (State)—History—19th century. 5. New York (N.Y.)—
Intellectual life—19th century. 6. Novelists, American—19th century—Biography.
7. New York (N.Y.)—Biography. I. Title.
PS2386.E94 2006
813'.3—dc22
2005018490

British Library Cataloguing in Publication data are available.

This book is published with the support of the University of Missouri–Columbia.

CONTENTS

PREFACE

In October of 1849, at a crucial juncture in his career, Herman Melville wrote to his former guardian and current father-in-law, Massachusetts Supreme Court Judge Lemuel Shaw, and predicted the reaction to his latest works:

> For Redburn I anticipate no particular reception of any kind. It may be deemed a book of tolerable entertainment; —& may be accounted dull. —As for the other book [*White-Jacket*], it will be sure to be attacked in some quarters. But no reputation that is gratifying to me, can possibly be achieved by either of these books. They are two *jobs*, which I have done for money—being forced to it, as other men are to sawing wood.[1]

After the success of *Typee* (1846) and *Omoo* (1847), the fact-based South Pacific travel narratives that had made his literary reputation, Melville received poor reviews and lamentable sales for the first time in his career for his third book, *Mardi* (1849). In response, he returned to the travel–adventure mode with his next two, *Redburn* and *White-Jacket* (both 1850). Melville's dismissal of these has been read as a romanticized rejection of the marketplace, reflecting his post-*Mardi* vision of himself as a literary "artist," a vision that fits a critical narrative of Melville's literary career as a trajectory from naïve opportunism (*Typee* and *Omoo*) to romantic ambition (*Mardi* and *Moby-Dick*, 1851) to bitter cynicism (*Pierre*, 1852) which has dominated Melville criticism since its emergence in the 1920s. Over the course of this book, I explore another critical narrative, one that locates Melville's work and career not merely within the literary history of American romanticism, but also within the larger social history of professional middle-class vocational and cultural distinctions. As a consequence, this book places Melville's work within a new class landscape in antebellum New York City.

My title reflects Melville's begrudging assessment to his father-in-law that *Redburn* "may be deemed a book of tolerable entertainment." The term "tolerable entertainment" not only specifies the level of enjoyment to be derived from reading the novel (presumably a modest one), but it also implies a level of social acceptability, especially in contrast to *White-Jacket*, which Melville predicts "will be sure to be attacked in some quarters." In assessing his prospects not so much on aesthetic merit or sales but by social standards, Melville draws attention to the emergence of new social distinctions associated with works of literature and other cultural productions in antebellum America. This new drawing of social lines in "entertainment" was particularly notable in the cities of the antebellum North, especially New York City, where Melville pursued his trade as author. As a range of cultural historians have shown, what constituted "entertainment" in New York City from the mid-1840s to mid-1850s became an issue of heated social conflict.[2] Increasingly, antebellum New Yorkers found themselves asking: entertainment for whom, and for what political or social purpose? Antebellum New Yorkers began to acknowledge openly that newly apparent social divides were made manifest in differences in entertainment forms and audience expectations. These entertainment forms, whether theater, literature, painting, or music, were used, both consciously and unconsciously, to help articulate and solidify emergent class identities in the period. As a writer in antebellum New York City, both in his literary work and his public persona as an author, Herman Melville modeled an evolving sense of cultural distinction, helping to shape the lines of demarcation between "high" and "low" culture that became central to class identity in American life over the course of the nineteenth century. My analysis traces Melville's engagement with the diverse forms of antebellum New York cultural life, from *Typee*'s reflection of the profitable lessons learned from P. T. Barnum and his American Museum to *Moby-Dick*'s meditation on the Astor Place Riots (in which Melville was a notable participant), the American Art-Union, and the emergent "middle-brow" cultural institutions such as the lyceum. Dismissive as he might have been of the social criteria that went into defining the world of aesthetics and entertainment in antebellum America, I demonstrate that, through his literary career in New York City from *Typee* to *Pierre*, Melville himself helped shape what we Americans might now see as "tolerable entertainment"—the professional middle-class–oriented social values used to define a formalized realm of "Culture" in modern American life.

Just as Melville's comment to his father-in-law hints at new distinctions between "high" and "low" culture and the emergent class identities that lie beneath those divides, his dismissive characterization of *Redburn* and *White-Jacket* also invokes new divisions in the world of work in the ante-bellum era. Proclaiming that his two rapidly produced books were merely "two *jobs*, which I have done for money—being forced to it, as other men are to sawing wood," Melville's distinction is not merely between "art" and "work," but also between kinds of work. At the time Melville was writing to his father-in-law from New York City, industrialization had begun to undermine the artisan system of labor in antebellum cities of the North, replacing its vocational structures of "trade" and "calling" with unskilled and disadvantageous "job" or "piece" work that offered little or no possi-bility of upward mobility. Melville's complaint that, owing to the demands of the marketplace, writing *Redburn* and *White-Jacket* was merely "two *jobs*" reflected not just an artist's anxieties, but widespread concerns among the new middle-class workers of antebellum cities who sought to formalize differences between their labors and those of the working class, for fear that their status would be reduced in a new industrialized economy that put every service and skill on the market.[3] The antebellum middle class responded to this threat by establishing new models of vocational identity. As social historians have argued, antebellum Northern cities, particularly New York City, became sites of dramatic reorganization of the forms of labor, modeling for the first time not only the de-skilled industrial work-er, but also the nonmanual manager and the modern professional during the 1840s.[4] Rejecting industrial labor, the new urban middle class sought to solidify its identity and status by establishing work values that embod-ied its members' social interests, most notably through a new model of professionalism, a meritocratic ethos of competitive specialization and expertise that rejected the older professional ethos of elite patronage.

In this book, I argue that vocational standards and distinctions were central to Melville's literary career and examine how his writing revealed issues of the new middle-class vocational model. From *Typee*'s meditation on initiations and demands required of individuals to enter into systems of exchange ("civilized" as well as "primitive"), to *Mardi*'s overdetermined search for an authoritative literary professional narrative form, and beyond to *Pierre*'s "ambiguous" unpacking of ideological discourses on professional vocational hierarchy, Melville wrote about writing, but in the process he also wrote about the reorganization of work in antebellum American life.

Recognizing the congruence of vocational and cultural formations as crucial elements in the new symbolic authority of professionals, I explore Melville's literary professional life and work in antebellum New York City within the context of the reorganization of the class landscape in nineteenth-century America. From marginally middle-class aspirant to literary professional to critical outsider, Melville's life and literary work function as both an embodiment of and a meditation upon the emergence of professional ideology in antebellum America. Although the insights of this book emerge out of the specific contexts of Melville's engagement with the forms of professionalism from *Typee* to *Pierre*, the issues and concerns of antebellum professional ideology resonate in profound ways within the contemporary American class landscape. Melville's negotiation of the complicated hierarchies of vocational and cultural distinction speaks to contemporary understandings of the ambiguous nature of American middle-class identity and the porous distinctions between "high," "low," and "middlebrow" culture. My assertion of Melville's relevance to contemporary understandings of class in the United States may open this work to charges of anachronism, but I believe it reveals the ways in which the promises and dangers of the ideological project of professionalism have been apparent from the start. Reading Melville's work allows us to see the best and worst possibilities of modern middle-class professionalism and, with that, consider our own investment and/or complicity in the distinctions of work and culture that structure our own class landscape.

ACKNOWLEDGMENTS

Research for this book has been generously supported by the American Antiquarian Society, the National Endowment for the Humanities, and the John C. Hodges Better English Fund at the University of Tennessee. Substantial portions of chapters 1 and 2 were published as "Made in the Marquesas": *Typee*, Tattooing and Melville's Critique of the Literary Marketplace," *Arizona Quarterly* 48:4 (Winter 1992): 19–44; and "'Every One to His Trade': *Mardi*, Literary Form, and Professional Ideology," *American Literature* 75:2 (June 2003): 305–33.

The interests (but not the writing) of this project were begun in graduate school, where a cadre of friends helped me to form and interrogate my understanding of professionalism. Thanks go out to Shelton Waldrep, Jane Kuenz, Phil Wegner, Susan Hegeman, Rob Seguin, Mike Maiwald, Glenn Willmott, Susan Weiner, Ted Hovet, and Babs Beck (an honorary egghead despite her best efforts). At the University of Tennessee, I enjoyed the companionship and intellectual example of my colleagues, especially La Vinia Jennings, George Hutchinson, Kenny Mostern, and Misty Anderson. My Americanist colleagues at the University of Missouri helped me to finish the undertaking. Phil Howerton assisted in the final stages: his organizational skills were much appreciated. Special thanks go out to Maurice Lee, a boon colleague and a professional in the best sense. I also have been especially lucky to encounter Sam Otter and

Paula Bennett in my scholarly sojourns: they have offered inestimable advice and support.

Emma Lipton read all and encouraged me throughout the writing. Our daughter, Margaret, appeared only as I was finishing this work, but she has been the best of all possible distractions.

TOLERABLE ENTERTAINMENT

Melville, New York City, and Professional Ideology

In 1857, Herman Melville's sister Augusta would assert in a letter to their uncle, Peter Gansevoort: "Herman is by birth & from his residence in the city of New York is known as a New Yorker; all his books are published in that city."[1] Her assessment has persisted and there is a long critical tradition for examining the influences of New York City on Melville's work, from Luther Mansfield's seminal dissertation "Herman Melville: Author & New Yorker" (1936), to Perry Miller's landmark study *The Raven and the Whale* (1956), to more recent studies such as Hans Bergmann's *God in the Street: New York Writing from the Penny Press to Melville* (1995) and Wyn Kelley's *Melville's City* (1996). Although these studies have sought to trace the literary, cultural, and political influences of New York City upon Melville's work, my intent is to reverse the process and look at Melville's literary career and community to understand larger trends within the social and cultural life of antebellum America. Locating Melville within the context of antebellum New York City, this project draws upon both the specificity of literary institutions and networks of acquaintance and influence and the larger contexts of economic and social change in city life. Life in antebellum New York City produced the nascent forms of modern American class identity, and it is important to trace how many of the issues and topics that galvanized Melville's writing were shared concerns not only of other New York City writers, but of New Yorkers in general and the emergent middle class in New York City in particular. Herman Melville undoubtedly lies at the center of this book, but his life and literary work become windows on the fascinating and tumultuous life of New York City and, beyond that, to the intersections of class and culture in antebellum America.

It was in the antebellum cities of the North, and most particularly New York City, where the urban and industrial forms that to this day shape American life first came to structure economic and social experience. The antebellum urban population of the United States grew at an unprecedented (and as yet unmatched) rate, increasing by 92 percent during the 1840s.[2] Although the number of cities in the United States rose dramatically during this period, the major cities captured the greater proportion of this new urban population, transforming rapidly into major metropolitan areas. No antebellum urban transformation was as notable as New York City's, where population grew at a staggering rate. In the second quarter of the nineteenth century alone, from 1825 to 1850, New York City's population tripled, and the cumulative growth rate over the first half of the century was 750 percent.[3] While early-nineteenth-century New York population growth came from New England and the surrounding rural areas, the period from 1825 to 1850 saw a notable rise in foreign immigration, so that by 1850, foreign-born whites, primarily Irish and Germans, constituted almost half of New York City's population.[4] The stunning growth and demographic shifts in antebellum New York City created a greater sense of social difference and fragmentation that would be emphasized further by transformations in the urban economy.

The economic developments of antebellum New York City made it a crucial site for the negotiation of modern American class identity. Already a long-standing trading power due to its port, New York City consolidated its dominance in American trade with the completion of the Erie Canal in 1825 and its superiority in rail-line construction in the 1840s and 1850s. At the same time, New York became an increasingly important manufacturing site for the raw materials entering the city. Unlike New England, antebellum New York City did not see such a dramatic rise of factory production, because the price of real estate and the primitive state of steam-powered generators limited urban industrialization. During this period, however, New York City manufacturing became increasingly specialized, depending upon subdividing and putting-out work in a fashion that dramatically altered traditional artisanal labor forms, thus producing what has been called "proto-industrial" laboring conditions.[5] Although it would be over-stating the case to see antebellum New York City as industrialized, geogra-pher Allan Pred argues that it "is clear that the functional transformation beginning to occur within the economy of most major centers [primarily Northern cities] between 1840 and 1860 was synonymous with the ongo-ing transition from commercially based capital accumulation to industrially based accumulation."[6] It was this transition to an urban industrial economy in cities like New York that paved the way for the rise of new class identities in the period.

The emergence of this new economic form reshaped social relations in the antebellum era, from the experience of work to socially differentiated experi-ences of city space, creating what historians have described as the rise of modern working- and middle-class identities.[7] Far from the traditional hier-archical, but integrated artisan's shop, the new urban workplace established different places in the economy and different social roles for workers, distinc-tions that were increasingly characterized by the hierarchical divide between "manual" and "nonmanual labor," "working" and "middle" classes.[8] The mid-dle-class investment in hierarchical vocational distinctions could be inter-preted as a response to the alienating reification of the new industrialized marketplace economy in which, as Georg Lukács describes it, "a man's activ-ity becomes estranged from himself, it turns into a commodity which, subject to the non-human objectivity of the natural laws of society, must go its own way independently of man just like any consumer article."[9] Seeking to escape the threatening disempowerment of industrialized manual labor, the antebel-lum Northern middle-class's investment in the nonmanual distinction did not, however, take its members out of the commodifying market, but instead put them into a different market, a different reified identity, within the urban economy. Increasingly separated from any act of production, the labor of these nonmanual workers—not simply the entry-level clerks and salesmen but also a whole range of the new professions—was oriented toward the more sym-bolic work of "management," directing the labor of others, and "marketing," the selling of their own services and products that others have produced.[10] Seeking to establish a hierarchical place in the nascent industrialized economy to escape the reifying threats of that new economic and social logic, the new antebellum middle class investment in nonmanual labor only more deeply implicated its members personally into the market.

Herman Melville's early life is a particularly revealing example of this complex process. My first chapter links his father's economic failure to the rise of the new market economy of New York City and examines Melville's own struggles to enter into and remain in this new urban middle class after his father's death and the Panic of 1837. In this context, I read his first book, *Typee* (1846), not only as a commentary on the South Pacific life he purports to describe but also as an ambivalent meditation on the personal costs and rewards of entering into this new market-oriented, middle-class world of work. The text's elaborate and shifting depictions of the "primitive" practices of tattooing and taboo demonstrate the threats to autonomy and self-hood posed by entering into symbolic economies—not just Marquesan, but also American. Hardly a true insider's view of Typee life, Melville's narrative explores the "personality market," in which the new middle class justified its place in the labor hierarchy of the antebellum economy. Chapter 1 considers not only Melville's first book, but also his meditations upon the new culture of "celebrity," P. T. Barnum, and the Mexican-American War as well as his status as author and celebrity after *Typee*'s publication. Far from a naïve first entry into the literary marketplace, *Typee* can be understood as a complex consideration of the personal consequences of being initiated into the middle-class world of work and the larger cultural consequences of the national transition into an American market society.

If antebellum urban centers like New York City saw the formalization of a divide between working and middle classes, they also saw a complicated negotiation of social position at the other end of spectrum, between the middle and the upper class as in the professional vocations. Just as the artisan system was a residuum of the eighteenth century, the American professions of the first quarter of the nineteenth century harked back to the past. During this period, members of the traditional trinity of professionalism—ministers, doctors, and lawyers—were typically educated but loosely trained, often unpropertied, members of the upper classes who depended upon the patronage of other wealthy members of the local community for use of their services.[11] The second quarter of the nineteenth century, however, saw a variety of threats to upper-class control over traditional professional authority that were tied to demographic changes and the dramatic rise of urbanization. Whether in the rise of the popular evangelicalism of the Second Great Awakening, the proliferation of nontraditional medical practices (such as homeopathy, Thomsonianism, and the long-standing threat of midwifery), or populist political acts to remove qualifications for admission to the bar, the traditional forms and constituency of the professions were dramatically altered.[12] These challenges democratized the professions, opening them up increasingly to the middle class.

This new influx of democratic values and middle-class members radically altered the traditional elite professional community and its ideological project.[13] For this reason, it was common in the period to hear nostalgic laments about the end of the professions, as this commentary from New York's *United States Magazine and Democratic Review* in 1846 illustrates: "Sustained by no special privileges or rewards, accessible to every class of society, every order of talent, and every degree of ignorance, the ancient dignity of their [the lawyers'] vocation has almost entirely abandoned it."[14] Similarly, in 1853, a commentator from New York's *Putnam's Magazine* argued that even women would find no increase in prestige in society by seeking employment in the "learned professions," because they were so diminished:

> Democracy has so shattered the dignity of the professions, it has so broken down the fences whereby their ancient respect was hedged in, and laid them open to every undisciplined vagabond who fancies that they may afford him a comfortable pasturage, that it is idle any longer to regard a man as respectable simply because he is a lawyer, physician or clergyman.[15]

Responding to these kinds of complaints from within the traditional professional ranks and the democratic attacks upon professional prestige from without, some historians have argued that the antebellum era constituted an "interregnum" or period of "stasis," a low point in professional status and authority.[16]

This antebellum attack on traditional professional status has justified historical claims for dating the rise of a modern professionalism from the late-nineteenth and early-twentieth century. In this model, a modern middle-class professionalism made itself known only in the late-nineteenth century through what has been called the "new class" or the "professional managerial class," an identity that became increasingly prominent in the Progressive era and a crucial element of the twentieth-century class landscape.[17] This association of a modern, middle-class version of professionalism with the Progressive era, however, neglects to acknowledge the antebellum origins of many of the roles and institutions that define modern professionalism. From the appearance of managers to the formation of professional associations, the antebellum era was the crucial matrix for the construction of a professional middle-class identity, not as a dominant form, but as an emergent ideology, setting the groundwork for an identity that would comprise an increasingly large portion of the U.S. population over the course of the second half of the nineteenth century and into the twentieth.[18] As Magali Larson argues, "the radical changes that affected American society after the Civil War were but the culmination of trends already discernible in the ante-bellum period."[19]

While many sociologists have studied the evolution of professionalism as simply a sign of the increasing complexity of modern society, others have explored this new professionalism as a vocational logic that established class or status distinctions in the new market capitalism of the nineteenth century.[20] According to Magali Larson, this new model of professionaliza-tion, the process of making one's self or one's work professional, can be understood as a social project "by which producers of special services sought to constitute *and control* a market for their expertise."[21] Out of the challenges to professionalism in the antebellum era came a new project of defending professional authority on the basis of specialized knowledge, an essential part of the meritocratic social logic that would justify middle-class vocational standing. For example, in *Putnam's* in 1853, a physician attacked the new competing medical forms as mere "quackery," and privileged the "true physician" as the rational man of science:

> The true physician guesses at nothing. He analyses all facts before him. By reading and long practice he learns to attribute to symptoms their true value. . . . Why . . . employ the doctor? Why draw down upon yourselves the phlebotomy of his bill? Because you are unskilled, you cannot estimate the importance of a symptom. The case that is trivial to-day, may be moribund to-morrow. Call your physician not as an apothecary anxious to sell his drugs, but as an observer careful to note, and quick to appreciate; forewarned and fore-armed, and ready to meet the first indication of danger with cautious skill, or Napoleonic energy, as the case demands.[22]

Drawing a line between the "true" professional and the "unskilled" lay-man, the doctor justifies his work not as a simple sale of service, but as the manifestation of specialized knowledge. Unlike the traditional elite profes-sionalism that depended upon local or communal patronage, antebellum professionalism's investment in specialized knowledge and discourse was not a rejection of the market per se, but an attempt to create what Magali Larson has called "the ideological and institutional bases for a special kind of non-physical property," a symbolic currency that some sociologists have termed "cultural capital."[23]

As promulgated through the work of Pierre Bourdieu, cultural capital is a form of knowledge that can be converted into symbolic value through social acceptance or prestige and authority.[24] Although there are many forms of cultural capital, Alvin Gouldner argues that the new middle-class professionalism can be distinguished from earlier class forms by its investment in cultural capital: "Underneath 'professionalism,' there is the political economy of culture."[25] Codifying authoritative forms of knowledge and professional practice within specialized fields that separate professionals from competitors, the new professionalism defined its relation to the market through its cultural capital. In this way, the new professionalism emerging in the antebellum era was directed toward the market, but with an eye toward entering the market from the privileged position that cultural capital could offer. As Gouldner suggests, this new professional middle class was "a new *cultural* bourgeoisie whose capital is not its money but its control over valuable cultures."[26] Professionalism's investment in cultural capital, manifested primarily through claims to authoritative knowledge and specialized discourses, acknowledges the new prominence of market demands to the modern professional's place in society, but seeks to defuse the socially leveling effects of the market by claiming monopolies on knowledge and discourse.

As an attempt to control the market for the newly middle-class services, professionalism can be understood as part of a social project for the new antebellum middle class, what Larson describes as "a collective assertion of special social status" and "a collective process of upward social mobility."[27] Simultaneously a justification of authority and status for a distinct segment of the population and an overarching logic for explaining the functioning of society, professionalism can be understood as an ideology in its nascent form during the antebellum era, and as a particularly potent ideology for the emergent middle class.[28]

This antebellum middle-class professionalization had a direct counterpart in the field of literary production, where the rapidly growing urban population constituted an unprecedented readership and new production and transportation technologies industrialized the publishing industry. This created new economic opportunities for authors, opening the way for men and women of the middle class who had previously been disenfranchised by the older model of literary production, which (like other older models of the professions) was based upon local patronage and associated with genteel, gentlemanly leisure. Antebellum authors found themselves in the same predicament

as other middle-class professionals in the period, benefiting from the economic opportunities brought on with the dramatic expansion of the marketplace, but also responding to its threats, particularly the decline in status that
involvement in the market could bring.[29]

The concept of professionalism first became a meaningful category of
analysis in American literary studies through the work of William Charvat.
His notion of antebellum authorship as an emergent profession is essentially an economic distinction.

> The terms of professional writing are these: that it provides a living for the
> author, like any other job; that it is a main and prolonged, rather than inter-
> mittent or sporadic, resource for the writer; that it is produced with the hope of
> extended sale in the open market, like any article of commerce; and that it is
> written with reference to buyers' tastes and reading habits.[30]

As such, Charvat's model reconceived the work of nineteenth-century
American authorship as shaped by economics: "[I]n so far as [the writer]
was dependent upon, and influenced, by the reader and the book trade, he
was not only artist but economic man. . . ."[31] Charvat's materialist history of
the interactions of nineteenth-century writers, readers, and publishers
paved the way for a reconsideration of canonical writers' engagement with
the marketplace as well as for new literary scholarship on popular and finan-
cially successful authors in the period, many of them women.[32] One influential critical model to emerge from Charvat's study of the effect of the
antebellum literary marketplace on authors has been the work of David
Reynolds. Exploring a remarkably wide range of antebellum writings,
Reynolds demonstrates the influence of "low" or popular literature upon the
writings of authors canonized in the twentieth century as "high" or literary
artists: Poe, Whitman, Emerson, Hawthorne, and Melville.[33]

Although attentive to the economics of the marketplace and particularly
helpful to exposing the complex interaction of gender and economics
within the period, this materialist scholarship on antebellum literary professionalism has largely neglected the social context in which professionalism has strongly figured as a subject of study and debate among social
historians and sociologists: as a middle-class response to the social pressures of urban–industrial capitalism in the nineteenth century.[34] As a result
of this, it is the central thrust of this book to consider antebellum literary
professionalism in the context of professionalism's broader ideological project to legitimize and bolster the status of the new urban middle class. At the
same time, however, this book locates the ideological project of profession-

alism (literary and otherwise) within the local frame of antebellum New York City, understanding that ideological movements are born out of local formations, connections, and institutions that shape individual experiences.

There is little question that New York City was the best place to pursue a professional literary career in this era. While literary pursuits remained a local and genteel activity for much of the nation during the antebellum period, the publishing industry of New York City followed the city's general move into trade dominance during this time, becoming the nation's literary capital for the business of writing.[35] As the Bostonian Henry Wadsworth Longfellow would proclaim in 1839, "New York is becoming more and more literary. It will soon be the center of everything in this country; —the Great Metropolis. All young men of talent are looking that way; and new literary projects in the shape of Magazines and Weekly papers are constantly started, showing great activity, and zeal, and enterprise."[36] The dominance of New York City's trade and publishing industry made it the center for a new literary professionalism that paralleled the broader emergent movement of middle-class professionalism.

Just as antebellum professionalism more broadly struggled in its negotiation of its residual premarket genteel associations and its emergent market orientation, New York literary professionalism in the period was an ideology in transition. Marking the shift between the residual form of local, genteel dilettantism of the previous generation of authors and the emergent industrialization of publishing tied to the profit-driven culture of reprinting (the practice of republishing English and American works outside of copyright), the new literary professionalism sought a middle ground where authors could address the larger marketplace while also retaining their distinctive authority.[37] Like doctors, lawyers, and a host of other professionals, some antebellum authors turned to the persuasive force of the cultural capital of specialized expertise to respond to the promises and threats of the marketplace.

This was particularly true of the small coterie of New Yorkers associated with what was called "Young America," a group of literary and political writers affiliated with the populist wing of the Democratic Party. In its literary configuration, Young America is most strongly linked to an exceptionalist nationalism and calls for new copyright protection for American authors.[38] However, one can also see Young America's literary stances as part of the larger class project of legitimating versions of the new professionalism. In 1847, the Young American editor Evert Duyckinck used the prospectus to the first edition of his magazine *The Literary World* to ask: "There is a religious, a political, a mercantile world, why not a literary one?"[39] Repudiating the amateurism of his genteel predecessors, Duyckinck's rhetorical question demonstrates how antebellum writers began to consider ways to define their fields and denote their specialized skills. Similarly, in an 1845 *United States Magazine and Democratic Review* essay "Amateur Authors and Small Critics," William A. Jones, a critic associated with the Young America literary movement, distinguished between the "two classes" into which "the trade of authorship is divided": "authors by profession, and amateur writers: those who regard study and composition as the business of their lives, and those who look upon them merely as incidental occupations."[40] In this distinction, Jones models what Burton Bledstein identifies as a broader cultural transformation in understandings of the term "amateur" in mid-nineteenth century America. It shifted from its eighteenth-century association with "a person who pursued an activity for the love of it," to connotations of "faulty and deficient work, perhaps defective, unskillful, superficial, desultory, less than a serious commitment, the pursuit of an activity for amusement and distraction."[41] In the Young American discourse of authorship, vocational specialization became a justification or legitimation of work, not only for doctors and lawyers but for authors as well.

Since *The Raven and the Whale*, Perry Miller's 1956 study of political conflict among antebellum New York writers, Herman Melville's New York literary context and community has been strongly associated with the Young Americans. But when Melville moved to New York City in 1847 to compose his third book *Mardi* and take up the profession of authorship in earnest, he joined Longfellow's "young men [and women] of talent," who flooded into the city seeking literary success, becoming part of a vital and active professional literary community, one that covered an ideological range from poses of genteel amateurism to specialized professionalism. In Chapter 2, I position Melville's 1849 novel as an exploration of his commitment to literary professionalism. Signaling his new investment in authorship as a vocation or profession, Melville recasts *Mardi* in a number of different narrative forms, each revealing a model of authorial authority present in antebellum New York City, from the residual Knickerbocker literary "idler" of Washington Irving and his descendents, such as N. P. Willis and Ik Marvel (Donald Grant Mitchell), to newer models, such as the socially activist, reformist city observers Lydia Maria Child and Margaret Fuller, through to Duyckinck's Young American literary expert or aestheticized specialist. *Mardi*'s problematic journey through different narrative forms encapsulates not only the shifting models of antebellum literary professionalism, but also more generally the new professionalism, as it shifted from its residual genteel orientation to the emergent modern, middle-class, conjoined, and potentially contradictory investment in reform and specialization.

Literary professionalization, like the broader movement of professionalization generally, was not simply about commercial success, but authority, prestige, and specialized expertise. As with the new middle-class movement of professionalism more broadly, literary professional specialization was not imagined as a rejection of the market, but rather as an assertion of hierarchical status that would allow the literary professional to enter the market from a privileged position. Developing his distinction between amateurs and professionals, Jones's 1845 article "Amateur Authors and Small Critics" justified the need for the specialization of authors and critics through comparison to other professionals and for the marketing of their services: "Now we all know very well how absurd a thing it would be for a client to ask the services of an amateur lawyer, with an air of confidence in the request, and, indeed, the analogy holds in every walk of life."[42] Far from dismissing the market, Jones uses the literary professional's dependence upon the market as a sign of his commitment and as a testament to his seriousness. The "amateur," by contrast, "rarely puts his heart or invests the whole stock of his faculties in a pursuit which he takes up casually to while away an hour or two of an idle day."[43] For Jones, the literary amateur, a wealthy idler, "injures the true author who unites a love for his profession, deep interest in his subject, and an honest independence, with the aim of procuring a sufficient livelihood."[44] Here, the "true author" must procure an income; he is not independently wealthy.

The Young American democratic vision of professional authorship, however, is not designed to open up writing and criticism to all, but instead to legitimize the writer's specialized labor:

> People of sense in ordinary matters, and men intelligent in their own walk of life, but who have never received any tincture of literature, make the most opinionated of all critics. . . . Thinking to bring everything to a common standard, the illiterate imagine themselves as good judges of right and wrong in morals, as of the beautiful and odious in aesthetics. . . . The same people who talk pertly of Milton and Wordsworth, would think it absurd for a blacksmith to attempt to take a watch to pieces. Yet the difference of difficulty, between the two operations, is by no means great.[45]

Although Jones attacks wealthy literary "idlers," he also attacks the judgment of the democratic "illiterate" who seek "to bring everything to a common standard," establishing a place between the economic poles of the upper class and the working class for the skilled or trained member of the middle class, who recognizes that reading Milton and Wordsworth is a complex task. In this way, Jones invests special social meaning in the work of cultural distinction, making it a crucial device for legitimating the authority of the middle-class literary professional. Simultaneously egalitarian and hierarchical, Jones's specialized logic of social and cultural distinction captures precisely the ambivalent project of middle-class professionalism.

This complex position of the literary professional between egalitarianism and hierarchy would play an important role in the formation of cultural distinctions in antebellum America. Long recognized as a crucial site for the negotiation of models of "high" and "low" culture, antebellum New York City was home to such cultural institutions as the American Art-Union, an art lottery that encouraged the masses to embrace American art (and Whig values), and the American Museum, where P. T. Barnum tried to entice the entire city's population with his displays of freak-show exhibits, panoramas, and "moral dramas" as well as the site of such crucial events as the Astor Place Riots, the period's most famous theater riot, and the start of the Jenny Lind tour; each has been read as a symbolic commentary on the negative and positive trajectory of American cultural life. Ambivalently positioned between the egalitarianism of democratic audience sovereignty and patrician aesthetic stewardship, New York's literary community played an active role in this cultural life as committee members of art and cultural institutions, as participants in conflicts, and as public commentators on cultural trends and events.

Although Melville moved out of New York City in 1850, he played an important role in the Astor Place Riots and was an eagle-eyed observer of the city's cultural life which filters in a variety of ways into his work. None was more perceptive than his 1851 novel, *Moby-Dick*, a text carefully marked by its cultural references and distinctions, all reflecting the complex social negotiation of status and authority in New York's cultural life. I argue that *Moby-Dick* participates in a broader ideological project to establish new terms for cultural hierarchy in American life, shifting authority from the earlier dominant forms—both Jacksonian working-class cultural democracy and patrician cultural stewardship—to a new professional, middle-class dominance. In Chapter 3, I trace how Melville's novel invokes the context of the most famous theater riot of the era when Shakespeare became the medium for violent confrontation over cultural authority. Through his use of Shakespeare in *Moby-Dick*, Melville seeks to create a "new" cultural politics, one that models a sophisticated balancing of social inclusion and exclusion that reorients the cultural hierarchy to privilege professional training and social standing. Similarly, Chapter 4, examines how *Moby-Dick*'s "cetology," in which Ishmael famously mocks and unsettles various epistemological discourses, critiques the new antebellum popular and "middlebrow" culture industry. This "middlebrow" culture was most famously embodied in the new institution of the lyceum circuit, where a stunning range of cultural voices—from Emerson to phrenologists, naturalists to reformers—competed for the attention of a status-aspiring middle class. Ishmael's "cetological" appropriation of the oratorical mode and interpretative approaches of the lyceum works to undermine the middlebrow lecture circuit's production of "useful" knowledge. In this way, my chapters chart how *Moby-Dick* is defined by its professionalization of culture, reflecting the ideological project of transforming professionals into gatekeepers over knowledge and taste, taking control over a form of cultural authority converted into prestige and status within nineteenth-century American social life.

Crucial to the modern model of professional authority has been its vision of the professional community or collective. No longer simply dependent upon the skills of individual practitioners, modern professionalism was quick to note a collective basis for its claims to authority and status within the industrializing American workforce. Reflecting this, Thomas Haskell has described modern professionalization as a "three-part process": a community is established, "distinguishes itself from other groups and from the society at large, and enhances communication among its members, organizing and disciplining them, and heightening their credibility in the eyes of the public." For Haskell, "[a]ny act which contributes to these functions," should be understood as "a step toward professionalization."[46] Despite the common association of professional organizations with the Progressive era, many of the most important professional organizations in modern American life were founded in the antebellum era, from the American Medical Association (1847), to the American Legal Association (an ancestor of the American Bar Association, 1849), to the American Society of Civil Engineers (1852), to the National Education Association (born as the National Teachers' Association in 1859).[47] Faced with the breakdown of the local communities of gentleman–practitioners from all disciplines that had supported professional endeavors previously, the new professionals found support within their own disciplines and fields of study. Drawing upon specialized discourses and seeking to formalize their difference from "quacks," amateur practitioners, and laymen, the antebellum professions, with their increasingly middle-class constituency, turned to voluntary associations, organizations, and narrowly defined professional communities as the best way to legitimize themselves. A characteristic example can be taken from the sciences. In 1846, Joseph Henry, scientist and head of the Smithsonian Institution complained, "We are over-run in this country with charlatanism. . . . Our newspapers are filled with puffs of Quackery and every man who can burn phosphorous in oxygen . . . to a class of young ladies is called a man of science."[48] Henry's response was to institutionalize as "a community of the competent," constructing the Smithsonian as a scientific community with set criteria for establishing the merit or validity of scientific research. In a similar fashion, the new national professional association or community was envisioned as the best way to uphold standards of professional knowledge and conduct. This professional community formed over a range of fields: no longer just the traditional triad of lawyers, physicians, and the clergy, all different sorts of skilled nonmanual laborers began to conceive of their work as "professional" and sought to establish "communities of the competent" that formalized their place within the larger society during this era.

And authors were no exception. Like other professionals of the period, antebellum New York literary professionals also found legitimation through association. Of course, there were no "American Authors' Unions" formed then. In fact, there was a fair bit of critical venom directed at the idea of such an association; for example, in 1845, the *Broadway Journal* published Charles Briggs' satires under the title of "The American Authors' Union," burlesquing the petty claims of failed authors who form a secret society. One episode concludes with the reading of one member's play, "The Author's Tragedy, or the Perfidious Publisher, A Drama in Six Acts."[49] Despite this ironic attack, many writers cited the existence of a substantial literary community to legitimize the authoritative claims of individual writers. A telling example can be found in the work of one of the more notable literary immigrants to New York City: Briggs' coeditor at the *Broadway Journal*, Edgar Allan Poe. Poe may seem like a particularly perverse example of professional collectivization, due to his legendary status as a loner and outsider, who was constantly attacking adversaries and alienating allies.[50] Yet Poe, whose drive for literary professionalism carried him to New York in 1844 after stints in

Richmond and Philadelphia, offers a particularly striking example of the ways in which the notion of a specialized literary community could be used to generate cultural authority in the antebellum era.[51] One of Poe's most successful literary ventures in the several years before his death in 1849 was his 1846 profile series "The Literati of New York City," published in the Philadelphia magazine *Godey's Lady's Book*. Poe justified his selection of New York writers as the subject of his profiles by proclaiming New York's literary prominence: "New York literature may be taken as a fair representation of that of the country at large. The city itself is the focus of American letters. Its authors include, perhaps, one-fourth of all in America, and the influence they exert on their brethren, if seemingly silent, is not the less extensive and decisive."[52] This community, standing in for "that of the country at large," legitimizes Poe's claim to authoritative literary judgments. Poe's profiles, then, become the voice of this authoritative literary community:

> In this series of papers which I now propose, my design is, in giving my own unbiased opinion of the *literati* (male and female) of New York, to give at the same time, very closely if not with absolute accuracy, that of conversational society in literary circles. It must be expected, of course, that, in innumerable particulars, I shall differ from the voice of the public, that is to say, from what appears to be the voice of the public—but this is a matter of no consequence whatever.[53]

Poe's logic is essentially professionalizing, placing the voice of the expert with the private community of authorities behind him against "the voice of the public." Poe's autonomous vision of literary criticism is based upon a model of specialization that, like other professionalizers, posed the community of skilled practitioners against laymen and "quacks":

> The very editors who hesitate at saying in print an ill word of an author personally known, are usually the most frank in speaking about him privately. In literary society, . . . the quack is treated as he deserves—even a little more harshly than he deserves—by way of striking a balance. . . . For these reasons there exists a very remarkable discrepancy between the apparent public opinion of any given author's merits and the opinion which is expressed of him orally by those who are best qualified to judge.[54]

Drawing a distinction between "popular opinion" and the views of "private literary society," Poe set out to reproduce the voice of "those who are best qualified to judge," the community of the competent in antebellum New York literature who know which author is or is not a "quack." In introducing his

series with illustrative examples, Poe compares the private literary community's opinion of Hawthorne ("he *is not* an ubiquitous quack") to Longfellow
("although little quacky *per se*, has … a whole legion of quacks at his control"),
to conclude with the unity of opinion within the literary community: "In fact,
on all literary topics there is in society a seemingly wonderful coincidence of
opinion."[55] Poe leverages this vision of a unified literary community, a shared
set of values and judgments, to legitimate an authoritative literary critical
assessment. In doing so, he mirrors the antebellum middle-class impulse to
find legitimation for cultural authority and status through vocational association or group identification.

In 1846, Melville had only just published *Typee*—too late to be included as
a member of Poe's *Literati*—but his name was often cited in contemporary
discussions of the antebellum New York literary community and of American authorship more generally, despite the steadily decreasing sales of his
books over the course of his career. Melville himself largely refrained from
commenting upon the literary community in his work. His most notable
exception is the "Young America in Literature" chapter in his 1852 novel
Pierre. This chapter is, understandably with that title, typically seen as a
satire on his Young America associates. Yet, when one examines the content
of Melville's ironic attacks, we do not find any particular critique of Young
America's distinctive interests—literary nationalism or the copyright—but
rather a general attack upon the practices and abuses of the New York literary community. Chapter 5 culminates my design here by examining this
novel as a thorough rejection and unpacking of professional ideology, a
recantation of Melville's vocational project up to this point. In his famous (or
infamous) transformation of his protagonist Pierre Glendinning into a professional author, Melville mocks not only his former New York literary colleagues, but also the broader ideological thrust of professionalism. From its
puncturing of the self-serving and contradictory privileging of nonmanual
over manual labor, to its savage attack on the professional vision of vocational
calling, to its depiction of the mental labor of writing as nothing more than
punitive self-denial and self-discipline, the story of Pierre's literary work
skewers the logic that legitimates professionalism in the antebellum era.

Like many single-author literary studies, this study of Herman Melville is
oriented around the concept of his "career," an embracing vision of his work
used to narrate a critical history. Perhaps more than that of any other writer
of the nineteenth century, Melville's work has been understood primarily

through the context of his career: from his supposedly naïve beginnings at authorship to his later neglected silence. My undertaking not only revises this narrative of his career but also rethinks the meaning of "career," examining the works that had the most significance for Melville's vision of his own "literary career" and exploring these works as part of a process of thinking through the meaning of his labor and the social understandings of work constructed in the period.

After all, the whole notion of a career was being constructed as Melville began writing. Beginning in the mid-nineteenth century, the "career" supplanted older models of work as a divinely determined "calling," embodying a teleological model of the work experience as a consistent movement upward in status and authority that became central to middle-class notions of selfhood.[56] As historian Burton Bledstein suggests:

> Career meant scheduled mobility, from the distinct and ascending levels of schooling, to the distinct and ascending levels of occupational responsibility and prestige. What formed a career was not disconnected ends, not conditioned habits, not ad hoc actions, not practical good works, *not an infinite series of jobs*, but the entire coherence of an intellectually defined and goal-oriented life. That coherence was manifested at every stage of a career.[57]

Melville's complaint in the letter to his father-in-law cited in the Preface, his claim that *Redburn* and *White-Jacket* were "two *jobs*," was precisely that they stopped him from being able to construct his literary labor as a "career," forcing him to treat writing not as a privileging form of work, but as akin to the lowest forms of manual labor such as "sawing wood." Although Melville's literary career has become stereotypical as an aesthetic or artistic narrative, Melville himself first struggled to articulate his work experience as a career and then, later, came to question the social logic and values behind work as a career. From his adjustments to the demands of a new industrializing urban market economy in *Typee*, to his articulation of and investment in new vocational and cultural hierarchies in *Mardi* and *Moby-Dick*, to his savagely disappointed recognition and critique of professionalism's interpellation into the restrictive industrial–capitalist order in *Pierre* and "Bartleby, the Scrivener," this study presents Melville's literary career in New York City as a microhistory of the emergence of modern professional ideology in American life.

As a result of his deep involvement in professionalism, Melville's New York City literary work becomes the ideal window upon the ideological project of professionalism. This claim does not imply that Melville was the exemplary literary professional of his era. Quite the contrary: depending upon one's definition of professionalism (commercial and/or critical success, personal commitment to vocation, standing within the literary community, cultural authority among the larger public, etc.), a number of other authors seem more appropriate. A critical consensus on the subject seems to have adhered to Nathaniel Hawthorne (a consensus seemingly formed in the antebellum era), but arguments about exemplary literary professional status can and have also been made on behalf of Longfellow, Poe, and Whitman.[58] Melville was neither the first nor the most successful literary professional of his era, but due to the particularities of his literary career—not only the form and content of his work, but also his status within the literary community—his work represents a singular engagement with the nascent worldview of modern middle-class professionalism. Although he is now legendary for his commercial failures—most famously *Moby-Dick* and *Pierre*—the fact is that from *Typee* through *Pierre*, Melville's works were published by important New York houses (and by London houses up to the publication of *Pierre*), and his works were widely reviewed both in Great Britain and across the nation. Admittedly, his works were hardly recipients of universal acclaim, but even in critical failure they became important sites for debates about the nature of authorship in the period. In fact, one could argue that the wide range of the genres and subjects of Melville's literary production during the period from 1846 to 1852, in which a self-sustaining professional literary career seemed within his reach, explores the limits of the antebellum literary field in a manner unmatched by any other author of the time. Apart from the range of his literary production, Melville became a notable figure of the author in antebellum public life after the success of *Typee*—as revealed by the intrusive press coverage of his 1847 wedding and his notably public role in the 1849 Astor Place Riots. Whether or not his works were commercially successful, Herman Melville was a prominent New York literary figure and, in this role, helped to articulate professional models of literary work and culture in the era. Moreover, no other antebellum author's work explores with the same focus the issues that galvanized Melville's literary production—adaptation to new modes of exchange and new distinctions within the worlds of work and culture—issues that were central to the new definition of a modern, professional middle-class identity over the course of the nineteenth-century and into the present.

Although I focus on Herman Melville and antebellum New York City, this book aims also to trace the ways that certain individuals and groups become specially empowered to spread visions of social order, hierarchy, and status within a culture. In this way, Melville as author is not understood simply as an isolated artist or merely as a representative of or analogous to a class position, but rather as an active agent in the shaping of a class ideology.[59] As Nancy Armstrong and Leonard Tennenhouse argue, authors have had a special cultural agency since the rise of print culture, speaking on behalf of the community constituted by the reader and the reader's imagined connection to other readers.[60] No longer writing for an audience defined by people living in the same town or region or even coming from the social class, antebellum New York City's professional authors addressed a public whose geographical boundaries had grown exponentially and whose demographic character had become increasingly urban, a public that was less and less frequently enacted in embodied collectivities or communities beyond work and home, a public more likely to find community in the intimate, but imaginary bond between reader and author.[61] In this setting, it is hardly surprising that authors took on ever more important significance as embodiments of a national identity, even if they were only expressing the deeply personal perspective of the emergent professional middle class, seeking to justify their specialized labors as skilled nonmanual workers in an industrializing urban setting. In this way, antebellum New York City literary professionals played an important role in shaping, not just mirroring, the beliefs and social understandings of Americans in the mid-nineteenth century.

This study defines the ideological significance of Melville's professionalism not only within an antebellum context, but also in a twentieth century one as well. In the twentieth century, Melville's ideological role has been recapitulated through literary canonization, the formal academic critical recognition that bestows official status upon an artist or work of art. Melville's work was recovered via *Moby-Dick* in the 1920s, and he was canonized as one of great literary artists in F. O. Matthiessen's 1941 *American Renaissance,* and since then he has been at the center of critical understandings of the American literary tradition.[62] In fact, one could argue that no author has withstood the shifting modes of twentieth-century American critical interest as well as Melville.[63] It is one of the central premises of this book that Melville is so important to twentieth-century visions of nineteenth-century American literature, because he, more than any other writer, embodies and works through the tenets of professionalism, the values that have guided the twentieth-century and present-day American literary academy.[64] Melville's centrality to the canon of American literature in the twentieth century reflects the ideological process whereby the paradox-ical social and cultural values of the relatively few, the emergent professional middle-class of the mid-nineteenth century, were translated into an embod-iment of national identity in the twentieth century. The form and nature of Melville's literary professional career as constructed by critics works to val-idate and legitimize the professional project of the American literary acad-emy. As a result, the status of *Moby-Dick*, Melville's most famous book, as a "masterpiece," is tied to its being understood by its contemporary American readership as a celebration of our national values, even if those values were hardly recognized as "national" at the time it was published.[65] In this way, while this study examines how the literary career of Herman Melville inter-vened within the social and cultural life of antebellum New York City, it also examines the ways in which his work has been appropriated—as artistic tra-dition or heritage—into the class project of twentieth-century American professionalism.

For this reason, I conclude with an epilogue on Melville's "Bartleby, the Scrivener" (1852) and the professional project of the twentieth-century American literary academy. As his first short story published anonymously in *Putnam's Magazine*, "Bartleby" in a number of ways signaled the end of Melville's status as a hierarchically privileged professional author (even if he received more money for writing stories than for publishing his books). Couching his story through the lawyer–narrator's self-justifying logic of hierarchy, Melville exposes the inextricable class interest within profes-sional authority in the antebellum era. Although the Epilogue frames Melville's critique of professionalism in "Bartleby," it focuses more centrally on the staggering critical interest in the story for the twentieth-century American literary academy, tracing the critical and contextual frames that have served to defuse and redirect Melville's criticisms away from the pro-fessional investment in discourse and authority toward a legitimation of lit-erary critical professionalism.

In reading the work of Herman Melville through the ideological project of professionalism, I do not mean simply to turn Melville into an ideologue. As an ideology, professionalism is not merely a self-interested logic that jus-tifies middle-class hierarchy, it is also an attempt to make meaning out of middle-class economic and social experience. As Louis Althusser famously posited of all ideology, professionalism can be understood as "the imaginary relationship of individuals to the real conditions of their existence."[66] In its "imaginary" form, professionalism undoubtedly justifies middle-class status and authority, but it is not simply reducible to "self-interest" and "false consciousness": professionalism is also a "utopian" vision, a dream of meritocratic collective unity.[67] The gap between the utopian goals of professionalism and the real conditions of middle-class existence, however, marks the "unevenness" of ideology, so that professionalism can be simultaneously experienced as a "description" of, a "goal" for, and a "judgment" upon the experience of the new antebellum urban middle class.[68] In this light, the literary career of Herman Melville in antebellum New York City serves to explore the unevenness of professional ideology, with different texts embodying different stages of Melville's relationship to that ideology. As such, Melville's deep personal investment in professionalism over the course of his literary career in New York City makes him alternately an aspirant to, an ideologue, and a fierce critic of professional ideology.

CHAPTER ONE

Typee and Melville's Initiation into the World of Middle-Class Labor

Herman Melville's first book, the travel adventure *Typee* (1846), became something of a cause célèbre when it first appeared. In addition to its glimpse into the exotic lives of South Pacific islanders (its subtitle is "A Peep at Polynesian Life") and its racy hints of the narrator's sexual experience among the natives, *Typee* presented a rather controversial attack on the Protestant missions to the region. Despite his disputatious comments in the narrative, *Typee* does show every sign of being carefully constructed for the antebellum literary marketplace, appealing simultaneously to the American readership's preference for "fact" and to that readership's emergent romanticism, drawn to the exoticism of Melville's encounter with the primitive islanders. As a popular fulfillment of the demands of the American literary marketplace, *Typee* could be seen as the twenty-five-year-old Melville's first successful venture into the antebellum world of middle-class work.

Herman Melville had struggled to find a secure place in the antebellum economy since he first entered it at thirteen, after the death of his father in 1832. Melville had failed to catch on in a variety of entry-level, nonmanual occupations such as clerk and teacher, and finally, at age twenty-one, signed on as a common sailor on a whaling ship. Upon coming back to the United States after his exotic travels, Melville may have turned to writing for lack of any other option. Melville's first biographer, J. E. A. Green, described

Melville's vocational quandary upon returning from his voyages: "One could not well see to what profession he was adapted."[1] Despite the fact that authorship was hardly seen as a secure vocation in the period, Melville clearly applied himself to the task of converting his experiences into a saleable narrative. Responding to the complaint of a prospective publisher that "it was impossible that it could be true and therefore was without real value," Melville augmented his narrative with additional information from a variety of other narratives by travelers to the Marquesas, ironically bolstering his narrative's factuality (and "value") through a kind of plagiarism.[2] Drawn from his exotic experiences as a sailor and based upon his careful study of the literary marketplace and other texts on the subject, *Typee* could be seen as his initiation into the demands of the antebellum world of urban middle-class labor.

Given this personal context, it is perhaps no small coincidence that the plot of Melville's first narrative is itself largely structured by the question of whether or not his narrative persona, Tommo, will be initiated into the Marquesan culture. Puzzled by the Marquesan religion–exchange system of "taboo" and its related representational system of tattooing, Tommo struggles to understand his role among the islanders (favored guest or possible feast?), just as he wavers in his comparison of the relative merits of "civilized" and "primitive" life. Far from a naïve recounting of exotic experiences or even a workmanlike pilfering from previous sources to form a cohesive and authoritative narrative, *Typee* is a complex, if indirect, meditation on the consequences of entering the middle-class world of work in the antebellum era. As a narrative, *Typee* considers what it means to perform the nonmanual labor of writing, entering into the symbolic exchanges of the middle-class service economy and transforming oneself into a marketable good. As a result, *Typee*'s representations of the "primitive" contexts of taboo and tattooing could be said not just to depict Marquesan life but also to comment on the penetration of capitalist exchange in antebellum America. This new penetration of capital transformed the cultural landscape of America, opening new opportunities for middle-class authors and artists like Melville and creating a new relationship between artist and audience through the emergence of the celebrity system in American cultural life. This chapter reads Melville's *Typee* and responses to it as well as his earliest journalistic satires, "The Authentic Anecdotes of 'Old Zack,'" as deeply engaged considerations of the personal and social consequences of the antebellum initiation into marketplace values.

Melville's Youth, the Market Economy, and Middle-Class Labor

Born in New York City in 1819, Herman Melville was descended from distinguished aristocratic and merchant families with notable Revolutionary War heritages from upstate New York and Boston. Melville's father, Allan Melvill (Herman's mother would add the "e" after her husband's death—a relatively common practice), had moved his family from Albany to New York City in 1817 with visions of surpassing the mercantile success of his Boston family. At that time he wrote to a relative justifying his choice of New York City:

> I have been induced by the advice of my commercial Friends here & at home, & various important personal considerations, to establish myself permanently at New York, a City of unexampled growth & prosperity, & of unrivalled local resources & foreign intercourse, which must become the great Emporium of the western World—my acquaintances there are numerous and respectable, and my Wife's Family and Connexions who are among the first People in the State . . . will afford me the same consideration I enjoy in my native town.[3]

Addressing the economic opportunities occasioned by New York City's expansion and foreseeing the spread of a national market economy with New York at its forefront, Melvill's decision to establish a shop for European luxury goods there seems prescient. In 1817, New York Governor DeWitt Clinton secured financial backing to begin construction of the Erie Canal. The canal, completed in 1825, established New York City's trade dominance, setting the stage for its role as "the great Emporium of the western World," as Allan Melvill predicted. His plan to establish himself as a merchant in foreign luxury goods in a city that was to become the nation's richest seemed promising.

If Melvill's plan seemed foresighted, however, the terms under which he imagined his future success also looked backward to an eighteenth-century notion of exchange and business mediated by local communities of prestige and influence, tying his business future to his "acquaintance" and his wife's "connexions" to the city's elite. Unfortunately for Melvill, the dramatic expansion of trade in New York City in this period was directly tied to its shedding of the older, more patrician model of business and replacing it with a far more free-market exchange system.[4] The building of the Erie Canal solidified New York City's role as the center for the exportation of domestic goods from the interior, but another bill, passed on the same day as that which funded the canal, dramatically altered the business Allan Melvill imagined starting in New York City: importing. New legislation required imported goods up for auction to be sold on the day offered, regardless of the price offered. This meant that importers could not withhold goods if bidding was low, forcing them to sell only at the market rate. This new market-oriented legislation, along with the establishment of a scheduled weekly packet ship line from Liverpool to New York City, quickly established New York City's preeminence as the nexus of American trade even before the Eric Canal was completed.[5] Allan Melvill's shop for imported luxury goods quickly suffered in this new market economy, competing as it did against the auction houses that could undersell him and escape the extra costs of a more fixed business establishment. In 1822, Melvill reported to his brother-in-law Peter Gansevoort, "Business at private sale is rather dull, for the Auctions engross more than ever, & injure us most essentially."[6] Caught between his vision of the "intimate" eighteenth-century city with its system of exchange based upon "acquaintance" and "connexions" and the emergence of a bustling, anonymous city of the market-oriented nineteenth century, Allan Melvill depended upon family money for ever more ambitious ventures and larger domestic arrangements for his growing family, all of which strained his finances beyond their limit. By 1830, he was forced to clear out of his New York City home at night to avoid creditors, aided by his second son, the eleven-year-old Herman. In 1832, Allan Melvill died in Albany in a feverish state of dementia, driven to exhaustion and illness by his effort to repay the debts he had incurred. His life was, in many ways, a lesson in the workings of the new urban economy and the breakdown of the older models of business and community. More than anything else, though, Allan Melvill's life revealed the new precariousness of status and authority in the burgeoning market ethos of the antebellum era, a lesson that clearly had an impact on the life of his son, Herman.

If Allan Melvill had earlier imagined himself entering the intimate world of the New York City elite that dominated the eighteenth-century city, Herman Melville's adolescence and young adulthood modeled the uncertain place of the new middle class in antebellum cities. While living the life of the son of a (supposedly) successful merchant during his childhood in New York City, Melville had a large home and expensive schooling. After his father's death, Herman Melville's education became sporadic, and he quickly found himself working in a series of entry-level, nonmanual-laboring jobs, such as clerk in an Albany bank and at his elder brother's short-lived furrier shop. It was precisely these kinds of jobs that began to proliferate in cities during the period, reflecting the industrialization and specialization of labor that formalized a distinction between manual and nonmanual work in antebellum America. This distinction became a crucial signifier of the differences between working-class and middle-class identity.[7] Despite his prestigious family heritage, Herman Melville entered the antebellum world of work as a marginal member of the middle class.

Melville's experiences as neophyte worker reflected the uncertain labor conditions for the middle class in that era, transitioning from the older apprentice system to a system not yet in place, which would delay entry into the nonmanual workforce by means of extended public-funded education.[8] Like many young clerks in antebellum cities, Melville augmented his education by joining a lyceum (the Albany Young Men's Association for Mutual Improvement) and participating in a debating society, institutions designed to inculcate values and skills that would encourage economic and social improvement among young men on the bottom rung of the middle class. Self-improvement and social mobility were crucial beliefs in the Jacksonian era, especially for members of the new middle class who imagined themselves, in the words of Karen Halttunen, "on a social escalator to greater wealth and prestige."[9] However, twentieth-century historians have demonstrated that the Jacksonian "era of the common man" was characterized more by the persistence of social hierarchies and the consolidation of older wealth than by the "self-made man" envisioned by ideologues.[10] In fact, statistics show that the young middle-class men entering the antebellum urban economy were as likely to fall in status as they were to rise.[11]

Like many of his generation, Melville struggled to find a place in the economy instead of steadily rising and clung to middle-class standing by only the barest thread throughout his early adulthood. Just as he reached adulthood, the Panic of 1837 hit New York City, and the economic downturn spread throughout the nation. Melville worked as a schoolteacher in rural New England, gained additional training as a surveyor, and unsuccessfully sought employment out west, and, as a temporary break from his search for steady employment, worked a stint as a common sailor on a merchant ship from New York to Liverpool. After returning from his short voyage, Melville worked again as a rural schoolteacher, then joined his elder brother Gansevoort in New York City in 1840, seeking a job in an economy still recovering from the Panic of 1837. There, Gansevoort complained to their mother, Maria, about Herman's inability to fit into this market economy, blaming Herman's continued unemployment on "laziness . . . which consists in an unwillingness to exert oneself in doing at a particular time, that which ought to be done."[12]

Whether due to his own "unwillingness" to fit himself to market demands, as his brother suggests, or to the constraints of the post-Panic economy, Melville was unable to find work in New York City and signed on as a common sailor on a whaling boat. This act, a long-term commitment with little hope of substantial financial gain, signaled Melville's failure to find steady work in the realm of nonmanual vocations. In the volatile economy of the period, this could have signified Melville's permanent fall from the middle class, but it was probably intended as yet another delay to his permanent entrance into a more stable vocation, with hopes of a better chance in the future. Although his father had failed in New York City due to his nostalgic dependence on an intimate, familial eighteenth-century world of elite business and social exchanges, Herman Melville's early work experiences demonstrated just how little the new middle class could depend upon in the increasingly market-oriented world of antebellum Northern cities.

Melville hardly escaped these concerns by becoming an author when he returned from his voyages. Though he sought to convert his experiences into narrative, it is likely that he did not imagine authorship as a viable career option. Hershel Parker suggests that family friends, particularly his guardian and future father-in-law Massachusetts Supreme Court Chief Justice Lemuel Shaw (to whom *Typee* is dedicated) may have encouraged Melville to publish a narrative, as "the reputation as a man who had written a book might be very useful in advancing a career in some other area of life. . . ."[13] This logic justified authorship not as an end unto itself, but as having a testamentary quality: it signaled the author's fitness for a variety of nonmanual labors, particularly in government service.[14] Shaw's plan for Melville's authorship is in many ways a literary counterpart to Allan Melvill's earlier plan for his mercantile success. Here, authorship was seen as being about reputation and status, marking one as a gentleman.

Like his father's experiences in importing, however, Herman Melville would discover that publishing was very much a business in the antebellum era, increasingly driven by market values. Previously, the American literary market had been limited by the regionalism of trade in the United States, with different regions served by only one printer/publisher or by itinerant booksellers (and even they were often limited by seasonal conditions that closed waterways or primitive roads).[15] The same transportation revolution that solidified New York's trade preeminence benefited New York publishers, transforming the city into the nation's literary capital. In contrast to the other cities whose trade remained largely regional, New York City's publishers increasingly began to reach a truly national audience, a growth highlighted by the fact that some New York publishing houses even began to pursue distinctive marketing practices for different regions.[16] When Alexander Mackay, one of many foreign travelers to the United States during the period who wrote narratives of their trips, sought to explain the differences in the literary cultures of the northeastern cities he visited in 1846–47, he explained that in Boston "the literary circle of the place" formed the "nucleus on which [society] turns," and in Philadelphia "literature is cultivated as an ornament," but in New York it is "pursued as a business."[17] This was most notably the case with the Harper and Brothers publishing house, whose extensive Cliff Street plant became something of a tourist attraction, with its thorough mechanization of printing in the period. In 1846, Walt Whitman, then editor of the Brooklyn *Eagle*, would describe the Harper headquarters and proclaim, "If the reader was never in the Cliff street establishment, he can have little idea of the immense business done there. . . ."[18] Though Judge Shaw may have viewed Melville's publication of a narrative as a decidedly nonmercantile project, designed to establish his ward's status as a gentleman and ease his entry into a government appointment, Melville's writing of *Typee* would become instead a "business" venture, with the text shaped to the publisher's demands for marketability.

The first draft of *Typee* was rejected by Harper and Brothers, that colossus among the New York publishing houses, in the late spring or early summer of 1845. Harper's reader, Frederick Saunders, recalled praising the manuscript, asserting that "this work if not as good as Robinson Crusoe seems to me to be not far behind it."[19] Without denying the reader's claim to literary merit, Harper's publication board rejected the manuscript, claiming that without more proof of "truth" or factuality, "it was without real value." This decision put "value" against merit. No one denied *Typee*'s merit, but Harper's decision was a market one, based upon an understanding of the logic that guided sales in that period. As William Charvat explains, "The most successful writers of the time were those who made alliances with history and other kinds of factual evidence."[20] Without more convincing proof of its factuality, publishing *Typee* would have been a risky business decision for the Harpers.

Soon after this rejection, Melville's brother Gansevoort took the manuscript of *Typee* along with him to London, when he was posted to the U.S. Consulate, hoping to find an English publisher for the narrative. While Gansevoort was shopping the narrative around, Melville did further research on the Marquesas in previously published travel narratives, writing new chapters and adding new material to existing chapters. This material, much of it touching upon the meaning of the system of "taboo," but also adding a variety of different details about Marquesan islander life, was designed to bolster the factuality of the narrative and thus augment its market "value." Recognizing that he needed to do this to get his narrative published, Melville readily acceded to the publisher's demands for what was ultimately a false truth—adding a veneer of plagiarized evidence that bestowed a commodifiable value upon his writing.

In this way, Melville's revision of his narrative was a kind of initiation to the marketplace, demonstrating his willingness to enter into the new market economy of the antebellum era. The narrative of *Typee*, however, can be read in a very different light, as a critical commentary on the very processes of symbolic exchange and initiation that Melville entered into in writing his first book, making his pseudofactual depiction of the exotic Marquesan life a depiction of antebellum America as well. As a result, *Typee* both fulfills Melville's initiation into the market exchanges of the antebellum economy and critiques that act at the same time.

Taboo, Tattooing, and Initiation into the Marketplace

Herman Melville's first book, *Typee*, is the story of a sailor abandoning ship in the Marquesan islands, escaping into a captivity–idyll among a tribe of islanders, his attempts to understand and adapt to their ways of life—their dress, their diet, their tattoos, their social codes, and their structures of exchange—only to reject them and return to "civilized" life. Explicitly presented to his antebellum readers as a factual narration of Melville's experience, *Typee* has been revealed to be an elaborate construct, a collage of personal narrative, secondhand research, and pure fiction by twentieth-century scholarship on Melville's process of writing, research, and publication.[21] Critical interest in *Typee*, since Melville's canonization as an important American literary artist, has taken it primarily as a work of fiction, focusing on the story as an exploration of a variety of symbolic dichotomies: primitive vs. civilized, good vs. evil, individualistic freedom vs. social conformity.[22] More recently, critical interest has returned to the context of the colonial encounter between the islanders and Westerners, reading *Typee* for its articulation of an ethnographic or postcolonial perspective.[23] Melville's discussions of the "primitive" practices of taboo and tattooing, presented as mysterious systems of exchange and inscription, however, show little evidence of being reflections upon actual

Marquesan practice, but can instead be read as important commentaries on the equally mysterious system of exchange under the newly emergent urban capitalism. Though certainly a work constructed for profit in the literary marketplace, *Typee* is also a consideration of the personal costs of an individual's adaptation to the new social and economic forms of antebellum market capitalism.

Throughout *Typee*, there is a symbolic doubling between Melville the author adapting to the demands of the literary marketplace in writing his book and his narrative persona, named "Tommo," attempting to adapt to the lifestyle of the Typees. It is suggestive of the importance of the theme of adaptation to *Typee* that Melville's name for his narrative persona, "Tommo," is the Marquesan verb meaning "to enter into, to adapt well to."[24] And, indeed, Melville as author did adapt well to the demands placed upon him, both in his selection of subject matter and his willingness to adapt his narrative to publishing's demands. Revising the narrative to dispel doubts of its factuality, Melville augmented the story of *Typee* with materials from a variety of other travelers' reports on the Marquesas, including G. H. von Langsdorff's *Voyages and Travels in Various Parts of the World*, Charles Porter's *Journal of a Cruise Made to the Pacific Ocean, in the U.S. Frigate Essex* (1815), Charles Stewart's *Visit to the South Seas* (1831), and William Ellis's *Polynesian Researches* (1833). Melville used these texts to bolster his narrative, turning his three-week stay and his limited understanding of Typee language into four months with substantial commentaries on language and rituals among the islanders. Hershel Parker describes Melville's writing process as "plundering sourcebooks" to "eke out his brief impressions" into a full-length narrative.[25] Charles Anderson, the earliest scholar on Melville's use of sources, claims that he was so dependent upon the work of others for his insights into the South Pacific that "Melville might have written *Typee* without ever having seen the Marquesas Islands."[26] Ironically, in its newly bolstered form, *Typee* was accepted as a factual narrative for publication by John Murray, one of the most prestigious English publishing houses, and would become a success, thus setting the stage for his future literary career. But, in the story itself, Tommo does not "adapt well to" Typee life, as his anxieties about the symbolic practices of taboo, tattooing, and cannibalism lead to his fearful rejection of and escape from the Typee.[27] This divide between the narrator and the author's responses to demands may suggest the ambivalence Melville experienced in writing *Typee*. As a compelling narrative that offered its author's life story front and center, but also rejected the notion that the narrator was required to submit to demands upon his identity, *Typee* is not just about the encounter between "primitive" and "civilized" cultures, but also a commentary on the adaptations required of authors by the new urban-industrializing market capitalism.

Far from being a naïve narrative of Melville's experiences of Marquesan culture, *Typee* is marked in a variety of ways by the publisher's demand for marketable fact and reveals the author's rather canny understanding of the processes of marketing or promoting himself and his narrative. Throughout *Typee*, Melville entices, asserts his authority, and engages with reader's skepticism—all demonstrating his careful consideration of the complicated demands placed upon the writer of the fact-based narrative by the literary marketplace. In doing so, Melville seems to immerse himself in the marketplace logic of "humbug," the part-scam, part-advertising marketing discourse that P. T. Barnum made so famous in the antebellum era. Like the antebellum interest in machinery, how-to manuals, and travel literature, Barnum's "humbug" exhibits such as the Feejee Mermaid (parts of a fish and a monkey sewn together and embalmed) exploited what Neil Harris has described as the appeal of the "operational aesthetic." The operational aesthetic reveled in popular interest in process, seeking to understand how something worked. In the case of Barnum's "humbug," the operational aesthetic "narrowed the task of judgment . . . to a simple evaluation" of "real or false, genuine or contrived. . . ."[28] Barnum framed the experience of humbug as a relatively unthreatening consumer choice. As Barnum asked of the Feejee Mermaid: "Who is to decide when *doctors* disagree? [Whether] the work of *nature* or *art* it is decidedly the most stupendous curiosity ever submitted to the public for inspection. If it is artificial the senses of sight and touch are ineffectual—if it is natural then all concur in declaring it *the greatest Curiosity in the World*."[29] Under the appeal of Barnum's operational aesthetic, the Feejee mermaid was worth the price of admission whether it was authentic or not. Barnumian humbug turned the often trying and important decisions and choices required of urban subjects of the new antebellum marketplace into a game: Barnum's audiences were as interested in observing the nature of the deception as they were in seeing an "authentic" oddity. Whether "humbug" or "authentic," the consumer could find enjoyment or learn something and Barnum could profit.[30]

Given the complications of Melville's balancing act between authenticity and duplicity in *Typee*, it is not surprising that in introducing his story, he comes to sound a great deal like Barnum.[31] In his preface to *Typee*, Melville seems to be following Barnum's "humbug" marketing modus operandi when he concludes by stating:

> There are some things related in the narrative which will be sure to appear strange, or perhaps entirely incomprehensible. . . . [The author] has stated such matters as they occurred, and leaves every one to form his own opinion concerning them; trusting that his anxious desire to speak the unvarnished truth will gain for him the confidence of his readers.[32]

Like Barnum, Melville begins by addressing his audience's skepticism, then avers the truth of his narrative, then doubles back and leaves it to the audience to decide. Like Barnum, Melville can profit from skepticism or belief in his readers, as long as they purchase the book to decide for themselves. Melville closes out his preface with the carefully worded hope that his "anxious *desire* to speak the unvarnished truth" will persuade his readers; he does not claim to speak the truth, but to have the *desire* to speak the truth.[33] Melville's preface to *Typee* capitalizes on the profitable liminal space of the "anxious desire" between truth and falsity, earnestness and duplicity that characterized the Barnumian humbug. This stance would fuel *Typee*'s success as an object of literary controversy, a major source of its popularity and interest to Melville's readers.

While the preface established his narrative's marketable tension of humbug, Melville quickly set out to validate the exotic content of his story in the first chapter. The appeal of Melville's narrative was, of course, the allure of the exotic and the primitive. As a result, the reader is promptly supplied with a list of all that they will encounter in the narrative, as the narrator summons up a suggestive mental picture of the Marquesas: "The Marquesas! What strange visions of outlandish things does the very name spirit up! Naked houris—cannibal banquets—groves of cocoa-nut—coral reefs—tattooed chiefs—and bamboo temples; sunny valleys planted with bread-fruit trees—savage woodlands guarded by horrible idols—*heathenish rites and human sacrifices*" (1: 5). Given its suggestive nature, it is not surprising that this passage was used as advertising copy for the second American edition.[34] And, indeed, Melville is careful to include all of these elements in his book: *Typee* is full of long descriptions of Marquesan landscapes, the types of clothing worn (and not worn) and how they are produced, as well as of diet and eating habits. Functioning as authentic experience, but also, ironically, derived almost entirely from other books, these details and information establish Melville's authority to speak on such matters.

Although Tommo's elaborate explanation of Typee culture formed the basis for his authority, Melville was aware of the possible skepticism with which his narrative would be received. As a result, he was also careful to not seem too authoritative and claimed ignorance of the meanings of the all-important practice of "taboo," the rules and strictures that governed Marquesan religion: "For my own part, I am free to confess my almost entire inability to gratify any curiosity that may be felt with regard to the theology of the valley" (24: 171). Far from disempowering his narrative, this disavowal takes a stance of authenticity and integrity against what he calls the "vast deal of unintentional humbuggery" of the other studies of Marquesan life (24: 170):

> [Scientific men] generally obtain the greater part of their information from the retired old South-Sea rovers, who have domesticated themselves among the barbarous tribes of the Pacific. Jack, who has long been accustomed to the long-bow, and to spin tough yarns on a ship's forecastle, invariably officiates as show-man of the island on which he has settled, and having mastered a few dozen words of the language, is supposed to know all about the people who speak it. A natural desire to make himself of consequence in the eyes of the strangers, prompts him to lay claim to a much greater knowledge of such matters than he actually possesses.
> . . . This is not a supposed case: I have met with several individuals like the one described, and I have been present at two or three of their interviews with strangers. (24: 170)

Addressing the "unintentional humbuggery" of other texts on the Marquesas, Melville distracts the reader from his own necessarily intentional "humbuggery," the plagiarized authority of the other writers' materials he adapts to his narrative purposes. Certainly, Melville himself would be open to charges very similar to those he attributes to the other narratives: "the natural desire to make [oneself] of consequence" leads to "greater claims of knowledge . . . than [one] actually possesses." Although Melville himself probably never "mastered [more than] a few dozen words" of the Marquesan language and was greatly indebted to the ethnographers and travelers whom he dismissively termed "learned tourists" (24: 170), his disavowal of authority is a canny strategy for persuading readers. Disavowing complete authority and shifting accusations that could be made against him in the direction of his competitors, Melville deflects potential threats against his narrative's truthfulness and value.[35]

But if the uncertainty about taboo paradoxically functions to legitimize Melville's claims to narrative authenticity (and thus value), Tommo's understanding of the arbitrarily imposed social code of taboo is closely linked to the "primitive" practice of tattooing, a representational form, which is experienced as a threat to Tommo's identity in the novel, ultimately leading to his phobic rejection of the islanders. Like taboo, the practice of tattooing among the islanders becomes the object of extensive commentary by Tommo. Tattooing was part of the exotic content advertised in the first pages ("tattooed chiefs" being one of the attractions), but the practice of permanent adornment through working ink into patterns beneath the skin becomes an overdetermined and conflicted symbol of both the "primitive" and representation in *Typee*.[36]

Early in the narrative, Tommo reports how French efforts to bestow Westernized regal pomp on their chosen "King" and "Queen" of Nukuheva are undermined by tattooing. The King's tattooes, "a broad patch . . . stretch[ing] completely across his face in a line with his eyes, ma[de] him look as if he wore a huge pair of goggles" (1: 7–8). This tattooing matched poorly with the "magnificent military uniform, stiff with gold lace and embroidery" that the French imagined would solemnize their puppet ruler. Even more horrifying to the French in the mocking tale, are the actions of the "Queen," who admires the tattooing of "an old *salt*, whose bare arms and feet, and exposed breast were covered with as many inscriptions in India Ink as the lid of an Egyptian sarcophagus" (1: 8). Not to be outdone by the sailor's display, the "Queen" lifts her skirt to show her tattooed buttocks, leading the colonizing French to flee "the scene of so shocking a catastrophe"(1: 8). Here, tattooing undermines the French attempt to impose European political hierarchies upon the South Seas, yet Tommo consistently ponders the social meanings of tattooing during his stay with the Typees. After describing the tattooing of a Typee in one of his first close examinations of an islander, Tommo asserts: "The warrior, from the excellence of his physical proportions, might certainly have been regarded as one of Nature's noblemen, and the lines drawn upon his face may possibly have denoted his exalted rank" (11: 78). But tattooing can also be merely homely ornamentation for Tommo, its "lines and curves and figures" likened to "the crowded groupings of quaint patterns we sometimes see in costly pieces of lacework" (11: 78). Similarly, the tattooes of Kory-Kory, Tommo's Typee attendant, are seen as "embellishments, . . . perhaps prompted by a desire to add to the engaging expression of his countenance" (11: 83). The ornamental display of tattooing is taken to its fullest form when the artful tattooing of the messenger Marno is described as an aesthetic accomplishment, "executed in conformity with some general design" (18: 136). In much of *Typee*, tattooing is simply a mode of signification that offers an added level of representational meaning to bodies.

Late in the narrative, however, Tommo witnesses the process of tattooing. Initially, just another example of the ethnographic evidence that bolstered the authenticity of the narrative, this encounter opens up to a threat that ultimately leads to Tommo's phobic rejection of Typee culture. The process of tattooing is described as a kind of torture: "I beheld a man extended flat upon his back on the ground, and, despite the forced composure of his countenance, it was evident that he was suffering agony" (30: 217). "His tormentor," the tattooist named Karky, sees Tommo and is "suddenly all eagerness to begin the work" of tattooing him. Tommo discovers that Karky is particularly intent upon tattooing his face, rejecting his offer of his arm for inscribing: "[H]e rejected the compromise indignantly, and still continued his attack on my face, as though nothing short of that would satisfy him" (30: 219). This demand recalls the early warning given by the captain of the *Dolly*, the ship Tommo and his companion Toby abandon for the Marquesan island:

> Plenty of white men have gone ashore here and never been seen anymore. There was the old Dido, she put in here about two years ago, and sent one watch off on liberty; they never were heard of again for a week . . . and only three of them ever got back to the ship again, and one with his face damaged for life, for the cursed heathens tattooed a broad patch clean across his figurehead. (6: 34)

The captain's threat plays upon the fear of being permanently damaged by contact with the Marquesans, and Tommo's reaction to the request that he be tattooed on the face reemphasizes this: "This incident opened my eyes to a new danger; and I now felt convinced that in some luckless hour I should be disfigured in such a manner as never more to have the *face* to return to my countrymen, even should an opportunity offer" (30: 219, *my italics*). Like the captain's threat, Tommo's realization plays upon the disfigurement of facial tattooing on multiple levels: it affects not merely facial appearance, but also one's symbolic "face," the status or prestige one holds in society. Both literally and figuratively, a facial tattoo would transform Tommo. In this way, Tommo's exclamation against Karky's plan resonates on multiple representational registers: "What an object he would have made of me!" (30: 219).

In this context, Tommo's uncertainty in regard to Typee practices becomes not a source of authenticity or authority, but a phobic anxiety.

Tommo imagines Karky plotting "a conspiracy against me and my countenance" (30: 219) that is taken up by the Typee leadership: "nothing but the
utter ruin of my 'face divine,' as the poets call it, would, I perceived, satisfy
the inexorable Mehevi and his chiefs" (30: 220). The demand that he be tattooed transforms Tommo's experience of life with the Typees. Early in his
stay, Tommo had highlighted the difference between the Marquesas and
the United States:

> There were none of those thousand sources of irritation that the ingenuity of
> civilized man has created to mar his own felicity. There were no foreclosures of
> mortgages, no protested notes, no bills payable, no debts of honor in Typee; no
> unreasonable tailors and shoemakers, perversely bent on being paid; no duns of
> any descriptions; . . . or to sum up all in one word—no Money! That "root of
> all evil" was not to be found in the valley. (17: 126)

If Tommo's idyll in the Marquesas is initially associated with its precapitalist freedom from the dunning demands of exchange, the threat of tattooing reveals the similarities between "primitive" and "civilized" life:
"Hardly a day passed but I was subjected to their annoying requests [to be
tattooed], until at last my existence became a burden to me; the pleasures
I had previously enjoyed no longer afforded me delight, and all my former
desire to escape from the valley now revived with additional force"
(30:220). Although the Typee valley may have been free of money, Tommo
discovers that Typee life is hardly free from demanding exchanges. Tommo
comes to recognize that it is his "face," his identity, that is the medium for
exchange, with tattooing as his initiation into Typee religion and life: "A
fact which I soon afterward learned augmented my apprehension. The
whole system of tattooing was, I found, connected with their religion; and
it was evident, therefore, that they were resolved to make a convert of me"
(30:220). Speculating on the nature of the tattooing designs, Tommo
admits, "Although convinced that tattooing was a religious observance,
still the nature of the connection between it and the superstitious idolatry
of the people was a point upon which I could never obtain any information.
Like the still more important system of the 'Taboo,' it always appeared
inexplicable to me" (30: 220–21). In the context of tattooing as a "conspiracy" against Tommo's control over his identity, its association with taboo
transforms the Typee valley from an Eden of innocent freedom into a rigid,
even tyrannical, but inexplicable system:

> Situated as I was in the Typee valley, I perceived every hour the effects of this
> all-controlling power, without in the least comprehending it. Those effects

were, indeed, wide-spread and universal, pervading the most important as well as the minutest transactions of life. The savage, in short, lives in the continual observance of its dictates, which guide and control every action of his being. (30: 221)

Over the course of the narrative, taboo and tattooing are transformed from mysterious, but authenticating information on a liberating primitive culture into signs of the arbitrary, but inscriptive structures that fix the identity of the islanders (and any who might join them).

Reactions to Melville's understandings of the Typee culture from modern ethnographers on Marquesan culture, whether on tattooing or taboo, have ranged from bemusement to dismay.[37] Melville's interest in tattooing and the evident falsity of his description of its cultural meanings have led a number of literary scholars to read tattooing's metaphoric and symbolic resonances as a commentary on the "scene of writing," a statement about Melville's attitude toward his own literary practice. Throughout *Typee*, tattooing is a system of inscription and signification; the tattooed body becomes a text, replete with meanings. Tattooing is likened to writing, whether as "inscriptions in India Ink" or "hieroglyphics" (1: 8), or art, with Karky ironically termed "A Professor of the Fine Arts" (30: 217) who turns his "painter's enthusiasm" upon "the human canvas before him" (30: 219, 218). For Mitchell Breitweiser, tattooing shows Melville the limitations of authorship, "that the writer may be written upon," reversing the authority of the writer to "impos[e] . . . a shaping will onto the lives of others. . . ."[38] For Elizabeth Renker, *Typee*'s anxieties about its narrator being tattooed comments on Melville's own anxieties about his vocational identity as author and the threat of being discovered at being nothing more than a copyist, due to his extensive dependence on others' texts.[39] Both Renker and Breitweiser's readings of tattooing in *Typee* suggest that Melville understood that writing both enabled authority and threatened one's self by making it an object of exchange. For both Renker and Breitweiser, the process of tattooing is symbolic of the tension between empowerment and disempowerment in writing. Rather than seeing this as simply about the trials and tribulations of Melville's personal experience of authorship, however, we can also see it as a commentary on how writing, albeit admittedly Melville's personal experience of it, fits into the larger system of exchange within the culture.

Tattooing is, above all, a reification ("what an object he would have made of me!"), transforming the self into an object of exchange, a commodity. Likening writing to tattooing as a reifying form of labor or production connects

Melville to the Marxist critique of labor under capitalism. Georg Lukács describes the experience of the laborer under capitalism in the following manner: "*Subjectively*—where the market economy has been fully developed—a man's activity becomes estranged from himself, it turns into a commodity which, subject to the non-human objectivity of the natural laws of society, must go its own way independently of man just like any consumer article."[40] The effect of this alienation of labor under capitalism is not simply to reify the product of labor, but also to reify the producer. Learning to see the product of their labor as a commodity, workers under capitalism come also to see themselves as commodities, as objects that they themselves offer up for sale, as Marx explains: "The *free labourer* . . . sells himself and, indeed, sells himself piecemeal."[41]

This process of reification was becoming dramatically evident for manual laborers in antebellum cities of the North, especially in New York City, where manufacturing became increasingly specialized, depending upon subdividing and putting-out work in a fashion that dramatically altered traditional artisan labor forms, producing what has been called "proto-industrial" laboring conditions.[42] While taking a different form, a similar implication in the reifying logic of capitalist exchange was enacted for the new middle class of the Northern city. Increasingly separated from any act of production, the labor of these nonmanual workers—not simply the entry-level clerks and salesmen but also a whole range of the new professions—was oriented toward the more symbolic work of "management," directing the labor of others, and "marketing," the selling of products and services.[43] In his influential study *White Collar*, C. Wright Mills describes the effect of a "marketing mentality" on the nature of middle-class work. Dematerializing the act of production, middle-class labor depends upon the worker's ability to embody personally the desirable traits of the market. This reification of the marketing self transforms the field of middle-class labor into a "personality market": "Whenever there is a transfer of control over one individual's personal traits to another for a price, a sale of those traits which affect one's impressions upon others, a personality market arises."[44] If the manual laborer is reduced to the reified labor task or product produced under capitalism, for Mills it is the personality of the nonmanual laborer that is reified, offered up for marketing and sale: the "personal and even intimate traits of the employee are drawn into the sphere of exchange and become of commercial relevance, become commodities in the labor market."[45] As author–subject of his narrative, Melville is forced to market his experiences and his personality, to put himself up quite literally as a commodity. Tommo's phobic narration of the threat of being tattooed ("What an object he would have made of me!") could be read as a rejection of precisely that association with a middle-class commodification of self and Melville's implication in this process through the writing of his narrative. *Typee*'s depiction of the meaning of tattooing, hardly accurate as representations of Marquesan practices, could be said to reflect Melville's discomfort with his own effort to "market" his life story and his body itself to secure capital in the exchange economy of antebellum capitalism.

Yet, if we want to see Tommo's fear of being tattooed paralleling Melville's feelings about writing *Typee*, Tommo's resistance to the Typees' proffered initiation stands in stark contrast to Melville's own initiation into publishing practices. This was clear from his additions to the narrative after the Harper rejection but also in his response to the controversy generated by the first American edition of *Typee*. When his American publisher John Wiley pushed for changes in *Typee* after the first edition's sexual content and critique of missionaries created a scandal, Melville famously agreed, justifying expurgation on the grounds that his narrative was written to maximize sales, as he explained to John Murray, his British publisher: "The book is certainly calculated for popular reading, or for none at all. If the first, why then, all passages which are calculated to offend the tastes, or offer violance [*sic*] to the feelings of any large class of readers are certainly objectionable."[46] Although Melville understood that to benefit from writing, *Typee* had to be "calculated for popular reading, or for none at all," his response to the threat of being written upon by the Typees reveals his understanding of the threat to his identity engendered by writing the book. In fact, contrary to Melville's acceptance of his publisher's demands, *Typee* is a narrative that can only reject: Tommo rejects both life at sea and life with the Typees, both the rules of civilization that bind his actions aboard ship and the code of taboo that governs the islanders' lives. Although Melville can generate positive endorsements of the serenity of Typee life in the novel, they are countered by his narrator's "shudderings" and Tommo's final blow against the Typee chief, Mow-Mow: "it was no time for pity or compunction, and with a true aim, and exerting all my strength, I dashed the boat hook at him" (34: 252). Although there is a consistent effort to translate the Marquesan experience into some form of coherent narrative, *Typee*'s energies are again and again expressed through the violent rejections, denials, and negations of Tommo's reactions, rather than any acceptance of a mode of living or exchange. These consistent rejections on Tommo's part are directly opposed to Melville's acquiescences to market and editorial demands.

In this way, *Typee* may have been written for the marketplace, but it was also written *about* the marketplace. Although Melville's first narrative was written for the purpose of satisfying a perceived community of readers, the energies of rejection and the anxieties about entering into a system of exchange are bound into the text. As a narrative, *Typee* marks lines of inquiry and critical energy that are representational not only of Melville's life among the "cannibals," but also of the new market culture of the antebellum Northern city. *Typee* ultimately fulfilled its hoped-for role, establishing a place for Melville within the antebellum economy, but perhaps it did so not simply because his experiences were so "exotic" or "foreign," but rather because, in their essence, Tommo's experiences in the Marquesas reflected the problematic choices Melville's readers, the antebellum middle class, themselves were required to make in their new lives in the capitalizing, industrializing northern cities. In the next section, I explore how Melville fared as the commodified object of his narrative in the literary marketplace, tracing his sudden fame as a literary "celebrity" and the role of the new phenomenon of celebrity in antebellum culture. Just as with my reading of *Typee*, I argue that Melville's engagement with his new place in American culture post-*Typee* reflects the ambivalent middle-class response to the spread of capitalist exchange in American life.

Typee, *Author of* Typee: *Celebrity and the Inscriptive Exchanges of the Marketplace*

Typee was a gratifying success for Melville. Though certainly not a "bestseller," *Typee* was widely and well reviewed, except when the sexual content and commentary on missions garnered critiques from newspapers or magazines that espoused conservative stances or were associated with Protestant denominations tied to missionary activities. Read as both light entertainment and serious ethnographic source, *Typee* was the book of the moment in 1846.[47] On the basis of his success in *Typee*, rapidly followed by its successor *Omoo* (1847), Melville became a notable figure on the American literary scene. In 1849, Nathaniel Parker Willis would place Melville prominently within a movement that represented what he described as a "change in authorship" in American letters: one in which writers no longer depended upon literary artifice, but simply performed themselves. Willis saw this new mode of authorship as a "democratic" turn as it meant that men (it is notable that this vision of authorship was distinctly male), whose stories once entertained only a circle of acquaintance, now could entertain all. But the effect of this transformation that Willis applauds is that writing is understood as simply a publication of the self.

> Conversational literature, or books written as agreeable people talk, is the present fashion with authors and passion with readers. Herman Melville, with his cigars and his Spanish eyes, *talks Typee* and *Omoo*, just as you find the flow of his delightful mind on paper. Those who have only read his books know the man—those who have only seen the man have a fair idea of his books.[48]

Thus, for Willis, Melville "*talks*" his travel adventures, and the books are transparent reflections of his identity, available to any reader: "Those who have only read his books know the man. . . ." In this way, Melville came to exemplify for many the new cultural form of the literary celebrity in antebellum America.

The celebrity, the public figure Daniel Boorstin circularly defined as being "known for his [or her] well-knowness," has been seen as a uniquely modern or even postmodern construction.[49] But the forms of the culture of celebrity made their first appearance in American life in the late 1840s and early 1850s and can be understood as a distinctly cultural response to the spread of an urban industrial capitalist exchange system.[50] As the capitalist market penetrated work and living conditions and a large-scale urban experience replaced the "walking city" and its "close-knit culture of face-to-face relations," antebellum Americans struggled to understand their place within an increasingly alienating public life.[51] In place of the rituals and commitments of extended family and community of village life, antebellum urbanites turned to commercialized entertainment in their leisure time. These increasingly isolated urban individuals sought replacements for affective bonds lost in the economic and social transformations of the period through the culture of celebrity, where the bond between the artist or cultural producer as "celebrity" and consumer as "fan" constituted what Leo Braudy has called "a new psychic connection."[52] What Thomas N. Baker calls "the dream-work of celebrity" offered an imagined compensation for whatever dissatisfactions were generated by the new social formations of antebellum life.[53]

Given the new importance that print had in the newly industrializing entertainment industry of antebellum American life, it should not be surprising that authors became some of the most important celebrities of the period.

With their books as a notable presence in the solitary moments of their audiences' lives, the private lives and personalities of antebellum authors came to be seen as a "natural" object of curiosity. An 1842 article for *The Knickerbocker Magazine* by Caroline Kirkland describes the inevitable interest antebellum readers had in writers' lives: "Nothing can be more natural than the desire to enjoy the society of authors whose writings have pleased us."[54] Charles Briggs, writing in the *Broadway Journal*, would mock this "natural" desire of readers to have contact with authors:

> No person of proper feeling can peruse the works of a distinguished author or authoress . . . , without an instantaneous desire to make his (or her) personal acquaintance. . . . [A]s a general rule, we are always inquisitive about the physical appearance of a celebrated author; and it is but a corollary from this proposition, that if we are prevented by unhappy circumstances, from beholding the author himself, we still entertain a longing to see his portrait. If we cannot see this, we get his autograph if possible—but if this again is not to be discovered, we then regard ourselves as unfortunate beings and subject to an especial dispensation on the part of Providence.[55]

To be denied access to an author, whether in actual sighting, portrait, or autograph is satirized as a tragedy, reflecting writers' perceptions of the demands of the antebellum readership.

Offering a commodified affective compensation to new urban cultural consumers, this culture of celebrity also bestowed new authority and higher social status upon artists, writers, and performers who could be made into celebrities. In antebellum America, celebrity was understood as a social distinction, used, as cultural historian Peter Buckley explains, "as a conscious opposition, or at least distinction, to people of aristocratic status or mere notoriety."[56] In this sense, the period's celebrity was famous for having done something, having achieved prominence for an accomplishment: celebrity was a meritocratic distinction that could be used to justify bourgeois social insurgency. In his book *English Traits*, Ralph Waldo Emerson would critique the English aristocracy for making "A man of wit, *who is also of the celebrities of wealth and fashion*" feel "that he could not enter [aristocratic] houses without being made to feel that they were great lords, and he a low plebian."[57] Emerson would extend this critique to English aristocratic attitudes toward *artistes*: "When Julia Grisi and Mario sang at the houses of the Duke of Wellington and other grandees, a cord was stretched between the singer and the company."[58] For Emerson, the English aristocrats made artificial and specious social distinctions between their own prominence, merely the result of inherited status, and "celebrities," whose prominence was tied to their skills or accomplishments. In this way, the culture of celebrity legitimated the new prominence of middle-class artists, writers, and performers.

In fact, it could be argued that the bond between the fan and the celebrity could only exist because there was no aristocratic "cord" stretched between performer and audience. The notable celebrities of antebellum America were typically seen as supportive or kindred spirits of their predominantly middle-class audience. This includes the Norwegian singer Jenny Lind, who experienced unprecedented success in her tour of the States at the beginning of the 1850s, the product of P. T. Barnum's tireless promotion of her as "private" and "domestic" along with her carefully planned "artless" performances of folk songs and opera arias, and Emerson himself, who would achieve celebrity status as "America's philosopher" in the 1850s on the national lecture circuit when his idealistic self-reliance became associated with a kind of entrepreneurial individualism.[59] The connection between cultural producer as celebrity and reader–listener as fan would be a lucrative one for the new antebellum celebrity, offering the possibilities of substantial profit to a range of middle-class artists and intellectuals for the first time in American life.

Despite the economic and social rewards of the culture of celebrity, middle-class cultural producers quickly came to recognize the threats involved in their implication in this cultural exchange. The deeply personal nature of the bond between fan and celebrity encouraged interest in the private lives of celebrities. N. P. Willis, another of the period's great celebrities, would describe this problem:

> The price of more admiration from the world than falls ordinarily to one person's lot, has, by immemorial usage, included one inconvenience—a forfeiture of privacy as to conduct, and a subjection to public criticism as to manners, habits, and personal appearance. Authors, artists, orators, and men high in office, must stop at the very threshold of Fame, and take leave of privacy of heart and home.[60]

Willis situates the consequences of "Fame" as an "immemorial" threat, but his commodified metaphor ("The price of . . . admiration") draws attention to the newly mercantile form of the celebrity's prominence, with its association of exchange both in profitable benefits but also the personal costs of alienation. If celebrity offered profit and social prominence to middle-class artists and cultural producers, this explicitly came at the cost of "privacy" and "home," a trait and place commonly held to be crucial to the formation of a middle-class identity in nineteenth-century America.[61] While the middle-class "cult of domesticity" insisted upon the private "sanctity" of women's lives in the period, even middle-class men were encouraged to find satisfaction at home, as Stuart Blumin suggests: "[I]t is clear that the home . . . was becoming the most characteristic and significant meeting place for middling folk. . . ."[62] In this way, celebrities, while meant to represent the middle class, also transgressed against its own valorization of privacy.

The result of this was a deeply ambivalent social relationship for both celebrities and fans. Celebrities, while desiring the new income that their public prominence produced, frequently expressed deep concerns about their public roles and the demands of their audiences. Seemingly innocent, the celebrity–fan relationship was also tinged with the threat of the fan's demands, which oversteps all social conventions in its prying interest in the celebrity's life. As Caroline Kirkland suggests, the condition of literary celebrity was premised on an unnaturally intimate relationship:

> We love the intelligent and suggestive companion of our quiet hours. We rank him among our benefactors, and we long for a nearer acquaintance. His person, his voice, his every-day habits and ordinary sentiments acquire a certain kind of importance, and for this reason those biographies which let us most completely into these minutiae have ever been esteemed the most precious. . . . [The reader] seeks the writer with a feeling of ready-made intimacy; he is a friend before he is an acquaintance; and he goes, with his heart in his hand, to find another heart which he knows to be congenial.[63]

The "importance" of the author as a "companion of our quiet hours" speaks to the celebrity's surrogate role, replacing lost affective bonds with "ready-made intimacy." But this "ready-made intimacy" transgresses against normal social relationships: the author is "a friend before he is an acquaintance." The eager reader "long[s] for a nearer acquaintance" and eagerly searches for information about the "minutiae" of the author's life, turning the author into the object of potentially painful public scrutiny.

As a result, the benefits of fame were very much offset by their drawbacks for many celebrities in the period. Michael Newbury argues that it was the negative elements that defined celebrity for authors in the period: "The celebrity was defined not by the audience's desire for his or her cultural productions or by the possibility of economically profitable exchange between the celebrity and audience but, rather by the audience's irrational drive to see, touch, hold, possess, and consume the celebrity body itself."[64] This ambivalence, however, cut both ways. Fans, while craving the new, more personal connection with artists and writers, often pondered the legitimacy of the celebrity's prominence and questioned whether or not the celebrity was simply a kind of "humbug." Did the celebrity honestly step forward for the public benefit, or was the celebrity simply driven by a desire for notoriety? Accusations would follow a range of antebellum celebrities, from the reformer Fanny Wright to Willis. The contradictions at the heart of this culture of celebrity, deeply enmeshed in middle-class interests and values, reflected a fascination with *and* an anxiety about exchange that, in turn, reflected the ambivalence of the middle-class adjustment to urban industrial capitalism.

Evidence suggests that Melville was aware of some of these complicated consequences of authorship and its implication in cultural exchanges of celebrity as he wrote *Typee*. Well into *Typee*, the narrator describes his encounter with an "old chief" from Maui who touts his participation in the cannibalistic consumption of Captain Cook. More than just an ironic sidenote, the anecdote of Cook and cannibalism in *Typee* can be read as a commentary on a number of processes of cultural production central to Melville's own experience of writing in the antebellum era:

> A few years since there was living on the island of Mowee . . . an old chief who, actuated by a morbid desire for notoriety, gave himself out among the foreign residents of the place as the living tomb of Captain Cook's big toe!—affirming, that at the cannibal entertainment which ensued after the lamented Briton's death, that particular portion of his body had fallen to his share. . . . The result was the making of his fortune; ever afterwards he was in the habit of giving very profitable audience to all curious travelers who were desirous of beholding the man who had eaten the great navigator's great toe. (32: 234)

The chief's marketing of his own cannibal celebrity reflects the changes brought upon South Seas culture by the arrival of Europeans and the capitalist exchange of the market. Where once cannibalism had been a ritual element of Hawaiian religion and culture, especially given the complications of Cook's semidivine status, it is now transformed into a marketable narrative, something to trade with the tourists.[65] Under the pressure of the marketplace, the meaning of the chief's life has been reduced to his status as "the man who had eaten the great navigator's great toe."

It is no small coincidence that when Melville would comment on his literary career and the lingering effects of his authorship of *Typee* in a famous 1851 letter to Hawthorne, he would complain that his "reputation" had been fixed forever as "a 'man who lived among cannibals.'" Like "the man who had eaten the great navigator's great toe," in *Typee*, Melville had willingly offered himself up as "a 'man who lived among cannibals,'" providing himself with some measure of literary success—"the making of his fortune"—but not without long-term consequences, consequences that his telling of the Hawaiian chief's story suggest he was aware of as he wrote his first narrative. Certainly, Melville would quickly experience the benefits and the constraining personal costs of his own literary celebrity after the publication of *Typee*. Although this passage does not mean that Melville predicted his own literary success, it does suggest that, even while writing *Typee*, he might have understood the consequences of his authorship.

Given the widespread attention to his first book and the controversy over the factuality of his adventures within it, it is not surprising that Melville became a celebrity. Responding to a request for an autograph from a correspondent, Melville presented himself like Byron, suddenly cast out of his conventional life by his literary production: "You remember someone woke one morning and found himself famous.—And here I am, just come from hoeing in the garden, writing autographs."[66] While some fans solicited autographs, Ellen Astor Oxenham, an Englishwoman in New York City and a passing acquaintance of Melville's sister, wrote feverishly requesting far greater intimacy with Melville as "Tommo" or "Typee":

> Why don't you live in New York & then I could see your bright eyes, & mayhap a small ray of Typeeian felicity might fall on me from Tommo's. . . .
>   Mr. [Fitz-Greene] Halleck says he knows your brother Mr. Allan Melville but I think he said he had not the pleasure of knowing Typee of pleasant memory. . . —you know I long to see you & Typee. . . . Typee, you dear creature, I want to see you amazingly.[67]

Here, Herman Melville as "Tommo/Typee" functions as an object of antebellum sexual fantasy, an embodiment of primitive, unrepressed sexual fulfillment. For this Miss Oxenham, as for some other antebellum fans, merely reading the book was not enough: "Typee, you dear creature, I want to see you amazingly." Throughout his adult life, Melville would be associated with Typee, with many people, whether close acquaintances or total strangers, hailing him interchangeably by the name of his book, "Typee," or the book's narrative persona, "Tommo."

Even Melville's 1847 wedding would be affected by his literary celebrity and its transformation of him into a notable exotic. The threat of public attention forced him and his fiancée, Elizabeth Shaw, to opt for a private ceremony when planning their wedding in the fall of 1847. She described the decision in a letter:

At first I had some idea of being married in church . . . but we all thought if it were to get about previously that "Typee" was to be seen on such a day, a great crowd might rush out of mere curiosity to see "the author" who would have no personal interest in us whatsoever . . . —So I determined to have it in the house, as privately as possible. . . .[68]

The alienating effect of Melville's celebrity is such that even his fiancée can name him alternately by his book ("Typee") or his vocational identity ("the author").

As the Oxenham letter suggests, Melville's celebrity was very much linked to publicity over his narrative's sexual content, with the press consistently invoking his "sexual history" with the island maiden Fayaway. After his wedding, the *Daily Tribune* reported: "BREACH OF PROMISE SUIT EXPECTED. —MR. HERMAN TYPEE OMOO MELVILLE has recently been united in lawful wedlock to a young lady of Boston. The fair forsaken FAYAWAY will doubtless console herself by suing him for breach of promise."[69] Melville's association with *Typee* and his (surmised) sexual experiences on the Marquesas would continue to shape response to him. When Nathaniel Hawthorne's wife Sophia met Melville for the first time in 1850, she wrote her sister: "Mr. Typee is interesting in his aspect—quite. I see Fayaway in his face."[70] Producing *Typee* converted Melville into "Mr. Typee" and transformed his "aspect" into a text of his sexual history: fulfilling the very concern that Tommo expressed about tattooing, "What an object he would have made of me!" Melville's early experience as celebrity–author is an object lesson in the simultaneously rewarding and damaging exchanges at the heart of the cultural marketplace of antebellum America.

This lesson was one that Melville would take to heart, as his writings in the immediate aftermath of *Typee* show him exploring the larger social and political ramifications of the rise of a culture of celebrity and its commodification of American public life. During the summer of 1847, Melville tried his hand at some satirical writing for the new magazine, *Yankee Doodle*. Edited by Evert Duyckinck's closest friend, Cornelius Mathews, *Yankee Doodle* aimed to be an American *Punch*, but failed within a few months. In the midst of his impending wedding and increasing celebrity, Melville wrote a series of humorous sketches on General Zachary Taylor and the Mexican War. Melville's nine "Authentic Anecdotes of 'Old Zack,'" published between July 24 and September 11, 1847, are basically ephemeral, spur-of-the-moment topical satires to which little critical attention has been paid.[71] But what is most striking about the "Anecdotes" is that Melville seems not as much interested in satirizing the Mexican War, an imperialist land-grab for which he had little sympathy, as in commenting on the processes of promotion, marketing, and celebrity that dominated the American nation's experience of the war and of Taylor, that war's chief officer.

Introducing the series, Melville offers that "a few authentic anecdotes may not be unacceptable to [*Yankee Doodle*'s] numerous readers" given that, "At the present time . . . everything connected with the homespun old hero [Taylor] is perused with unusual interest, and unprincipled paragraphists daily perpetrate the most absurd stories wherewith to titilate public curiosity concerning him. . . ."[72] If *Typee* was seriously engaged in marketing authenticity and generating profit from "public curiosity," the 1847 "Anecdotes" spoofed those same processes. Introducing the series, Melville produces a fake authenticating certificate, which (mocking the jingoism of the national war mood) was "placed in a brass frame cast from a captured Mexican forty-two brass shot," prominently displayed at the *Yankee Doodle* office, "where it may be seen from 9 A.M. till 3¾ P.M. every day, Sundays excepted."[73] This certificate asserted "our columns to be the only true source where an anxious public can procure a correct insight into his private life and little personal peculiarities."[74] In a comical antithesis to *Typee*, the "Anecdotes" mocks the litigious atmosphere that encouraged his publishers to demand further authenticating documents of Melville's presence in the Marquesas and led him to write his carefully worded avowals and disavowals of authority throughout *Typee*. In these anecdotes, Melville belittles the antebellum interest in "private life and little personal peculiarities," satirizing the construction of celebrity as a democratic right of the Jacksonian "anxious public."

If Barnum was a hidden influence in *Typee*, in the "Anecdotes" he becomes the writer's obvious competitor and kindred spirit. At one point, Barnum is reported dropping by the *Yankee Doodle* offices and getting ideas for jingoistic displays at his American Museum. In another anecdote, Melville sends a "draught of a placard" for a display of a torn pair of Zack's pants to Barnum:

PRODIGIOUS EXCITEMENT!!!!!!
OLD ZACK'S PANTS!!!
GREAT SIGHTS AT THE AMERICAN MUSEUM!!!
OLD ROUGH AND READY!
UP TOWN EMPTIED OF ITS INHABITANTS!
TOM THUMB FLOORED![75]

In yet another anecdote, Barnum seeks to hire Taylor as an exhibit for his Museum. Invoking Tom Thumb's fake status as "General," the satire points out that Barnum "had already possession of one General and hoped soon to get another. . . ."[76] Melville includes a letter of solicitation from a representative of Barnum, encouraging Taylor to take up residence at the Museum: "Think General, of yourself reclining on the poop of the Chinese Junk [another of Barnum's famous exhibits of the period], receiving visits of your friends; adopt this course and you must be elected president; reject it and perhaps—but I forbear to press this matter."[77] Taylor would indeed become the next president, cynically nominated by the Whig Party after winning a popular war that the Whigs had not even supported, but Melville's satire plays on the politics of celebrity and the ways in which an acquiescence to the demands of the market was seamlessly integrated into democratic political and social ideals: "You will be associated with all that is curious in nature and art, . . . and more than all you will gratify the lawful desires and advance the happiness of myriads of your countrymen and countrywomen. Can a philanthropist doubt? No, my dear General! I wait with confidence your determination."[78] The Barnumian sales pitch transforms the possibility of Taylor's exhibiting himself as a "freak" exhibit into a philanthropic service. Under the new logic of the market, the celebrity's "gratify[ing] of lawful desires" becomes the best way to serve the public as well as the only way to public prominence.

Both *Typee* and the "Anecdotes" demonstrate Melville's understanding of the new culture of the market and of celebrity in the antebellum urban economy as a kind of freakish self-exposure.[79] By associating public figures with freaks, Melville comments on the market and capitalist exchange. But, despite its association with freakish self-display, celebrity allowed middle-class individuals like Melville to take a significant place in the market culture, to profit from their own commodification. In *Typee*, Melville shows his awareness of writing as an entry into the market-exchange economy through his careful managing of demands for narrative authority, while also signaling his anxieties about the inscriptive demands placed upon one's identity within that system through his narrative's negations. In the "Anecdotes," Melville was able to make this critical consciousness more overt, demonstrating the ways in which market logic penetrated and weakened American political and social ideals, turning our highest elected office into the equivalence of a freak-show exhibit. And yet the new cultures of the market and celebrity were more democratic, creating a more prominent place in the national public life for middle-class Americans and their values, allowing opportunities that benefited

Melville himself. Marked by a radical ambivalence, Melville's earliest writings show a profound meditation on the consequences of the capitalist reorganization of American public life and the complex adjustments that the members of the middle class made to see themselves both as prominent within and critical observers from without the new market culture.

As Melville's early writing suggests, the antebellum urban middle class viewed this new market culture with decidedly mixed feelings. This new culture may have validated middle-class values, but it also put them "on the market," subject to economic and social forces that were very much out of their control. As a result, members of this new middle class would begin to seek new ways to carve out a more secure place within the American urban economy and social hierarchy. Constructing new public roles for themselves and new legitimating discourses of social authority, the upper end of the antebellum middle class began to articulate a new vocational discourse of professionalism, emphasizing specialization and autonomy to counter their implication in the market logic. Melville would also participate in this process, seeking to transform his status as a writer from "a 'man who lived with cannibals'" into what was for antebellum America a new construct: the serious and ambitious literary professional. Next, I explore how Melville's 1849 novel *Mardi* reflects and comments upon the antebellum middle-class articulation of a discourse of professionalism.

CHAPTER TWO

"Every One to His Trade"

Mardi, Literary Form, and Professional Ideology

In 1847, as part of a series on "Copyright, Authors and Authorship," Grace Greenwood published a satire on Herman Melville, after his success with *Typee* and *Omoo.* This satire hints at some of the pressures at work in defining authorship in antebellum America. Mocking Melville's "impromptu" forays into authorship, Greenwood questions his right to comment on literary matters, despite the commercial success of his first works.

> My own authorship was an impromptu affair, and as far as my experience goes, I have nothing about which to complain; my book having met with a sale beyond my expectations. But it is my *belief* that *Poets* are not properly esteemed and recompensed in our country . . . in this connection, I will give a brief account of how they manage these matters in Typee. . . .
>
> One afternoon, while stretched upon the mats, taking my luxurious *siesta*, Kory-Kory ran in, shouting, "Clingy Lingy," (the poet's name,) "makee rimee!" and hoisting me on his back, trotted up to the "charmed circle," who were listening to the wild chantings of our Improvisatore. . . .[1]

In fact, Melville did not substantially address the copyright issue at any point in his career, despite his personal connection to Evert Duyckinck and other members of the "Young America" literary coterie who made copyright a central issue in their push to elevate the status of American literature. However, by the time of the publication of Greenwood's satire—whether or not Melville had actually read it—he had begun to write his ambitious third book, *Mardi*

(1849), which implicitly seemed to respond to Greenwood's criticism of the limitations of his authority. Melville would explain to his skeptical British editor John Murray that *Mardi* was intended as a distinct departure from his fact-based narratives and thus should be understood "as a literary acheivement [*sic*], & so essentially different from those two [earlier] books."[2] The production of *Mardi* has long been understood as a pivotal episode in Herman Melville's literary career, signaling his commitment to pursue authorship as a profession. The novel's sprawling, digressive, and fragmentary form that would doom it commercially and critically is, I will argue, derived from Melville's investment in a professional vision of authorship and demonstrates how the idea of professional authorship underwent changes in this period.

William Charvat's *The Profession of Authorship in America, 1800–1870* (1968) helped institute professionalism as an important category in the study of antebellum authorship. Charvat's definition of literary professionalism as the economic negotiations of the American author, seeking to achieve self-sufficiency through writing within the often-threatening confines of the literary marketplace, dominates critical work on the subject.[3] As Greenwood's satire of Melville suggests, however, that professional status in the antebellum literary field was not defined solely by sales, but also by a symbolic economy determined by the practitioners' own efforts to define literary skill, knowledge, and authority, definitions that were shifting as Melville wrote.

In balancing specialized skills, cultural authority, and the demands of the marketplace, antebellum literary professionalism mirrored the emergence of a new concept of professionalism generally, one which encompassed a range of vocations from doctors, lawyers, and ministers to teachers, engineers, and businessmen. Professional standing in the United States had once been the exclusive domain of traditional urban elites, who depended upon patronage within the small, wealthy communities of American cities; in the antebellum era, however, the swelling urban population led to an increased market for professional services at the same time that populist politics led to new demands for democratization of professional privilege. These challenges to older professional forms led to a new market-oriented professionalism that became associated with the antebellum urban middle class, whose members used this new authority to stabilize and legitimate their place in a new industrializing economy. With its focus on Melville's professionalization, *Mardi* allows us to chart not only some of the shifts in antebellum understandings of authorship, but also the ideological shifts and contradictions at the heart of the formation of American middle-class identity in Northern cities.

The new market culture of the urbanizing and industrializing cities of the antebellum North led to a collision between older notions of elite professional authority and a new middle-class market professional identity, especially in New York City, which became the largest city and the dominant center of U.S. trade during the antebellum period. Following this trend, New York City became the first national center of publishing, taking advantage of its emerging trade dominance to supplant the traditional regionalism of the American book trade.[4] Melville's decision to move to New York City while writing *Mardi* clearly reflected its prominence as the new American literary capital, and he joined an unprecedented number of authors in a substantial New York City literary community. Critical understandings of this community have been largely shaped by Perry Miller's *The Raven and the Whale* (1956), which depicted a literary landscape dominated by the divide between the genteel and Whiggish *Knickerbocker* and the market-oriented and nationalistic Democratic "Young Americans."[5] But Miller's politicized split of antebellum New York City authorship ignores a range of writers who came to New York City to pursue professional careers as authors. The antebellum New York City literary community revealed a remarkable range of vocational identities available to writers during the period. In the mid-1840s, Washington Irving continued in his Knickerbocker mode, writing from the pose of a gentleman idler and depending in part on the patronage of John Jacob Astor, while, at the same time, writers such as the sensationalist city-profiler George Foster and the transplanted Transcendentalist Margaret Fuller, both working for Horace Greeley's *Tribune*, understood their literary efforts as tied to their status as "employees."[6] Thus, just as the new commercial possibilities of the antebellum urban marketplace put pressure on understandings of the traditional professions, they also affected notions of authorship, which were now expanding across an ideological spectrum from residually aristocratic to emergent market to corporate professional.[7] We can read the work of antebellum New York City literary professionals and the ways they understood their labor as participation in the ideological debate over the form of professional identity in the new economy.

This complicated context is reflected in *Mardi*. Over the two years Melville invested in writing it, the sprawling novel variously took the shape of at least three distinct literary genres: romance, allegorical travelogue–satire, and self-reflective symbolic meditations on aesthetic practice. Critical attention to the novel once focused primarily on dating and tracing these shifts in the narrative.[8] Since the 1950s, however, the most important critical readings of *Mardi* have tended to emphasize one certain textual form for the novel. The influential readings by Richard Brodhead and Charles Feidelson, for example, focus on the novel's symbolism, and more recent work by Cindy Weinstein and Wai Chee Dimock emphasizes the allegorical nature of the novel.[9] Rather than identifying any one form as dominant, I will argue that *Mardi*'s disjunctive combination of a variety of narrative forms reflects the wide range of models of authorship available in New York City, with Melville shifting from the genteel Knickerbocker persona, to the more ambitious reformist professional, and finally to the specialized professional artist. But if these elements of *Mardi* seem disparate and incongruous, they point to more than just divisions in the New York literary community. By reflecting Melville's evolving notion of what constitutes the proper narrative form and content for professional literary work, *Mardi* also comments on key problems in middle-class vocational identity in the antebellum era, such as the limited effectiveness of gentility in a market society and the conflicting impulses to reform and specialize in the middle-class search for legitimacy and authority. *Mardi*'s disjunctions document the conflicting impulses of the antebellum professional middle class in its attempt to define its place and status in mid-nineteenth-century American life.

Mardi *and Romance: Knickerbocker Authorship and the Authoritative Amateur*

Greenwood's satire reminds us of Melville's dominant contemporary literary reputation as a recorder of exotic facts in *Typee* and *Omoo*. To prove himself among his literary peers, Melville needed to produce a work that would demonstrate his artistry and ambition. Although Perry Miller's study and others situating Melville in New York City link him to the Young America literary movement, the early section of *Mardi*, his first novel with explicitly professional intentions, would show a surprising investment in the antithesis of the Young American ethos: Knickerbocker authorship. As Evert Duyckinck, the architect of the Young America literary platform, wrote in his diary on July 31, 1847, after meeting with Melville at the time *Mardi* was getting under way, "Dined with Herman Melville at the Astor House. He is to be married next Wednesday. He is cheerful company without being very [illegible] or original and models his writing evidently a great deal on

Washington Irving."[10] Irving's pseudoaristocratic, reverie-oriented sensibility narrative persona, in fact, dominates the first third of *Mardi*.[11] Melville gradually revealed his intention to write Irving-inflected fiction to Murray, his censorious editor, shifting his description of *Mardi* in the winter of 1848 from a possibly factual narrative that "combines in one cluster all that is romantic, whimsical & poetic in Polynisia," to an overtly fictional narrative, a "Romance of Polynisian Adventure," by that spring.[12] Melville's investment in the Irvingesque Knickerbocker mode of romance in *Mardi* is directly tied to his commitment to authorship as a profession and to his search for a legitimating authorial persona.[13]

Irving was at the center of early nineteenth-century literary life in New York City, both as the writer of the first American transatlantic success, *The Sketch Book* (1819), and as part of the Knickerbocker school. Paradoxically, by embracing Irving's Knickerbocker mode as a sign of his new professional ambition, Melville had to ostensibly eschew ambition and regard authorship as the product of leisure. The Knickerbocker school, which included such writers as James Kirke Paulding and Fitz-Greene Halleck, espoused a vision of authorship as "an avocation rather than a profession and seldom...a means of earning one's livelihood."[14] The literary personae of these writers, who nostalgically associated literary pursuits with aristocratic indolence, tended to fall into elaborate reveries, favored erudition in light doses, and regarded travel as a type of avoidance of commitment. In *Tales of a Traveller* (1824), for example, Irving's character Buckthorn, a writer-manqué, elaborates on his literary propensities: "that is to say that I have always been an idle fellow and prone to play the vagabond."[15] In spite of the increased commercial opportunities in the 1840s compared to the 1820s, a variety of popular antebellum New York writers of the next generation, including Nathaniel Parker Willis, Donald Grant Mitchell ("Ik Marvel"), and George W. Curtis emulated Irving's Knickerbocker anticommercial narrative persona. Called the "male sentimentalist" by Ann Douglas, this person seemed to model an anachronistic figure, out of touch with his increasingly commercial time. Ironically, it was one of the most popular and commercially successful conceptions of the writer in the antebellum era.[16]

Given Melville's new commitment to authorship as a profession, it is perhaps not surprising that the early parts of *Mardi* show the imprimatur of the popular Irvingesque, male sentimentalist model of authorship. Melville was quick to signal the differences of his narrator in *Mardi* from his earlier fact-based narratives. Although *Mardi*'s story begins, as his others did, with a sailor–narrator abandoning ship, Melville's new ambitions required that *Mardi*'s narrator be genteel rather than a regular sailor, as this opening passage illustrates: "[A]board all ships in which I have sailed, I have invariably been known by a sort of drawing-room title.... [S]uffice it to say, that it had gone abroad among the [ship's] crew, that at some indefinite period of my career, I had been a "nob."[17] Melville's narrator emphasizes the genteel traits that distinguished him from his fellow sailors: "an occasional polysyllable; an otherwise incomprehensible deliberation in dining; remote, unguarded allusions to Belles-Lettres affairs; and other trifles superfluous to mention" (1: 14). If the narrator complains of the "annoying" perception of his social difference, he does not disavow the validity of the judgment that he "had been a 'nob,'" a person of wealth or social distinction.

Embracing Irvingesque conventions, Melville transforms his narrator from a sailor into a genteel aesthete, whose literary taste is a mark of distinction that may be, it is implied, a reason for his abandoning ship. If the other sailors do not match his genteel "sympathies," neither does the captain: "Could he talk sentiment or philosophy? Not a bit. His library was eight inches by four: Bowditch, and Hamilton Moore" (1: 5). Whereas the captains of Melville's previous narratives had been tyrants of various sorts, here the captain's failing is his inability, despite his social status, to be a literary companion to the narrator.

As if responding to Grace Greenwood's criticism of the narrator of *Typee* for the limitations of his knowledge of literature, Melville seems determined in the first chapters of *Mardi* to invoke a wide range of literary sources, many of which he had read in recent months.[18] The narrator invokes *Frithiof's Saga*, for example, in his description of his shipmate, Jarl: "Ah! how the old sagas run through me!" (3: 12). The early chapters of the novel also offer citations of Sir Thomas Browne (13: 39), "my Right Reverend friend, Bishop Berkeley" (20: 63), and "my Peloponnesian friend Thucydides" (32: 104). No longer simply the exotic traveler, Melville's narrative persona is a well-read, casual name-dropper.

Throughout this display of erudition, the narrator of early sections of *Mardi* is careful to take a mildly mocking tone, reflecting Irving and the male sentimentalists' adaptation of the eighteenth century litterateur's habit of displaying his knowledge lightly to avoid pedantry. Like the ostentatiously modest claims of Irving, Willis, or Marvel, Melville entitles an early chapter "Containing a Pennyweight of Philosophy" (26: 83). Similarly, the narrator explains one character's dropping of the ship's log overboard as a display of "an aversion to literature" and mockingly speculates on its fate: "Doubtless, it met the fate of many other ponderous tomes, sinking quickly and profoundly" (29: 94). Ironically, as his vision of *Mardi* changed, Melville remade it into the very sort of "ponderous tome" that writers like Irving or Marvel (and critics whose taste would follow them) might scorn.

Like the work of male sentimentalists in the wake of Irving, the early part of Melville's *Mardi* is filled with meditations on the nature of reverie, the privileged starting point for these writers who joined romanticism with a conservative sensibility. Ik Marvel, for example, introduces *Dream-Life* (1851), his follow-up to *Reveries of a Bachelor* (1850), with this praise of dreams as source of self-knowledge:

> Married or unmarried, old or young, poet or worker, you are still a dreamer, and will one time know, and feel, that your life is but a Dream. Yet you call this fiction: you stave off the thoughts in print which come over you in Reverie. You will not admit to the eye what is true to the heart. Poor weakling, and worldling, you are not strong enough to face yourself![19]

For the male sentimentalists following Irving, dreams and indolence are the sources of literary inspiration, a romantic spin on the construction of authorship as the privileged result of aristocratic leisure.

The narrator of *Mardi* also seems to find the source of insight and imagination in reverie. After he and Jarl jump ship, he describes his encounter with an abandoned ship they discover. In a "quiet strolling and reverie" (31: 100), he evokes Irving as he universalizes and idealizes the receptive state of dreamy wandering: "Every one knows what a fascination there is in wandering up and down in a deserted old tenement in some warm, dreamy country; where vacant halls seem echoing of silence, and the doors creak open like the footsteps of strangers" (31: 100). This generative dream-state characterizes the first third of *Mardi*, which covers a substantial part of the entire novel's plot development, including the narrator's jumping ship, the sudden appearance of the Pacific Islander's canoes bearing a white maiden, Yillah, to a whirlpool for ritual sacrifice, the narrator's murdering of the head priest Aleema, and the romance of the narrator and Yillah.[20]

If *Mardi* had sustained this Irvingesque mode, we could confidently claim that Melville considered it the best way to forward his career. But Melville quickly changed direction: after Yillah's mysterious kidnapping, the rest of *Mardi* loosely narrates an allegorical, episodic journey through the Mardian archipelago, interrupted only by occasional self-reflective chapters on the nature of his aesthetic work. These alternate literary forms hint at the new models of literary authority to which Melville was drawn.

Before launching these new narrative modes, however, Melville went back, I believe, and augmented *Mardi*'s first section, adding a new chapter that demonstrates his revised sense of his project and his critique of the Irvingesque mode in which he had already written. Chapter 2, "A Calm," introduces an additional, superfluous explanation for the narrator's desire to abandon ship and represents a change in narrative voice, switching from the first person that relates the rest of the early section of the novel (and disappears after the Yillah romance) to an omniscient third-person narration. More important, this chapter seems to chart a new course for Melville's thinking. No longer citing genteel tedium and aesthetic disdain as cause for the narrator's jumping ship, "A Calm" finds a more complex reason. The ship's calm is experienced as a philosophical crisis: "To a landsman a calm is no joke. It not only revolutionizes his abdomen, but unsettles his mind; tempts him to recant his belief in the eternal fitness of things; in short, almost makes an infidel out of him" (2: 9). Reverie stops being a source of gentle philosophy and insight, and Melville suddenly presents the calm aboard ship as an identity-threatening stasis, a crisis that threatens the easy-going complacency that Irving and his followers modeled. Far from embodying some "warm, dreamy country," the calm generates neither imagination nor ease, but an existential uncertainty that requires effort to exist within:

> Vain the idea of idling out the calm. He may sleep if he can, or purposely delude himself into a crazy fancy, that he is merely at leisure. All this he may compass; but he may not lounge; for to lounge is to be idle; to be idle implies an absence of anything to do; whereas there is a calm to be endured; enough to attend to, Heaven knows. (2: 9)

As Melville suggests, writing as enduring the calm is not an avoidance of work, not "leisure" or idleness, but the challenging task of coming to terms with the philosophical questions that earlier models of philosophy no longer answer: "enough to attend to, Heaven knows." In this chapter, we can see Melville replacing the older model of authorship as generative leisure with a new grounding in active mental work, a nonmanual labor that is not "idling," but confronting mental tasks that require skilled attention.[21] *Mardi*'s transformation from the light romanticism of dreaminess to the serious philosophical "work" of 'enduring the calm' speaks to a change in Melville's vision of authorship.

This shift to mental labor as a new literary professionalism mirrors the shifts in antebellum professional ideology more generally. Like Melville, many new professionals came to reject professionalism's anachronistic or residual investment in patrician or aristocratic social standing, finding a new authoritative persona in the marketing of skilled, nonmanual services. The new allegorical and metacritical forms that *Mardi* takes after the Yillah romance reveal Melville's commitment to an emergent vision of professional authority and expose the contradictions at the heart of the new modern American professional ideology.

Mardi *and Allegory: Professionalism and Social Reform*

"All benevolent persons, whether deeply thinking on, or only deeply feeling, the woes, difficulties and dangers of our present social system, are agreed that either great improvements are needed, or a thorough reform," claimed Margaret Fuller in the *New-York Tribune*, February 6, 1846.[22] In line with this reformist movement, Melville's turn to an allegorical mode in *Mardi* suggested that he sought to adopt a more active, politically and socially engaged vision of authorship. Suddenly casting aside the Yillah romance, Melville transformed his story into an episodic travelogue through the imaginary Mardian peninsula. For the rest of the novel, the first-person narrator of the first part is transformed into the character Taji (the name of a demigod for whom he is mistaken by the Mardian islanders), who joins with a troupe of island characters embodying perspectives Melville wanted to explore, including a monarch, an older conservative historian, a young poet, and a philosopher. The troupe travels from island to island, ostensibly in search of the kidnapped Yillah, but more practically, allowing Melville to comment at length on a seemingly endless round of subjects, from religion to literary trends and from various forms of quackery to the political tumult of 1848.[23] In perhaps the most important recent critical commentary on allegory in *Mardi*, Cindy Weinstein has argued for the importance of Melville's investment in allegory as a commitment to a kind of literary mind-work.[24] Although I agree, it is important to acknowledge that this new model of mental work in *Mardi* was associated with the activist spirit of reformism, the political and social ethos encouraging what Margaret Fuller characterized as the need for "either great improvements...or a thorough reform" of American life. Just as reformism hinted at the important new role the professional middle class could take in changing and improving American life, Melville's turn toward reformist allegory in *Mardi* gave him a new authoritative literary persona. While *Mardi's* reformist mode demonstrates the new possibilities for middle-class authority, the course of *Mardi's* allegories, particularly its depiction of the European revolutions of 1848, also reveals the limits of professional middle-class investment in reform, exposing its larger investment in social hierarchy and the status quo.

This reformist sensibility spread rapidly during the antebellum era. From antiprostitution to temperance to the abolition of slavery, reform movements galvanized antebellum Americans, particularly in the Northern cities. Debating the causes of this phenomenon, historians have found sources in humanitarianism and altruism as well as class interest and social control.[25] Many of these movements began under the aegis of an elite leadership, but the constituency of reformers at the midcentury came to take on a decidedly middle-class air. Whatever their causes or motives, reform movements became sites of identity formation and political action. They gave members of the new middle class a public forum from which to express their values and make legitimate their place in society.[26] Professionals and nonprofessional members of the middle class alike, particularly women, found reform movements a potent way to reconstitute their cultural authority and to remake American life in their image.[27]

This activism was apparent also in the literary field, as the 1840s saw the rise of an alternative role to the writer as aristocratic dilettante: that of the professionalized literary reformer. This transformation was particularly visible in New York City, where a number of successful writers openly tied their literary professionalism to reform. In her *Letters from New-York* (published in the abolitionist newspaper *National Anti-Slavery Standard*, 1841–44), Lydia Maria Child, a prominent, if controversial, literary professional, used the letter's personal form to describe social conditions observable in the city. In one letter, Child observed the infamous New York neighborhood of "the Five Points," where "you will see nearly every form of human misery, every sign of drunken degradation."[28] In a similar fashion, Margaret Fuller, who came to New York from the Transcendentalist stronghold of Concord to pursue a career as America's first full-time book reviewer for Horace Greeley's *Tribune* (a notable step toward the professionalization of criticism), used the literary pages of the paper to forward a social reformist agenda.[29] In a piece supporting Thanksgiving as a national holiday, Fuller commented:

> And for this present day appointed for Thanksgiving, we know of so many wrongs, woes and errors in the world yet unredressed; . . . yet on the other side,

we know of causes not so loudly proclaimed why we should give thanks. For that movement of contrition and love . . . which calls . . . the Poet from his throne of Mind to lie with the beggar in the kennel, or raise him from it; [and] which says to the Poet, "You must reform rather than create a world."[30]

In the face of "so many wrongs" in American life, Fuller finds the new push toward reformist authorship something to celebrate in the new Thanksgiving. Both Child and Fuller come to define the work of authorship as distinctly tied to the reformation of social problems.

Although Fuller called for her fellow writers to eschew fictional creation for "reform," other New York City writers found ways to join the two. For example, William Starbuck Mayo, whose North African travel adventure *Kaloolah* (1849) was favorably compared with *Mardi* when they were first published, found time for reformist gestures in his description of Framazugda, an imaginary white African society of order and plenty. Mayo, a doctor as well as an author, describes at length the public hygiene system of Framazugda, favorably comparing it to New York City. Mayo ends his detailed description by highlighting the importance of this lesson to his "New-York readers": "There can be no doubt that similar means would produce like results in the cities of America, and it is in hope of stirring up some of the New-York readers to the importance of the subject, that I dwell upon it to the exclusion of more interesting details."[31] In Mayo's white African utopian community, a requirement for appointment to public office was to "have written a book, or perpetrated something in the literary way," as "an opportunity is thus afforded to the people of judging of the general capacity, the mental and moral tone of their rulers. . . ."[32] The new reformist model of authorship imagined writers transformed from inconsequential idlers and vagabonds to socially and politically important figures in the reform of American culture.

Like Mayo, Melville used an imaginary exotic setting to forward his reformist project, transforming his narrative into an episodic travelogue of thinly veiled allegories of social, political, and cultural issues, particularly reflecting the concerns of New York City and its new middle class. Before he had even arranged to make Yillah disappear, Melville signaled his new interests in social reform, describing the contrast of living conditions in the island of Oro, the home of Taji's future travel companion, King Media in Chapter 63, "Oro and its Lord." Here, Melville exoticizes Child and Fuller's reformist observations on city life, noting how the "higher classes" of Oro live in "separate households," whether in "the cool, quivering bosoms of the groves," or at the beach or "like the birds, build their nests among the sylvan nooks of the elevated interior; whence all below, and hazy green, lay steeped in languor the island's throbbing heart" (63: 191). But the "common sort" of Oro "lived in secret places, hard to find": "noisome caves, lairs for beasts, not human homes" (63: 191). Melville's allegory explores the increasingly common discussions of class distinctions in antebellum New York City, as housing became one of the most noted embodiments of the class divide in the city.[33]

Like sensational "mysteries of the city" profiles by writers like George Foster, Melville's allegory offers to expose the hidden truth of "island" (city) life.[34] The distinction between Oro's visible wealth and the hidden poverty creates the sense of a deceptive scene: "to a stranger, the whole isle looked care-free and beautiful" (63: 191). But if popular city writings like those of Foster demonstrated the allure of revealing a sordid underbelly to urban life, Melville's allegory reflects the more earnest reformist rhetoric of Child and Fuller, considering the economic and social causes beneath the scandalous behavior of Oro's poor:

> Toil is man's allotment; toil of the brain, or toil of the hands, or a grief that's more than either; the grief and sin of idleness. But when a man toils and slays himself for masters who withhold the life he gives to them—then, then, the soul screams out, and every sinew cracks. And so with these poor serfs. And few of them could choose but be the brutes they seemed. (63: 191)

In contrast to the idle reveries of the earlier part of the novel, Melville highlights the world of work in this allegorical mode. Although he mentions the distinction between manual and nonmanual labor that became crucial to antebellum middle-class identity, Melville's allegory invokes the solidarity of labor against "masters" (63: 191).[35] Like the reformism of Child and Fuller, Melville's allegory simultaneously marks his social and moral elevation above the poor, while still seeking to reform the status quo.

If Melville was eager to address New York City poverty in a tropical light, he was just as likely to comment on the other end of the social spectrum: the world of upper-class fashion in antebellum New York City. In allegorical encounters with the inhabitants of the island of Pimminee, Melville describes a community of clothing manufacturers who, having achieved wealth themselves, "resolved to secede from the rabble" and form their own island community (127: 399). Because much of the community's fortune was based upon their production of clothing and their standing as "capital judges of tappa [South Seas cloth] and tailoring," these islanders are called "Tapparians" (127: 399). In his depiction of the Tapparians, Melville allegorizes New York City's newly wealthy merchants and manufacturers who were often dismissively called the "shopkeeper aristocracy" in antebellum city profiles written by a range of social observers.[36] Drawing attention to the social habits and refined tastes of the *nouveaux riches* over the course of several chapters, Melville concludes by dismissing the wealth of Pimminee (and thus New York City) as in any way representative of the culture at large:

> They think themselves Mardi in full; whereas, by the mass, they are stared at as prodigies; exceptions to the law, ordaining that no Mardian shall undertake to live, unless he set out with at least the average quantity of brains. For these Tapparians have no brains. . . . They are the victims of two incurable maladies: stone in the heart, and ossification of the head. (131: 413)

Speaking on behalf of the poor and dismissing the cultural agency of the wealthy, Melville's allegories mirror conventional tropes of antebellum middle-class reform discourse on city life, particularly that of New York City. Melville uses his South Seas allegory to justify the importance of middle-class perspectives on the urban social scene.

While Taji's voyage allowed Melville to discuss a range of social-reform issues, *Mardi*'s allegories culminate in his depiction of the European revolutions of 1848. A chain reaction of uprisings in England, France, Germany, Austria, Italy, and Hungary emerged out of the combination of bourgeois and working-class activism. New York City was particularly enthusiastic in response to the revolutions, greeting news of the French uprising with a rally in City Hall Park on April 3, where thousands celebrated.[37] Although Melville was not in the city during the celebration, his initial response to the explosion of revolutionary fervor in Europe seems guardedly optimistic. In a span of chapters from 145 to 163, *Mardi*'s voyagers visit Dominora (England), Kaleedoni (Scotland), and Verdanna (Ireland) and witness the eruption of a volcano in Porpheero (Europe), particularly affecting Franko (France). While the conservative historian Mohi laments the effects of the upheaval, "This fire must make a desert of the land. . .; burn up and bury all her tilth," the poet Yoomy replies that "Vineyards flourish over buried villages" (153: 500). The philosopher Babbalanja extends this positive sentiment:

> True, minstrel . . . and prairies are purified by fire. Ashes breed loam. Nor can any skill make the same surface forever fruitful. In all times past, things have been overlaid; and though the first fruits of the marl are wild and poisonous, the palms at last spring forth; and once again the tribes repose in shade. . . . It may be, that Porpheero's future has been cheaply won. (153: 500)

Melville's agricultural metaphor for the European uprisings suggests the necessity of violent change. Like overfarmed land, the European political landscape requires "purification" that can only be brought about by dramatic reform. For Melville, the 1848 revolutions initially offered a fulfillment of the possibilities of reform.

As *Mardi*'s travelers continue on to Vivenza (America), however, Melville's narrative reflects on the later developments of the revolutions and seems to look upon the events far more skeptically, epitomizing the shift of middle-class attitudes more generally. By June of 1848, the alliance of the working class and the bourgeoisie in France broke down into violent conflict, as it did all over Europe. American sympathy for the bourgeois political struggle was far greater than that for the working-class social struggle. As a result, when the violence of the French June proletarian revolution arose (itself the product of bourgeois suppression of working-class insurgency), middle-class American support dwindled. In this way, American attitudes toward the revolution mirrored Georg Lukács's general characterization of the transformation of bourgeois attitudes to the revolutions from "revolutionary democracy into compromising liberalism."[38] Reflecting this new skepticism toward revolution, Melville shifts from praising the European uprisings to making critical observations on the enthusiasm of Vivenzans for the revolutions and the overall effect of Jacksonian populist egalitarianism. Melville then closes out his allegorical visit to Vivenza's north with the reading of a lengthy "scroll" that functions to encapsulate his views on politics.

The scroll, the most overt and sustained political commentary of Melville's career, is apparently written by one of his narrative's voyagers (it is left undetermined whether King Media or the philosopher Babbalanja is the author) and directly addressed to the Vivenzan/American crowd, who tear it into shreds after it is read to them. Drawing attention to limitations of reformism, the scroll refutes the efficacy of revolution:

> Now, though far and wide, to keep equal pace with the times, great reforms, of a verity, be needed; nowhere are bloody revolutions required. Though it be the most certain of remedies, no prudent invalid opens his veins, to let out his disease with his life. And though all evils may be assuaged; all evils can not be done away. For evil is the chronic malady of the universe; and checked in one place, breaks forth in another (161: 529).

The earlier agricultural metaphor of burning of exhausted fields here gives way to the more moderate medical metaphor of the "prudent invalid," who avoids the unnecessary letting of blood. This limited reformist theory, called Burkean by one of the more attentive reader of *Mardi*'s politics, reflects not merely a political attitude.[39] The scroll's devaluation of political change and the radically dehistoricized sense of social order ("evil is the chronic malady of the universe") turn capitalist competition into a universal, reflecting what Georg Lukács described as "a metaphysical history-dissolving mystique" that characterized the bourgeois response to the 1848 revolutions.[40] Melville's scroll demonstrates the limitations of antebellum middle-class reformism, which Burton Bledstein describes as its fear of "the excessive openness of American society, . . . and the failure of moral restraint."[41]

By this point in the narrative, Melville's social views have evidently changed, especially from his first allegorical chapter depicting the brutalization of the poor on the island of Oro, justifying class animus and proclaiming the need for reform. The 1848 revolutions were a test of middle-class reformism both in Europe and America. By the time they ended in the violent suppressions of working-class calls for social equality, the European revolutions had transcended the limits of most American reformist sensibilities, including, apparently, Melville's.[42] These chapters on the revolutions signal, in effect, the end of Melville's interest in allegory in *Mardi*, reflecting not just the end of its narrative efficacy for Melville's text, but also apparently the end of his belief in the merits of a reformist literary project. At the end of the visit to Vivenza (and the end of the revolutions of 1848), Melville shifts his narrative away from allegories and the reformist social thinking to which it seemed tied, to aestheticism, a move that reflects the major shift in European art at the time "from political radicalism and social realism into aestheticism."[43] With the close of the allegories of revolution, Melville would make self-reflexive writing and increasingly hermetic symbolic commentaries on the process of writing increasingly dominant near the end of the novel, signaling *Mardi*'s own parallel retreat into aestheticism.

Mardi *and Professionalism: Symbolism and Aesthetic Specialization*

At the same time that Melville redirected *Mardi* into an allegorical travelogue, he also began to include chapters on the nature and difficulties of the task of writing and engage his characters in long debates on philosophical issues touching upon the artist and literary production. Although these episodes are only occasional counterpoints to the allegorical encounters throughout much of *Mardi*, they become increasingly important in the aftermath of Melville's allegorical meditation on the 1848 revolutions, as he turns toward what has been called "symbolistic" writing, literary work that self-consciously deals with the terms of its own creation.[44] It is this fitful form that led Richard Brodhead to characterize the "real object" of the novel as "nothing [Melville's] characters seek but the mental world he himself discloses through the act of creating the book."[45] Criticizing the formalism of these readings of *Mardi* that cast the novel simply as Melville's symbolic narrative of aesthetic autonomy, Wai Chee Dimock insists that "the figure of the 'creative artist' is not without its own history" and calls for a "study [of] the emergence of [the creative artist] and the attendant elevation of his calling—to study it not just as an episode in literary history, but as a phenomenon concurrent with and perhaps connected to other historical events."[46] Connecting *Mardi*'s vision of artistry with history, we can read Melville's investment in an autonomous and hermetic mode of aesthetic practice by the end of his novel as not only a statement about authorship—"literary history"—but also a reflection of the professional middle-class project of vocational specialization. Just as the other literary forms of *Mardi* signaled Melville's investment in the legitimizing possibilities of a particular literary persona, which in turn reflects larger shifts in the ideology of professionalism, the novel's final self-conscious and self-reflective symbolic form reveals Melville's commitment to the professional project of specialization.

The late 1840s saw an unprecedented "wave of association," as professional groups such as the American Association for the Advancement of Science (1847), American Medical Association (1847) and American Legal Association (precursor to the American Bar Association, 1849)—to name only a few—began developing normative educational methodologies and establishing internal mechanisms for validating certain work practices and invalidating others.[47] These organizations were crucial mechanisms for the establishment of a new middle-class professionalism that emerged across the nation in the antebellum era.

The various professional associations that constituted themselves in the antebellum era all depended upon specialization to establish their authority. No longer tied to an elite patronage system, the professions were required to enter the marketplace. Association allowed the professions to "constitute and control a market for their expertise," defending their authority by establishing the terms that would define their practice.[48] Historian Thomas Haskell presents the Smithsonian Institution's head Joseph Henry as a prime example of this process, demonstrating how the antebellum scientific community created set criteria for establishing the merit or validity of scientific work, with the double effect of "insulat[ing] the practitioner of science from those least competent to judge him, and . . . bring[ing] him into intimate contact with—and competitive exposure to—those most competent to judge him."[49] Although professionals used private organizations and specialized discourses both to "test" ideas and to "insulate" them from outside competition, this autonomy was never an end unto itself. Autonomy and specialization produced what Magali Larson has called a "special kind of non-physical property," what other sociologists have called "cultural capital," that give professionals a privileged position in the markets of service, labor, and ideas.[50] Professionals, as Pierre Bourdieu asserts, "live on the sale of cultural services" and, as a result, "the accumulation of economic capital merges with the accumulation of symbolic capital, . . .[as in] the acquisition of a reputation for competence and an image of respectability. . . ."[51] Professional specialization may have been a withdrawal from an "open" marketplace of services and ideas, but it was designed inevitably to return to that marketplace from a new position of authority. Seemingly a rejection of the marketplace, specialization, in fact, reflected the middle-class interest in altering its highly vulnerable place within the new economy and social hierarchy by controlling the terms of its members' entrance into the marketplace.

It might easily be argued that antebellum authors were particularly resistant to the kind of formalized association that characterized professionalism. New York literary professionals, however, did gather together, in groups formal and informal, that were far more cohesive than suggested by Perry Miller's narrative history of the contentious Knickerbocker–Young America divide. The earliest organizational or trade meetings could be said to have taken the form of memorial dinners at the death of prominent authors, such as James Fenimore Cooper in 1852, or in trade festivals sponsored by publishers, such as the 1855 "Fruit and Flower Festival, Given to Authors, by the New York Publishers' Association."[52] More informally, however, the antebellum New York literary community came together and understood itself as a community in salons hosted by prominent women authors of the period, such as Anne C. Lynch, Emma Embury, and the Cary sisters. Like the European salons of the eighteenth and early-nineteenth century, which brought together writers and the aristocracy, antebellum New York literary salons used the private home as the site of association. Unlike European salons, though, the antebellum New York City gatherings were not so much an intersecting point between the arts and wealth or political power, but primarily a site for the association of writers, artists and other members of the middle class.[53] In this way, the form of literary socializing constituted a change from the Knickerbocker mode of clubbing, itself more reflective of the European model, where small groups of men—including writers, artists, politicians, and patricians—would gather in a bar or restaurant to read either edifying lectures or satires and to discuss (or gossip about) local and national politics.[54]

Although much of antebellum New York literary socializing was still all-male, the prominence of a salon like Lynch's Saturday evenings, which began in the late 1840s and ran into the 1850s, speaks first to the increasing importance of women in the literary field, but also to the cohesive and unified sense of a literary community that could be produced in the period. As the poet and travel writer Bayard Taylor put it, "nearly all the author-tribe" was likely to appear at Lynch's home. Melville attended a famous Valentine's Day Party at Lynch's in 1848, along with Taylor, Halleck, Duyckinck, Cornelius Mathews, William Cullen Bryant, John Inman (editor), Grace Greenwood (popular writer), Parke Goodwin (contributor to *The Democratic Review*, later publisher of *Putnam's Magazine*), Charles F. Briggs (novelist and editor of *The Broadway Journal* and *Putnam's*), Nathaniel Parker Willis and George Morris (editors of *The Home Journal*), Charles Fenno Hoffman (writer and editor of *The Literary World*), Mary E. Hewitt (poet), Rufus Griswold (editor and anthologist), Frances Osgood (poet), Catherine Maria Sedgwick (poet and novelist), Caroline Kirkland (writer and editor), and Seba and Elizabeth Oakes Smith (writers). Lynch is also known to have played host to such other disparate New York literary professionals as Poe, Margaret Fuller, Lydia Maria Child, and Lewis Gaylord Clark (famous editor of *The Knickerbocker*). As described by John Hart, the anthologist of *Female Prose Writers of America* of 1852, "[Lynch] has for many years opened her house on every Saturday evening to ladies and gentlemen of her acquaintance, connected with literature or the fine arts. Men and women of genius here meet, very much as merchants meet on the 'Change, without ceremony, and for the exchange of thought."[55] Likening Lynch's home to the Exchange, where New York businessmen met to discuss their work, the description identifies the salon as a place for specialized literary and artistic association. City sketch-writer George Foster profiled Lynch's salon for the *Tribune* in his "New York in Slices" series and used the existence of the New York literary salons to justify an argument for New York City's domination of American culture:

> These weekly *reunions,* of which during the Winter season there are three or four every week among the different literary coteries, are a peculiarity of New York society, which has not been imitated elsewhere to any considerable extent—simply because the materials are wanting. New York, as the grand intellectual focus

of the country, is the point at which concentrate the wandering rays of genius from all quarters; . . . It is this which adds the final embellishment and imparts the crowning charm to New York society—which sets a seal of unapproachable value, and confers indescribable force upon New York public opinion, before whose dicta the mind and intellect of the whole country unconsciously bow. . . . In civilization, every powerful nation must have one intellectual centre, as every individual must have a brain, whose motions and conceptions govern that entire system. In the United States, New York is that centre and that brain.[56]

In a fascinating reflection of the peculiarity of the new professional ideology more generally, Foster's claim for the representative nature and power of the New York literary community comes from its ability to be its own audience. It is the autonomy of not having to address a broader public audience within their own salons that enables them to become the "centre" and "brain" of the nation. The presence of a specialized literary community as a cohesive body in New York City is used to make it "the grand intellectual focus of the country," giving New York writers special authority to speak for the nation.

We can see Melville participating in this seemingly contradictory process of professional specialization, particularly in the final section of *Mardi* with its turn inward toward self-referentiality and metaliterary meditations. In turning his narrative focus increasingly toward the act and nature of writing itself, Melville transforms *Mardi* into a specialized text, one that defines its authority through a kind of literary autonomy, addressed not to a general readership, but rather to a specialized audience of other like-minded literary professionals. At interstices between different strands of substantial allegorical plotting in the second half of *Mardi*, Melville inserts philosophical interludes that defend or validate his own literary efforts and methods. These chapters are respites from the story, marked as different by their titles, characterized by grand philosophical and metaliterary themes ("Time and Temples" or "Faith and Knowledge") and by the invocation of nonallegorical contexts and sources. In the later chapters "Dreams" and "Sailing On," however, the commentary on Melville's act of writing will turn explicit. In "Dreams" Melville openly addresses the reader in the immediate act of writing: "My cheek blanches white while I write; I start at the scratch of my pen; my own mad brood of eagles devours me; fain would I unsay this audacity; but an iron-mailed hand clenches mine in a vice and prints down every letter in my spite" (119: 368). Imagining the writer as Promethean, Melville portrays himself as both heroic and suffering, serving the world and cut off from it as a result of his efforts. Melville's "Dreams" inscribes the act of writing and the author's feelings about it into the text, making it a dramatic action rather than a hidden effort. By drawing attention to the act of writing itself, Melville legitimizes the work of the author in *Mardi*.

If "Dreams" turns writing into a heroic act, "Sailing On" converts *Mardi*'s allegorical voyage into a metaphor for the progress of Melville's thinking. Again addressing the reader directly, Melville calls for the reader's attention to his own efforts:

> Oh, reader, list! I've chartless voyaged. With compass and the lead, we had not found these Mardian Isles. Those who boldly launch, cast off all cables; and turning from the common breeze, that's fair for all, with their own breath, fill their own sails.
> . . . That voyager steered his bark through seas, untracked before; ploughed his own path mid jeers; though with a heart that oft was heavy with thought, that he might be only too bold, and grope where land was none.
> So I. (169: 556–57)

Melville's vision of the writer as voyager, invoked in other chapters by other symbolic references to Marco Polo (75: 228), Columbus (97: 297), and Mungo Park (119: 368), goes beyond mere implication into heroic self-assertion in this new vision, where the writer trumps the explorer with his greater freedom: "But this new world here sought, is stranger far than his, who stretched his vans from Palos. It is *the world of the mind*; wherein the wanderer may gaze round, with more wonder than Balboa's band roving through the golden Aztec glades" (169: 557; *my italics*). Melville's announcement that his narrative has explored a "world of the mind" is, in a sense, a revision of the allegorical impulse. Certainly no reader, by this point in the narrative, can have imagined that *Mardi*'s voyage was in any way factual, but the earlier allegorical chapters drew attention to pressing issues in antebellum U.S. social and political life, speaking to the need for action and reform. In "Sailing On," however, Melville calls on his readers not to take action in the world, but to perceive his own autonomous role in constructing this "world of the mind," which is his text.[57] Charles Feidelson reads "Sailing On" as the central moment in *Mardi*, leading him to suggest of the narrative as a whole that: "What is thought *about* [in *Mardi*] is a relatively minor matter; Melville's ultimate question is *how*. In the largest view the book is a study of what it entails to regard thinking as a metaphysical journey."[58] If Feidelson's claim seems to simply forget 400 pages of reformist allegory, it does seem to capture the intensity of feeling that emerges in "Dreams" and "Sailing On," which leaps out at the reader after the fairly mechanical elaboration of allegory late in

Mardi. In effect, "Sailing On" rechristens *Mardi* yet again—this time as a symbolic and autonomous exploration of the writer's aesthetic authority.

This narrative shift is formalized at the end of *Mardi,* when in his lengthy discussion of the Mardian author Lombardo and his text, the *Kostanza,* Melville turns the novel completely in on itself and makes his own writing process its subject. In the discussion between the voyagers and the traditionalist King Abrazza, Melville clearly represents his sense of his own writing process and *Mardi* itself. As in "Sailing On," Melville rejects the light romanticism of his earliest work on the novel and transforms "reverie" and "idleness" into a rigorous self-exploration:

> When Lombardo set about his work, he knew not what it would become. He did not build himself in with plans; he wrote right on; and so doing, got deeper and deeper into himself; and like a resolute traveler, plunging through baffling woods, at last was rewarded for his toils. . . . "Here we are at last, then," [Lombardo] cried; "I have created the creative." (180: 595)

As *Mardi* is transformed into a novel that is about writing a novel and creativity, it distances itself from conventional narrative forms. Melville recognizes this and predicts his own skeptical readers' response to *Mardi* in King Abrazza's comment on Lombardo's work: "But the unities, . . . the unities! They are wholly wanting in the Kostanza. . . . [It] lacks cohesion; it is wild, unconnected, all episode" (180: 597). Melville also predicts the comments of *Mardi*'s critics in the reaction of Lombardo's contemporaries, "the professional critics" whose comments "betrayed such base, beggarly notions of authorship, that Lombardo could have wept" (180:599). Melville critiques the vision of authorship constructed by these critics:

> He is the great author, think they, who drives the best bargain with his wares: and no bargainer am I. Because he is old, they worship some mediocrity of an ancient, and mock the living prophet with the live coal on his lips. . . . Feelings they have none: and their very opinions they borrow. They cannot say yea, nor nay, without first consulting all Mardi as an Encyclopedia. And all the learning in them, is as a dead corpse in a coffin. Were they worthy of the dignity of being damned, I would damn them; but they are not. Critics?—Asses! Rather Mules!— so emasculated, from vanity, they can not father a true thought. (180:599)

Rejecting criticism, Lombardo claims a special authorial autonomy that relates to the professions: "For I am critic and creator: and as critic, in cruelty surpass all critics merely, as a tiger, jackals. For ere Mardi sees aught of mine, I scrutinize it myself, remorseless as a surgeon. I cut right and left; I probe, tear, and wrench; kill, burn and destroy" (180: 599). Here, Melville's association of authorship with surgery speaks to his fantasy of authorial autonomy, a vocational fantasy linked to the authority bestowed upon the medical profession. But Melville would also question his impulse to produce *Mardi*, having Lombardo ask:

> "Who will heed it," thought [Lombardo]; "what care these fops and brawlers for me? But am I not myself an egregious coxcomb? Who will read me? Say one thousand pages—twenty-five lines each—every line ten words. That's two million five hundred thousand *a*'s and *i*'s, and *o*'s to read! How many are superfluous? Am I not mad to saddle Mardi with such a task? Of all men, am I the wisest, to stand upon a pedestal and teach the mob?" (180:601)

Galvanized alternately by confidence and doubt about his authorial project, Melville is, in any case, still writing exclusively about writing by the end of *Mardi*.

No longer interested in fulfilling conventional narrative demands to reach a popular or general readership, *Mardi* becomes an embodiment of Melville's 1849 famous assertion to his father-in-law, posing the possibility of commercial "success" of his novels against his "earnest desire to write the sort of books which are said to 'fail.'"[59] With this logic, only commercial failure can guarantee the kind of success Melville truly longs for, the recognition of his artistry by his true peers and by posterity. In effect, Melville's final vision of *Mardi* is that of a specialist's, making his novel available to a limited audience suitably prepared or trained to appreciate his work.

It is perhaps inevitable that *Mardi*'s embrace of a symbolic autonomy is read as a significant moment in Melville's career as a "romantic" artist. But, as Raymond Williams and Lawrence Buell have argued, romanticism itself (whether British or American) was a vocational discourse of aesthetic specialization.[60] In fact, the construction of literary or art history as its own field of knowledge or study can itself be understood as a symptom of the ideological process of specialization. As sociologist Pierre Bourdieu suggests, the world of art as it has been constructed in modern life is dominated by a symbolic economy of cultural capital, becoming "a sacred island, systematically and ostentatiously opposed to the profane, everyday world of production, a sanctuary for gratuitous, disinterested activity in a universe given over to money and self-interest."[61] In this sanctified "anti-economy," the "pure artist" embraces a "professional ideology" that, far from being unique, simply embodies in its purest form the professional middle-class relationship to an industrial capitalist mode of production.[62] Rather than seeing Melville's narrowing of his ideal audience and drive for autonomy in *Mardi*

only as an oddity in the world of literary history, we can also read it as a crys-
tallization, perhaps even a concentration, of the larger process of professional middle-class specialization, a reaction to (but not a wholesale
rejection of) the emergent market economy of antebellum America.

Over the course of the novel, the form of *Mardi* changes dramatically, and
with it, Melville's vision of authorship and audience. From the general, but
implicitly Irvingesque genteel readership who might be drawn to "all that
is romantic, whimsical & poetic in Polynisia," to a reform-minded middle
class who might find their values seconded in the allegories, Melville shifts
to an increasingly narrower and more specialized vision of his audience, culminating in a text deemed inaccessible to a general contemporary readership, but one that will find its place in the pantheon at some future date.
Although *Mardi* was consistently meant to authorize Melville's sense of his
literary professionalism, his vision of what constituted that identity kept
changing and increasingly disassociating authorship from sales. By its end,
Mardi functions under the logic of what Bourdieu has called "the anti-
'economic' economy of pure art."[63] Although rejecting commercial and
short-term economic profit, this aesthetic logic is also tied to an economy,
Bourdieu argues—but to a "symbolic economy," where aesthetic ambition
and difficulty function as "a kind of 'economic' capital denied but recognized" that can lead to prestige and authority.[64] By its close, *Mardi* becomes
the embodiment of Melville's specialized professional authority, a text written against market demands but with an eye toward the legitimation that
would allow him to take up an authoritative position in the market.

Rather than viewing *Mardi* simply as a misguided expression of Melville's
new literary ambition, we should read it as an interrogation of what defines
literature, literature's audience, and professional work in antebellum American culture. The disparate and, at times, contradictory textual elements of
Mardi directly reflect the conflicting impulses of modern American professional ideology, revealing tensions within middle-class social authority. As
one key gesture of antebellum professionalism, specialization encouraged
autonomy by dividing fields of knowledge and separating experts from those
deemed unqualified to judge specialized discourses and effort. In contrast,
reform turned professional focus outward, both using and bolstering reformers' authority through their involvement with problems in the larger social
field. Although the two impulses could work in conjunction, they also tugged
in opposite directions, raising questions as to whether professionalism was
simply a self-interested class movement or a concerted effort at improving

conditions for knowledge and reforming American society as a whole. The text of *Mardi* exemplifies these opposing impulses: its socially engaged reformist allegory demonstrates middle-class desires to improve both professional practice and American society, while its self-referential symbolism turns away from social problems to focus exclusively on specialized literary concerns and discursive authority. Although *Mardi* has been traditionally read as part of Melville's journey into artistry, we can equally understand it as a journey through the evolving and contradictory ideologies of middle-class professionalism in antebellum America.

Mardi's Reception: Professionalism and the Literary Field in Transition

Completing *Mardi* in January of 1849, Melville had spent between a year and a half and two years writing his novel—expending far more time and energy on it than he had devoted to *Typee* or *Omoo*. Given what Melville called the "Antarctic tenor" of Murray's response to his enthusiastic plans for the novel in correspondence, it came as no surprise that the publisher did not find *Mardi's* overt fictionalizing suitable and rejected it.[65] Melville quickly found another British publisher in Richard Bentley, who had already solicited his work, to join his American publishers, Harper and Brothers, in publishing *Mardi*: Bentley's edition appeared on March 16 and the Harpers' on April 14, 1849. Within a few weeks, reviews began to appear. Though Melville was clearly disappointed in the response and *Mardi* is legendarily one of Melville's "failures," critical response was, in fact, mixed, with positive commentary generally outweighing negative.

The critical response to *Mardi* is informative, not so much for its aesthetic assessment, but for what it says about conflicting attitudes toward the role of the author and the critic and the relation of literary vocations to social ideologies in the period. As Bourdieu has commented, "All critics declare not only their judgement of the work but also their claim to the right to talk about it and judge it. In short, they take part in a struggle for the monopoly of legitimate discourse about the work of art, and consequently in the production of the value of the work of art."[66] The response to *Mardi* suggests that nearly all of the reviewers recognized Melville's substantial meditation on authorship, literature, and criticism, with both supportive and critical reviewers entering into lengthy metacritical discussions. More than just a reflection of cliquish literary conflict or shifting generic tastes in the literary marketplace, the critical divide over

Mardi reflects emerging distinctions between the labor of literary professionalism and the meaning of "literature" that comments directly on the
formation of modern professional middle-class social ideology.[67]

Both negative and positive critical assessments of *Mardi* dwelt upon the
amount of work or effort required to write and read it, reflecting divided
notions about whether literature should be difficult or not. The New York
Tribune's literary critic, George Ripley, began his negative assessment by
stating: "We have seldom found our reading faculty so near exhaustion, or
our good nature as critics so severly [*sic*] exercised, as in an attempt to get
through this new work by the author of the fascinating *Typee* and *Omoo*."[68]
Henry Cood Watson, writing for *Saroni's Musical Times*, commented on the
deceptiveness of *Mardi*'s form, metaphorizing reading as a journey (the
corollary of Melville's writing as journey):

> We were flattered with the promise of an account of travel, amusing, though
> fictitious; and we have been compelled to pore over an undigested mass of ram-
> bling metaphysics. We had hoped for a pleasant boat-ride among the sunny isles
> of the tropics; instead of which, we were taken bodily, and immersed into the
> fathomless sea of Allegory, from which we have just emerged, gasping for
> breath. . . .[69]

Both Ripley and Watson begin their criticisms of *Mardi* by associating reading it with extreme physical effort ("exhaustion" and "gasping for breath").
The aesthetic standard for writing here is, implicitly, leisure and ease, invoking the aristocratic/male sentimental model of literary labor.[70] Ironically, the
positive assessments of *Mardi* were just as likely to note the "work" in the text,
but to identify it as praiseworthy. It is, of course, no surprise that Evert Duyckinck lauded *Mardi*, but his praise reflects a wholly different notion of
authorship from Ripley's or Watson's. Listing some of *Mardi*'s literary precursors (characterized by the conjunction of wit and seriousness, including
Hood, Rabelais and Swift), Duyckinck's touts Melville's literary effort:

> Is it not significant that our American mariner, beginning with pleasant pictures
> of his Pacific Ocean, should soon sweep beyond the current of his isles into this
> world of high discourse: revolving the condition, the duties, the destiny of men?
> No vagrant lounger, truly, into the booths of literature, where frivolous wit is sold
> in the fashion of the hour, but a laborious worker, of a rare discipline, on our Amer-
> ican book shelves.[71]

Beyond the nationalist notion that "our American mariner" could enter the
"world of high discourse," Duyckinck's comment reveals the new value

placed upon authorship constructed, not as the product of leisure (the "friv-olous wit" of the "vagrant lounger" or aristocratic dilettante), but of "disci-pline" and "laborious" effort. Duyckinck praises Melville and his text as exemplars of the new professionalism, exhibiting the discipline and train-ing (using Duyckinck's books, of course) to construct an authoritative liter-ary specialist.

For both supporters and detractors, *Mardi* made specialized demands upon its readership. Duyckinck's praise of Melville's professionalism, in addition to highlighting the "exactly two years" Melville "devoted consci-entiously and laboriously to *Mardi*," noted, "There is 'something in it' every-where" and called it "a book of thought, curious thought and reflection."[72] Noting its thoughtfulness and symbolic ambitions, Duyckinck emphasizes *Mardi*'s demand for a sophisticated readership. William Young, writing for the New York journal *Albion*, praised *Mardi* and claimed that it would be of particular interest to reviewers: "The book invites study, and deserves the close investigation which appertains to reviewers, for whom indeed it will be a *bonne bouche*."[73]

If Young identified reviewers as the specialized audience of readers who would find *Mardi* a 'tidbit' as part of his praise of the novel, detractors were inclined to disagree with Melville's demands for a specialized readership. In his *Saroni's Musical Times* review, Watson notes that "Melville is hard upon the critics" in *Mardi* and "question[s] the good taste of his remarks," posit-ing, "The only difference between critics and other readers is that the for-mer *print* their opinions."[74] Watson's espousal of critical amateurism is endorsed by other reviewers who found fault with *Mardi*, including the *Examiner*'s reviewer, who mockingly suggested that "even the all-wise critic, somewhat sharing the reader's dullness . . . , thinks it safest to say as little as may be about the profundities of allegorical meaning which appear to be involved [in *Mardi*]."[75] In the *Athenaeum*, Henry Fothergill Chorley imagined *Mardi*'s readers deserting over the course of the narrative, leaving "The Critic" as "the one intrepid mariner who holds out to the end." Although Chorley sees his reading of *Mardi* as a professional duty, his critic as "intrepid mariner" mocks Melville's own demanding model of profes-sional authorship.

Criticism of *Mardi* highlighted the antebellum era's conflicted sense of authorship, criticism, and readership, and these issues were understood as not simply an aesthetic concern. The social nature of the critical issues raised by *Mardi* is made clear in William Jones's *United States Magazine and Democratic*

Review piece, which launches into a long disquisition on the specialization of labor before introducing Melville's book as his topic. Published in July 1849, Jones's review has a retrospective quality, explaining the social context that determined the poor reception received by *Mardi*:

> There are few men whose scope of vision extends over the area of human exis-
> tence. The view of most is confined to their trade, profession, or sect. Success
> in the lowest uses of life, in the competitive sphere in which we live, has made
> this limitation of sight a necessary fact. The boy's advice to the clergyman is
> too commonly quoted to need explanation, viz.: "Every one to his trade—you
> to your preaching, and I to my mouse-traps." A man cannot be expected to till
> his farm, build his house, and make his shoes, and his clock.[76]

Jones pictures Melville's novel within the broad context of a transformation of American society, the shift to what he calls a "competitive industry" that necessitates vocational specialization. Focusing on one task, the American worker has become both more interdependent and less secure: the worker must "exchange work" and keep a "sharp look-out" on his fellow workers not to be cheated.[77] In the meantime, traditional hierarchical forms of cultural authority, like the clergy, have been replaced by a horizontal model of specialization that establishes narrow fields of authority ("you to your preaching, and I to my mouse-traps"). Continuing, Jones links this vocational commentary to the world of aesthetics:

> There seems a sort of necessity that men should not see all over the field of
> human economy, or philosophy, when engaged to the limit of their strength, in
> making pegs, or shoes, heads or points of pins, six days out of the week. . . . And
> when their sight is thus abridged and confined, it would be gratuitous cruelty
> to blame them if they do not recognize and accept, as belonging to this mun-
> dane sphere, world-pictures made in high places, by the few of far-sight.[78]

For Jones, the competitive world of industrializing capitalism renders specialization necessary: society creates both the maker of "pegs" and the maker of *Mardi*. In this context, neither Melville nor the general readership should be blamed if *Mardi* is not widely appreciated. For Jones, the division between the literary professional and the general readership was inevitable under industrialization. The social and economic conditions of antebellum society made it necessary that the critic should no longer be different from the reader only in "*print*[ing] their opinions." Under this new social and economic setting, the critic must be a specialized reader, as Jones explains: for *Mardi* to be properly appreciated "it must be read carefully, and by those measurably imbued with the author's philosophy."[79] For Jones, the effect of

Mardi was to distinguish between kinds of readers, its demanding form marking those who are qualified to read and understand it from those who are not. In this way, Jones understands the failure of *Mardi* as simply the inevitable result of economically and socially determined distinctions within the literary and cultural field in antebellum America. Placing Jones's review in relation to other responses to *Mardi*, we can see that the critical divide over the novel was essentially a debate about whether the "labors" of writing and reading were socially meaningful acts and what kinds of social distinctions could be made through reading.

In effect, Jones's review, with its situating of aesthetic production within industrial capitalism and its articulation of social distinctions through aesthetic culture, sets the stage for what we could call the professionalization of culture. This process, which many scholars have recently described as beginning in the antebellum era, produced a transformation of the American cultural scene, setting cultural professionals in a new position of authority over definitions of art and entertainment. The next two chapters explore the ways in which Melville's 1851 novel *Moby-Dick* emerged out of the complex and deeply conflicted landscape of antebellum urban cultural politics and how the novel itself was enmeshed in the process of articulating this new model of cultural professionalism.

Ahab at the Astor Place Riots

Melville and Shakespeare

It is probably no overstatement to claim that in the last twenty years no cultural narrative has been as influential as Lawrence Levine's vision in his 1988 book, *Highbrow/Lowbrow: The Emergence of Cultural Hierarchy in America*, of the rise of a rigid divide between models of American "high" and "low" culture over the course of the second half of the nineteenth century.[1] Despite (or perhaps because of) its influence, scholars have noted the overdetermined nature of Levine's narrative that identifies high–low divides in antebellum events, such as the Astor Place Riots, when a conflict between popular and elite New York theater audiences led to over twenty deaths, at the same time that it imagines the high–low divide being born out of these antebellum cultural conflicts. Levine's "chicken-or-egg" dilemma has been exposed by a range of cultural historians and literary scholars who have delineated the distinctive cultural values of the different classes of the antebellum cities of the North, particularly in New York City. While the working class had its own "Bowery Republic," attending performances of minstrelsy and melodrama downtown, the wealthy of the uptown Fifteenth Ward attended exclusive performances of foreign-language opera at the expensive Astor Place Opera House, while also attempting to promulgate their values through cultural enterprises like the American Art-Union. At the same time, to further complicate Levine's model, some scholars have noted the rise of what could be called an antebellum "middlebrow" cultural form, embodied in institutions such as Barnum's American Museum, the Young Men's Institute, and the Lyceum Hall that occupied a careful middle position on the Northern city's cultural landscape, catering to a middle-class audience who sought through their entertainment the same legitimation of their values and reassurance of their importance as did the working class and the elite.[2]

While many quibble with Levine's narrative of origins, however, few scholars interested in American cultural hierarchy reject his culminating vision of a twentieth-century model of a formalized realm of "High Culture" dominated by an exclusionary social ethos. The course of the latter half of the nineteenth century reveals an unmistakable hardening of the distinctions between "high" and "low" culture and a dramatic expansion of the forms and institutions of "high" culture in American life. What, then, was added in antebellum America to begin the shift from an "old" model of the high–low divide to a "new" model? It is the central premise herein that the expansion of "high" culture was indicative, not of a dramatic expansion in the population or influence of the "upper ten," the antebellum city's wealthiest individuals who had dominated the earlier model of "high" culture, but in the rise of both population and influence of a new urban professional middle class who identified "culture" as a particularly effective locus of class identification and status affirmation. Just as doctors, lawyers, and a host of other nascent middle-class professionals turned to a model of vocational specialization to legitimize their standing, artists, authors, and critics would find a parallel legitimation in distinctions around culture—including art, literature, philosophy, and others—and, in the process, work to "professionalize" culture. In this way, the formation of a new model of cultural hierarchy reflects the investment of the professional middle class in the realm of art and aesthetics, the construction of an expertise and authority around a formalized notion of "Culture."

Faced with the prospect of the continuation of the kind of class conflict exposed by the Astor Place Riots and the possibilities for the disempowering commercialization of culture revealed by the "mass culture" industry of Barnum as well as the new-class aspiring forms of middlebrow culture such as the lyceum, antebellum professionals began to imagine an alternative model of aesthetic culture that would insulate them from the demands of the market while also assuring them a privileged place within American social hierarchies. Absorbing and synthesizing Jacksonian cultural impulses toward elite stewardship, popular sovereignty, and the new middlebrow culture, the professionalization of culture was both "elitist" and "democratic" at the same time, reflecting the ambiguous position of the professional middle class. The transformation of culture into a field of knowledge, a separate realm presided over by "experts," made culture a "symbolic" alternative to capital, giving professionals both a position from which to critique capitalism and a place within it. This professionalization of culture was an important part of the ideological project of legitimating professional authority in antebellum America.

As an aspiring literary professional in antebellum New York City, Herman Melville had a significant and material role to play in this ideological process. In 1849–50, Melville was working on *Moby-Dick*, and though he moved out of New York City during the drafting of his epic novel of whaling, the complex and conflicted cultural life of the city had left its impression on his life and his novel. Melville's 1849 reading of Shakespeare famously marks *Moby-Dick*. But that same reading, and his friendship with Evert Duyckinck, led to Melville's involvement in the Astor Place Riots, where he sided with New York City's elites against the Jacksonian tradition of working-class sovereignty over theater culture. Although Melville's use of Shakespeare in *Moby-Dick* has been read as a kind of aesthetic amplification, transforming the "poor old whale-hunter" Ahab into what F. O. Matthiessen called "a Shakespearean king," we can also read Melville's use of Shakespeare as an attempt to articulate an alternative to the dominant antebellum popular and elite appropriations of the Renaissance playwright manifested during the Riots, one that would privilege his own subtle and ambivalent position of professional middle-class standing.

If Melville's depiction of Ahab can be read as a meditation on the social and political possibilities of a professionalized alternative to the divides of antebellum cultural politics, so, too, can *Moby-Dick*'s other narrative voice, Ishmael. In his book-long project of analyzing the whale, Ishmael uses a variety of scientific discourses, scholarship in history and art, and philosophical speculation to unpack antebellum "middlebrow" entertainment forms. As narrator of *Moby-Dick*, Ishmael transforms the commercial forms of that middlebrow "self-culture," with its mercantile production of simplified "useful knowledge" and "respectable entertainment," into a philosophical open-endness and an ambivalent cultural stance that offers to include, but also threatens to exclude, readers.

In *Moby-Dick*, Melville draws his narrative personae as responses to the problematic cultural models available in the antebellum era, shifting them to articulate a professional model of culture and a vision of discursive authority that combines antithetical claims to democracy and hierarchy. Not simply a reflection of the cultural conflicts of the period, *Moby-Dick* is Melville's attempt to construct an alternative cultural politics, an ideological project that justified professional authority in a period of cultural crisis. As a result, *Moby-Dick*'s cultural significance has a kind of ideological trajectory: its special meaning or importance in twentieth-century American culture as a "masterpiece" or cultural touchstone owes its primary debt neither to antebellum "high" nor "low" cultural models, but to a new professionalized model of culture rising out of professional middle-class anxieties about position and status in antebellum America that had solidified by the twentieth century.

In twentieth-century America, Shakespeare has been most commonly associated with "high" culture, an elevated form of aesthetic expression requiring training and knowledge for understanding it appropriately.[3] As is well known now, however, when Melville was living and writing in New York City in the late 1840s, Shakespeare was far from a sacrosanct "high"-culture icon. His plays were as likely to be watched from the cheap seats of popular theaters as from the expensive boxes of the fancy new opera houses. In fact, the theater in which one watched Shakespeare performed in New York City then could be read as a marker of social standing. This was made most evident in the famous 1849 riots at the Astor Place Opera House in New York City where disagreements between two well-known Shakespearean actors led to a deadly street battle between a popular audience and a combination of armed city police and state militia forces acting at the behest of a wealthy elite audience. These Riots have become the subject of renewed interest to scholars as a crucial site of America's battle over cultural hierarchy, the beginning of the process whereby Shakespeare, once the most popular playwright on the American stage, came to be marked as a form of "high" or "elite" culture as opposed to "low" or "popular" culture.[4] Enacting the conflict between divided audiences, the Astor Place Riots suggest that Shakespeare and aesthetic values expressed deeply felt social antagonisms and divisions in antebellum America.

Beginning with a disagreement over the acting styles of the famous English actor Charles Macready and the equally famous American Edwin Forrest, the Riots took place inside and outside the Astor Place Opera House in early May 1849. Both Macready and Forrest were scheduled to perform *Macbeth* in New York City theaters on May 7, Forrest at the popular downtown Broadway Theater and Macready uptown at the new and exclusive

Astor Place Opera House. In return for what they perceived as an insult from Macready during Forrest's earlier tour of England that led to unfavorable audience response and reviews, Forrest's popular supporters prepared what they hoped would be a similar reception for Macready in New York. On the night of Macready's first performance, antagonistic working-class supporters of Forrest shouted and threw objects until Macready and his fellow actors abandoned the stage.[5] Like many other actors attacked by the popular New York audience, Macready vowed to end his run in New York after this protest.[6]

In an unusual gesture, however, a number of New York City's wealthiest men, banded together with lawyers, writers, and editors to publish a petition in several newspapers urging Macready to continue, claiming that "the good sense and respect for order prevailing in this community will sustain you on the subsequent nights of your performance."[7] Most commonly associated with the patrician values of the Whig Party, the signers of this petition, called "the Macready Card," included established and conservative figures such as the lawyer and real estate developer Samuel Ruggles and that Knickerbocker literary icon, Washington Irving. But the petition also included the names of Democratically aligned Young American literary-nationalist spokesmen Evert Duyckinck and Cornelius Mathews and their associate, Herman Melville, suggesting that political affiliations, while relevant, were not strictly determining of allegiances in the battle over Shakespeare and theater practices. Soliciting city police and state militia support for Macready's next performance, the petitioners were aware of the provocative nature of their stand against the sovereignty of the popular audience. The armed presence on the scene at Macready's return to the Opera House on May 10 ensured that the play was performed without interruption. Meanwhile, during and after the performance, a growing crowd, consisting primarily of downtown laborers galvanized by the Democratic Tammany Hall sloganeering, formed outside the theater and refused to disperse. The crowd began throwing stones at the armed force positioned in front of the Opera House, and eventually the militia opened fire, killing over twenty people and injuring many others.

The May 10 riot was only one in a long history of theater riots since the advent of popular theater in the United States, but never had such a conflict resulted in so bloody an end. As one contemporary journalist famously reported: "[The Riot] leaves behind it a feeling to which this community has hitherto been a strange—an opposition of classes . . . ; in fact, to speak right out, a feeling that there is now, in our country, in New York City, what every good patriot has hitherto felt it his duty to deny—a *high* and a *low* class."[8] Although some scholars have found this comment particularly suggestive, it would be misleading to identify the Astor Place Riots as simply a moment of class identification: the Riots were an important moment of ideological conflict and cohesion for the whole spectrum of intersecting urban social, cultural, and political interests in the period. Not simply a conflict between "high" and "low" classes, the Astor Place Riots entangled the traditional urban elites, downtown workers, and the new middle class, the New York City Whig and Democratic political machines, the traditional cultural prerogatives of the urban elite and the Jacksonian popular audience as well as the new professional-middle-class model of cultural expertise. Far from simply exposing the existence of "high" and "low," the Astor Place Riots could be said to reveal the importance of professional cultural authority for a new cultural model that would supplant the traditional forms of "high" and "low" that had dominated American cultural life in the previous era.

Those who protested against Macready on May 7 and 10—the ostensible members of the "low" culture—understood their actions in a complex nexus of social and political meanings. For the protesting working-class people participating in the Astor Place Riots, support for Forrest and antipathy to Macready were expressions of their vision of American political and social order.[9] Forrest had made a career for himself in such theatrical vehicles as *Metamora* (1829), *The Gladiator* (1831), and *Jack Cade* (1835), playing charismatic heroes set within a decidedly egalitarian political context—one theater historian describes him as "the Andrew Jackson of his profession."[10] Forrest's self-styled "heroic" mode appealed directly to his audience's vision of democratic individualism, and he freely adapted both the content and form of Shakespeare's plays when he performed them to fit the demands of his popular audiences. In reviewing Forrest's *King Lear* in 1848, Evert Duyckinck, soon-to-be petitioner on Macready's behalf, would complain about Forrest's adaptations: "Mr. Forrest's stage version of Lear is not that of Tate altogether, or of Shakespeare. It has the tragic close of the original, but the fool is not restored, and the language retains something too much of the stage commonplaces. Why not bring back the original altogether? The play would be far more effective."[11] Although Forrest's adaptation was a compromise—Nahum Tate's version of *Lear* (1681) transformed Shakespeare's tragedy into a happy story, with Lear and Cordelia surviving—part of his popularity could be associated with his willingness to give the popular audience what they wanted.[12] The working class saw support for Forrest as a means of advocating democracy and social equality against the preferences of the elite for Macready.

In contrast, many contemporary observers saw the crowd outside the Opera House as simply a jingoistic mob, galvanized by a simplistic nationalism. A broadsheet, plastered on downtown walls on May 9, hinted (falsely) at British sailors' plans to suppress the popular audiences' "express[ion of] their opinions" of Macready, proclaiming:

WORKING MEN,

SHALL

AMERICANS

OR

ENGLISH RULE IN THIS CITY?. . .

We advocate no violence, but a free expression of
opinion to all public men!

WORKINGMEN! FREEMEN!

STAND BY YOUR

LAWFUL RIGHTS!

—*American Committee.*[13]

The broadsheet was instigated by "Captain" Isaiah Rynders, a Tammany Hall operative, who sought to capitalize on the patriotism of the populist "Locofoco" wing of the Democratic Party and the anti-British feeling among its many Irish members. But this was not simply a partisan political divide. Whether or not this sheet in fact advocated "no violence,'" it did speak to the Jacksonian continuation of what E. P. Thompson has called, in a British context, the "moral economy of the crowd," the manifestation of a "public" identity through crowd protest.[14] Although historians have demonstrated how the rioting crowd was delegitimized as a valid expression of American political identity from the aftermath of the Revolution through the nineteenth century, one form in which the rioting crowd had retained "popular sovereignty" was in the tradition of theater riots.[15]

Since the rise of American theater culture in the 1820s, American audiences, particularly popular audiences, had protested against performers, often British, who had displeased them in some fashion, but also generally against mediocre or bad performances. Evert Duyckinck, who would later emerge as a key agent in the Macready petition and thus an antagonist to the popular crowd's response to the Briton, favorably invoked this audience activism in 1847: "At the Bowery, a farce, founded on Dickens' Battle of Life, has been hissed—an old fashioned prerogative of the audience which might be more generally restored to our theatres with great advantage. It frequently saves a great deal of time, anticipating the slower result of the mathematical calculations of the treasurer."[16] By signing and distributing the Macready petition in 1849, Duyckinck was refuting his own 1847 acceptance of that "old fashioned prerogative of the audience." Indeed, for many contemporary commentators who took the side of the rioters, the pro-Macready petition circulated in the city papers functioned as an attack on that prerogative. The *United States Magazine and Democratic Review*'s account of the Riot argued that "the right to suspend the performances of an offending actor is become as it were common law" and described the petition as "casting opprobrium upon them for the exercise of their indefeasible right of expressing that displeasure."[17] For the rioting crowd, the petition became an attempt to overcome the traditional voice of "the people," as an elite project to supplant the popular audience's cultural authority to which they responded with a more vociferous version of the same.

This conflict did not come out of nowhere. That the Forrest–Macready feud tapped into an emergent social divide in New York City theater culture is illustrated by a minstrel song performed in a popular theater earlier in the year of the Riots:

> Music now is all de rage;/ De Ministrel Bands am all engaged;
> Both far and near de people talk/ 'Bout Nigger Singing in New York.
> . . . .
> De Astor Opera is anoder nice place;/ If *you* go thar, jest wash your face!
> Put on your "kids," and fix up neat,/ For dis am de spot of de *eliteet*![18]

This song, with its direct address to the primarily working-class, minstrel-attending *"you,"* who needed to "wash your face" and put on kid gloves to be allowed into the Astor, clarified the new social distinctions implicit in the Opera House's presence in the cultural life of antebellum New York. This perception of the Opera House as the home of an exclusionary *"eliteet"* was clearly in the air on the night of the Riots, as the rioting crowd chanted "You can't go in there without kid gloves on!" and "Burn the damned den of the aristocracy!" as they pelted the theater with paving stones.[19] The Riots could thus be understood as a vehicle for expressing the beliefs of the downtown crowd's egalitarian vision of American social order and a defense of their traditional cultural prerogatives and authority against attack.

The elite response of the petition was just as deeply embedded in political, social and cultural traditions of the period. Just as Forrest's popular

audience identified with his performance of a heroic "self-made" individualism reflected in a freely adapted Shakespeare, Macready's elite audience of
uptown Opera House attendees was drawn to his unexpurgated or "faithful"
versions of the plays that invoked Shakespeare as a figure of unquestionable
authority. This Shakespeare was characterized by works which were, in the
words of prominent antebellum lecturer Henry N. Hudson, "but commentaries on the law written on the human mind; ... [Shakespeare's] genius rec-
onciles, in its own operations, perfect obedience with perfect freedom."[20]
Not simply an icon of aesthetic authority, Hudson's Shakespeare embodied
a vision of social authority, one that naturalized the perfect order—"obedience" and "freedom" ideally joined in a "perfect" status quo. This same vision
of a natural order of freedom joined "perfectly" to obedience and to the status quo, emerged in a sermon on the Riots by the Reverend Henry Bellows,
whose Unitarian church the Melvilles had recently begun to attend at the
time of the Riots. Evert Duyckinck quoted Bellows in the aftermath of the
riots. Defending the action of the authorities against the protesting crowd,
Bellows asserted: "It is the peculiarity and beauty of all true and just laws,
to tend to convert obedience into joyful acquiescence."[21] Not included in
Duyckinck's account of this sermon was a portion, commented upon by the
pro-rioter "American Citizen," in which Bellows asserted rather vindic-
tively: "We have done something to vindicate order and law; WE OUGHT TO
HAVE DONE MORE!" The pamphleteer, taking this as an example of "aristocratic hate," called Bellows "the oracle of a large class in this community."[22]
Surveying Bellows' lectures and writings, Thomas Augst identifies him as
a representative of Whig mercantilism, a "prophet of liberalism" bestowing
authority upon commercial success.[23] Linking Shakespeare to the authority
of a culturally and religiously sanctioned status quo, the wealthy develop-
ers, merchants, and lawyers who supported Macready envisioned themselves as defenders of a distinctly upper-class-oriented vision of American
social order.

This elite vision of culture bolstering the status quo was a traditional element of antebellum urban elite cultural politics, often associated with the
Whig Party, which manifested itself in a stance of stewardship and uplift. If
antebellum populist politics could be characterized by the "old fashioned prerogative" of hissing and rioting, antebellum elite cultural politics emerged in
forms like the American Art-Union, an institution begun in New York City in
1839 to promote American visual arts and to promulgate certain aesthetic and
cultural values. When Joel Tyler Headley proclaimed in an 1845 address to

the Art-Union, "*pictures* are more powerful than *speeches*," he articulated the logic that justified elite investment in aesthetic culture as a continuation of politics by other means.[24] Essentially an art lottery dependent on membership, the managers of the Art-Union selected paintings and prints that they believed were innately "American," validating their patrician values by emphasizing history, republican virtue, and a traditional vision of community.[25] By the late 1840s, however, the Art-Union was under attack from both the popular press, particularly Bennett's New York *Herald*, which identified the Art-Union as a source of exclusivity, and from artists and cultural professionals such as Nathaniel Parker Willis, who labeled the managers "merchant amateurs."[26] The Art-Union was dissolved by 1852, after being prosecuted as a gambling institution, reflecting the ways in which traditional elite cultural interests were particularly vulnerable in the antebellum era. The two groups that attacked the Art-Union were representative of some of the important challengers to traditional urban elite authority. Bennett's "penny paper" *Herald* is frequently identified as a symbol of the newspaper revolution of the antebellum era, representative of the "democratization" of printing, which undermined elite control over public opinion.[27] The other critics of the Art-Union, mostly artists excluded from Art-Union patronage, and cultural commentators such as Willis, represented a new professionalized group of artists and critics who sought to legitimize their own authority by making elite or patrician aesthetic judgments seem simply like dilettantish meddling. Although attacked from "below," the Art-Union was not being attacked by "low," "popular," or "working-class" cultural interests, but by an emergent group of middle-class professionals who began to assert their power and authority over cultural interests in urban life.

The Macready petition was, in many ways, a response to this disempowerment of traditional antebellum elite cultural enterprises, but it represented an effort to include this new professional element that had demonstrated its new clout.[28] The petition carried the standard range of Whig-oriented urban elites, mainly old-money patricians with prominent roles in public and private institutions.[29] But the group also included two other components that, while intersecting with the traditional world of elite Whig cultural stewardship, also marked the importance of the new professionalism of specialization and expertise, embodied here by lawyers and literary professionals.

Lawyers were, of course, part of the traditional trinity of the professions, and a sizeable contingent of lawyers, more than from any of the other professions, kept their traditional association with urban elite culture in the antebellum era. Hence, some of New York City's wealthiest citizens were lawyers, including Samuel Ruggles, one of the petitioners. However, Peter Buckley notes that among the many lawyers whose signatures were gathered for the Macready Card—22 of the 48 signers—several were among the "poorer" of the petitioners.[30] In addition to certain Whig affiliations or sympathies, however, the lawyers included in the petition were notable for what Buckley described as "an aggressive vision of legality, and in particular, a new belief in the administration of law as a science."[31] Including lawyers who were proponents of a new legal professionalism, Macready's defenders sought another kind of validation for their intervention in cultural life. Responding to what the *Democratic Review* had described as the "common law" practice of popular audience sovereignty, the Macrèady petitioners legitimized their claim by adding the names of lawyers who had committed their careers to what Buckley described as "the reduction of arbitrariness in the application of common law, the spread of codification and the elevation of the legal profession further above the strata of the Trades."[32] This new legal professionalism proved a helpful ally to Macready's advocates who sought to go against the cultural tradition of popular-audience authority.

The other notable group included in the petition, seven literary professionals, also marked a significant shift from the general wealth and traditional elite status of the signers. At one level, the presence of the writers and editors signals the residual persistence of the association of the author and literary pursuits with the elite status of "gentleman." Certainly, the signature of Washington Irving, exemplar of the increasingly archaic model of the "literary gentleman," marks the lines of affiliation between authorship and elite status within the petition. Similarly, editors such as Duyckinck and Mordecai Noah were members of boards of such institutions as the Art-Union. However, there was no question that the literary professional presence on this petition was seen as a notable departure from conventional practice. The pro-rioter "American Citizen" noted that among the petition's "serried ranks of superannuated *millionaires*, [and] their dawdling sons" were to be included "unfortunate authors."[33] This view that authors were "unfortunate" participants in the conflict was shared by others. If the Whig stalwart Washington Irving did sign the petition, the other prominent American literary figure of the earlier generation, James Fenimore Cooper, did not. Reporting to his wife on the emerging conflict, Cooper wrote that those who did sign the petition were making a grave error in participating in the social conflict: "There is a

McReady [*sic*] riot, and likely to be a fight to-night. As I am not in it, I shall not volunteer a broken head. Some of the *literati* have put themselves forward and won't stand 'the hazard of the dye.'"[34] "Putting oneself forward" was the description of someone running for political office, and Cooper clearly imagined no good result coming from such an active mixing of writers with public life. Understanding his writing career as still very much a genteel activity, Cooper saw himself above the fray. Despite the active role that Cooper's later work took in commenting on American social and political life, his comments here suggest that he felt that it was not the writer's place to involve himself so directly in public life, but rather to keep his interventions to the printed page. In distinction to Cooper's vision of the author as one who should remain distinct from public life (and allow only the texts to embody his political and social views), the literary professional's signature could be seen not simply as an "unfortunate" mistake or an indication of political naïveté, but marked a new vision of the author's place in American life. The presence of literary professionals on the petition was, like that of the lawyers, a sign of the authority that the new professionalism bestowed upon authors in the antebellum era.

As earlier chapters have demonstrated, antebellum New York writers and editors were developing new public relations with their readership and establishing new professional standards for their work in this period. No longer modeled on the republican eighteenth-century public sphere of print that privileged anonymous or pseudonymous publication, the explosion of books and magazines of the antebellum era actively represented writers, often including profiles and engraved portraits of authors along with their writing in the many literary journals that appeared in Northern cities during the period.[35] If the new public role of literary celebrity was experienced as potentially alienating by individual writers, as my reading of *Typee* suggests, it still gave authors newly important status as individual representatives of aesthetic culture.[36] Whatever their affiliation with Whig politics or traditional elite cultural authority, the writers signing the Mcready petition functioned not as disinterested republican citizens, but as newly minted "experts" on matters of aesthetic culture. The signatures of writers and editors, including Herman Melville, signaled the way that literary professionals, as part of a general movement of professionalism, became socially significant as producers of symbolic capital in the new industrial economy.[37]

The Astor Place Riots demonstrate the way that antebellum literary professionals, like lawyers, doctors, and scientists, could become important elements in the new social configuration of American life. Like other professionals, writers could become "experts" whose opinions could mediate or intervene in conflicts among the classes. That the legal and literary professionals would side with elite interests during the Astor Place Riots could be said to symbolize the "natural" or "inevitable" allegiances that would form between the new professionals and urban wealth and capital, but it would be a mistake to associate professional interests exclusively with capital. In fact, one could argue that the different groups signing the petition could be doing so with decidedly different social and cultural purposes. For example, when Duyckinck reviewed the aftermath of the Riots, he saw the Riots themselves as a way to reconfigure the definition of the city's and nation's collective identity to the benefit—not of the wealthy—but the new urban middle classes. In an editor's column in *The Literary World*, Duyckinck contrasted the behavior of the rioting popular audience to that of city schoolteachers who had attended a free reading by Macready earlier in the week of the Riot:

> There was not the least expression of public opinion against Mr. Macready; for there was nothing censurable in his conduct. If any class of persons represent the people in this city it is the large body of common school teachers, men and women; and these, a few days previous, had passed unanimous resolutions, in the Hope Chapel, expressive of their esteem of Mr. Macready. The people were not represented by the mob who brought tow and matches to fire the Opera House on Monday night. This was understood by everybody who thought or cared for the matter in the community.[38]

If the Riots were essentially an ideological conflict over cultural agency—whose social values define American culture?—Duyckinck suggests that the "winner" was neither the traditional cultural models of "high" or "low," but the new middle classes, urban nonmanual laborers, whose cultural values, taste, and behavior would come to represent the American "public" and "people." Duyckinck's proclamation hardly fixes or proves the reality of middle-class cultural dominance, but it does reveal some of the ideological stakes involved in the professional participation in the Astor Place Riots.

In fact, although the Astor Place Riots have been interpreted as a conflict between the two most prominent models of cultural politics in antebellum America, with the "low" popular sovereignty of the Jacksonian working-class audience battling the "high" patrician governance of urban wealth with "high" winning out, one could argue that the Astor Place Riots were truly the starting point for a new professional middle-class cultural hegemony. Indeed, in the aftermath of the Riots, it was a professional cultural politics, formed as a synthesis of antebellum "high" and "low" that made claims for "democracy" while promoting new hierarchies, which became increasingly dominant over the course of the nineteenth century.

As a signer of the Macready Card, Melville was an active participant in the construction of this new model of American cultural politics. However, no commentary on the Riots survives from Melville: no mention in correspondence and just a tangential reference in his published writings (only a reference to seeing Macready perform in London).[39] Despite this, I argue that Melville was deeply involved in thinking through the meanings of this cultural conflict. If the Astor Place Riots revealed the antebellum "high" and "low" versions of Shakespeare, we can look to the writings of Herman Melville and his complex engagement with the social and cultural meanings of Shakespeare to understand what a "professional" version of Shakespeare could look like.

Melville's Shakespeare: Forging a Professional Cultural Politics

Given the symbolic importance of the Astor Place Riots to antebellum New York City life, it is significant that Melville was himself a participant. This is a very material example of the way that writers can be deeply implicated in the political and social debates of their times. With the publication of Levine's *Highbrow/Lowbrow* in 1988 and its focus on the Riots has come increased, though still relatively scant, attention to Melville's involvement.[40] In his exhaustively researched biography, for example, Hershel Parker acknowledges Melville's participation, but attaches little significance to the act, asserting that he signed the petition "without thinking of the implications," adding parenthetically, "who expected anything to follow from an expression of principle?"[41] Far from being an unthinking, inconsequential act, though, Melville's participation in the Astor Place Riots reflected not only his friendship with Duyckinck, one of the major circulators of the petition, but also his involvement with Shakespeare's works and their social meanings from the moment he began reading (or rereading) the plays early in 1849. From his initial response to his reading, to his signature on the Macready Card, to his literary manifesto/criticism "Hawthorne and His Mosses," and beyond to *Moby-Dick*, Melville's thoughts on Shakespeare were filtered through the social meanings of culture in the antebellum era. Melville's signature on the petition and his meditations on the meanings of Shakespeare reflect the same class-divided associations of Shakespeare

revealed by the Astor Place Riots, but all demonstrate his attempt to articulate a synthesis of these different understandings, working to develop what
could be called a "professional" model of Shakespeare.

Writing to Duyckinck in the winter of 1849, Melville reported "loung-
ing on a sofa" in his father-in-law's Boston home "& reading Shakspeare
[sic]."[42] The reading experience led Melville to liken Shakespere to Jesus
Christ: "Ah, he's full of sermons-on-the-mount, and gentle, aye, almost as
Jesus. . . . [I]f another Messiah ever comes twill be in Shakespere's person."[43] Given Duyckinck's noted piety, such comments were potentially
offensive, and Melville's next letter to Duyckinck on March 3 seeks to
explain his enthusiasm: "To one of your habits of thought, I confess that in
my last [letter], I seemed, but only *seemed* irreverent."[44] Explaining this,
Melville quickly situates his understanding of Shakespeare within the complex set of social meanings and distinctions that emerged during the Astor
Place Riots three months later:

> And do not think, my boy, that because I, impulsively broke forth in jubillations
> [sic] over Shakspeare, that, therefore, I am of the number of the *snobs* who burn
> their turns of rancid fat at his shrine. No, I would stand afar off & alone, & burn
> some pure Palm oil, the product of some overtopping trunk.
>
> I would to God Shakspeare had lived later, & promenaded in Broadway. Not
> that I might have had the pleasure of leaving my card with him at the Astor, or
> made merry with him over a bowl of the fine Duyckinck punch; but that the
> muzzle which all men wore on their souls in the Elizebethan [sic] day, might not
> have intercepted Shakspere's full articulations. For I hold it a verity, that even
> Shakspeare, was not a frank man to the uttermost. And, indeed, who in this
> intolerant Universe is, or can be? But the Declaration of Independence makes a
> difference.[45]

This famous passage is often noted for its expansive citation of the Jacksonian exceptionalist notion that the democratic "Declaration" makes the
United States different from all other nations, making it a place where true
"frank[ness]" might be expressed for the first time. In this comment,
Melville seems allied primarily with the Democratic political values
espoused by Young American political and literary enthusiasts, but also by
Tammany Hall's working-class–oriented political machine.[46] This Shakespeare is no transcendent voice of obedience to the status quo, but instead
the advocate of heroic individualism: the Shakespeare understood by the
downtown audience to be embodied so forcefully by Forrest.

If the comment on the "Declaration" seems primarily political, with
decidedly egalitarian social connotations, Melville's differentiation of his

appreciation of Shakespeare from "the number of the *snobs*" who worship him is explicitly social, albeit this time not as an identification with egalitarian values, but from an elevated social status. The word *snob* has always been a derogatory term, but it was a term whose social meaning was in transition at precisely the moment Melville was writing. During the late 1840s and early 1850s, this colloquialism could mean either the specific social rank of "a person belonging to the lower classes of society" or the more vague social condemnation of "a vulgar and ostentatious person."[47] It is almost precisely at the moment that Melville uses the term "snob" that the Oxford English Dictionary marks the shift into its less directly lower-class associated meaning, the beginning of its eventual transformation into its more common present association, ironically enough, with the opposite class valence. In any case, given the brevity and isolation of the reference, it would be impossible to assert authoritatively which social group Melville was attacking, though commonality of usage in the period would suggest the lower-class association. If so, this passage pits Democratic, egalitarian political views against Whiggish or elite-oriented social values. This might seem a contradictory mix, but it is one that speaks not just to Melville's personal idiosyncrasies, but also to the complicated balancing act of the new professional cultural politics. In any case, it is important to note that from its earliest references, months before the Astor Place Riots, Melville's response to Shakespeare is inextricable from social distinctions in antebellum New York City cultural life.

Even the way Melville imagines Shakespeare as he would be if he lived in the antebellum era is deeply enmeshed in social and cultural distinctions of the period. To envision Shakespeare "promenad[ing] in Broadway" invokes one of the most widely recognized, yet complex acts of social distinction and hierarchy formation in antebellum New York City. When Melville imagines Shakespeare promenading on Broadway, he situates the Elizabethan playwright within a ritual that one historian suggests "symbolically negotiated the tension between class hierarchies and civic fellowship in a capitalist democracy."[48] Broadway was a street with enormous social significance in the antebellum era. It was, as Edward Spann describes, "the fashionable street of the nation, *the* place in democratic America for the successful to display their superior social status."[49] Promenading on Broadway was a new public act of distinction in the antebellum era, one that David Scobey claims "stabilized social position by making it *visible*, symbolically assuaging middle-class anxieties over the deceitful, occluded, illegible conditions of urban life."[50] In one of his city profiles for the *New-York Tribune*, later published in book form as *New York in Slices* (1849), George Foster wrote of the Broadway promenade: "It is above all other streets . . . the test of respectability. If you touch your hat to fifty people in Broadway, your character is 'O.K.'—you are an established man."[51] To imagine Shakespeare promenading on Broadway was not, thus, a particularly "democratic" vision: Broadway's working-class counterpart, the Bowery, had its own culture of display, where elaborately dressed Bowery "b'hoys and g'hals" enacted their own rituals and distinctions.[52] Melville's fantasy of Shakespeare promenading on Broadway could be said to highlight the ways in which social distinctions in antebellum America were writ across any attempt to understand the meaning of a cultural experience, whether reading Shakespeare or walking down a commercial boulevard.

On the one hand, imagining Shakespeare promenading on Broadway, so that his "full articulations" would be 'unmuzzled' seems to be a refutation of the Macreadyite vision of Shakespeare as a genius who links "freedom" and "obedience." On the other, the assumption that Shakespeare would be most comfortable striding about on Broadway, appears to locate him markedly within "respectable" society, fitting him into the petitioners' vision. Deeply enmeshed in the complications of cultural politics in the period, Melville's letter reveals his own ambivalent cultural allegiances and demonstrates that his participation in the Riots was part of a larger process of engagement with the social conflicts of culture in antebellum New York City.

Antebellum social distinctions were no less prevalent in Melville's published comments on Shakespeare. In the aftermath of the Astor Place Riots, Melville published his most important work of literary criticism in Evert Duyckinck's magazine *The Literary World*. Ostensibly a review of Nathaniel Hawthorne's *Mosses from the Old Manse*, the 1850 piece entitled "Hawthorne and His Mosses" comments extensively on Shakespeare as an exemplar of artistic excellence and demonstrates Melville's attempt to establish an understanding of his own aesthetic practice from the social divides of Shakespeare's antebellum meanings. From the first, Melville situates Shakespeare within the social context of theater, asserting that the playwright's success has come from his popular audiences' misunderstanding of his work:

> For by philosophers Shakespeare is not adored as the great man of tragedy and comedy.— "Off with his head! So much for Buckingham!" this sort of rant, interlined by another hand, brings down the house,—those mistaken souls, who dream of Shakespeare as a mere man of Richard the Third humps, and Macbeth daggers.[53]

The interpolated 'ranting' quotation "Off with his head" comes from Colley Cibber's adapted version of Shakespeare's most popular play in the antebellum era, *Richard III*, and was an example of what Melville calls later in the essay "the popularizing noise and show of broad farce, and blood-besmirched tragedy" of the popular Shakespeare (245).[54] It was precisely this version of Shakespeare, freely adapted ("interlined by another hand") and dramatically staged ("Richard the Third humps and Macbeth daggers"), that constituted Forrest's method and the Shakespeare most appreciated on the popular stage in the period.[55] Continuing to attack Shakespeare's popularity, Melville argues that the audiences who saw him only "on the tricky stage, (which alone made, and is still making him his mere mob renown)" experience only the "least part of [Shakespeare's] genius" (245). Criticizing Shakespeare's popularity as "mob renown" and his popular audience as "mistaken souls," Melville seems to claim the Shakespeare of the Opera House as his own.

While Melville critiques the working class misunderstanding of Shakespeare, he also excoriates the upper class for its attitude toward the English playwright. In contrast to the Macreadyite claim by the lecturer Hudson, "Great genius has in almost every instance approved itself a worshipper of the past, a cherisher of social order," Melville asserts that "great geniuses are parts of the times; they themselves are the times and possess a correspondent coloring" (246).[56] Far from Hudson's vision of Shakespeare as a static preserver of the status quo, Melville imagines artistic geniuses in dynamic engagement with their times. Melville dismisses the elite construction of Shakespeare as the transhistorical voice of the status quo, producing "commentaries on the law written on the human mind." Asserting, "Let us away with this Bostonian leaven of literary flunkeyism toward England," Melville could be said to chide the elite for their lack of patriotism:

> Besides, this absolute and unconditional adoration of Shakespeare has grown to be a part of our Anglo Saxon superstitions. The Thirty-Nine Articles are now Forty. Intolerance has come to exist in this matter. You must believe in Shakespeare's unapproachability, or quit the country. But what sort of a belief is this for an American, a man who is bound to carry republican progressiveness into Literature, as well as into Life? (245)

Here Melville highlights the hypocrisy of Americans who would praise the "republican progressiveness" of American politics, but refuse to see similar progressive possibilities in American literature.

Significantly, Melville's invocation of the Anglican Church's "Thirty-Nine Articles" and the Anglo-Saxon heritage of Shakespeare's worshippers refers to a decidedly different constituency from those who established his "mob renown." By 1850, the foreign-born population of New York City constituted over 45 percent of the total population.[57] This immigrant population, predominantly Germans and Irish Catholics, made up a high percentage of the city's poor and became identified with a host of social problems. Many of the city's earlier population, especially the city's traditional elite, but also many of its workers, who were predominantly Anglo-Saxon and Protestant, turned to nativism as a response to social problems and potential political disenfranchisement. Nativist political groups emerged in New York City in the 1840s and then reemerged later in the 1850s, running as reformers against the problems posed by immigrants and Catholics. Although it would be inaccurate to associate nativism with elite status, there is little doubt that in associating this group of Shakespeare's admirers of Anglo-Saxon racial heritage and a Protestant religious background, Melville is locating a group that would not be associated primarily with the working-class or the "mob." Using the language of republicanism, Melville questions the cultural politics of the tradition-bound ethnic and religiously distinct upper classes of the antebellum city.

Whether attacking the Bowery audience's misunderstanding of Shakespeare or the urban elite's self-serving appropriation of Shakespeare, Melville marks his aesthetic distinctions with social distinctions throughout "Hawthorne and His Mosses." But critical readings of "Hawthorne and His Mosses" have seldom acknowledged the conflicted antebellum social content of the essay's comments on Shakespeare.[58] Perhaps, though, we should blame Melville himself for this absence. The very vagueness of his assertions has allowed readers to see Melville's version of Shakespeare as simply romantic aestheticism.[59] After all, in the essay, Melville isolates a Shakespeare whose work expresses what he portentously, but obscurely, calls "occasional flashings-forth of the intuitive Truth."[60] These moments, which probe "at the very axis of reality," are said to make Shakespeare one of the "masters of the great Art of Telling the Truth."[61] For Melville, this "Truth" is expressed "through the mouths of the dark characters of Hamlet, Timon, Lear, and Iago," for what is said is "so terrifically true, that it were madness for any good man, in his own proper character, to utter, or even hint of them."[62] But other than imbuing this "Truth" with a vaguely subversive quality, Melville avoids suggesting why such "Truth" would be so unpopular.

But even these abstracted and vague terms cannot be wholly separated from Melville's political and social understandings. Although the social content of Melville's Shakespearean "Truth" remains unexplained in "Hawthorne and His Mosses," Melville returned to this topic in a letter to Hawthorne nearly a year later, written near the time of the completion of *Moby-Dick*. In this famous letter, Melville renewed the claim that "Truth" was dangerous, socially unacceptable, or mad: "Truth is the silliest thing under the sun. Try to get a living by the Truth—and go to the Soup Societies. . . . Truth is ridiculous to men."[63] Seemingly unconnected to the Shakespearean aesthetics of "Hawthorne and His Mosses," Melville uses the term "Truth" to address his own political beliefs, which he describes as a fusion of "political equality" and "an aristocracy of the brain."[64] His belief in "political equality" reflects the Jacksonian ideology of egalitarianism, but the notion of "an aristocracy of the brain" reflects an elitist validation of intellectual labor that justifies professional middle-class distinctions from the working class. In this way, Melville's letter recapitulates what one sociologist has described as the professional dilemma in antebellum American life: "The ideology of merit clashed in America with the ideological egalitarianism of the political system."[65] Like Melville's letter, which becomes a tangle of contradictory political and social stances, antebellum professionals faced an ideological crisis: wanting to justify hierarchical distinctions from the working class, they also needed the social logic of democracy to justify their equality (if not moral superiority) to the wealthy elite or capitalist class. It is the difficulties of explaining the conjunction of these apparently conflicting beliefs that leads Melville to speak of Truth's ridiculousness.

Attempting to dismiss the threat that an "aristocracy of the brain" posed for "political equality" in American life, Melville closes his discussion by asserting, "It seems an inconsistency to assert unconditional democracy in all things, and yet confess a dislike to all mankind—in the mass. But not so. —But it's an endless sermon, —no more of it."[66] Although acknowledging the ideological "inconsistency" of a view that attempts to join egalitarian belief to elitist distinctions from "the mass," Melville is unable to rebut imagined critiques of his "Truth." For Melville, Shakespeare could become the cultural expression of his paradoxical social politics, and in his major work after the Astor Place Riots, *Moby-Dick*, Melville would adopt Shakespearean literary forms to express this vision. For Melville, Shakespeare becomes a way to resolve the contradictory or "inconsistent" cultural politics of the antebellum professional model of culture.

Moby-Dick's *Shakespeare*

Moby-Dick is more than a famous American book; it has become a cultural touchstone, a common reference point in modern American life. Integral to this sanctification was the work of F. O. Matthiessen, whose critical study *American Renaissance* (1941) formalized a canon of nineteenth-century American literature for the post–WWII era.[67] Matthiessen made *Moby-Dick* the centerpiece of his study, but validated his reading of *Moby-Dick* and his defense of an American literary tradition through its "intimate kinship to the seventeenth-century [English literature's] metaphysical strain."[68] This allowed Matthiessen to unveil "Melville's extraordinary debt to Shakespeare," validating American literature by associating the American authors with the already established icons of the English literary canon, particularly Shakespeare.[69] Matthiessen was not the first to observe Melville's "debt to Shakespeare," but in the aftermath of *American Renaissance,* the most long-standing and prominent tradition of *Moby-Dick* criticism has used Melville's literary debt to Shakespeare, especially the novel's liberal use of intertexts of *Hamlet* and *King Lear,* to elevate its status as a sophisticated and profound work of art.[70] It could be argued, in fact, that *Moby-Dick* owes its importance in American literature and cultural life substantially to its association with Shakespeare.

The novel's use of the play's dialogue form, stage directions, and soliloquies as well as its direct invocation of Shakespearean intertexts are the basic elements of the critical apparatus that established *Moby-Dick* as one of America's cultural masterpieces. The Shakespeareanism of the novel is most consistently associated with Ahab, the mad whaling captain obsessed with a white whale. Melville initiates his use of Shakespearean language and dramatic forms in *Moby-Dick* in a sequence of chapters beginning with "The Quarter-deck" and closing with "Midnight, Forecastle," which introduces reader and crew to Ahab's project of revenge. Using language evocative of Shakespearean theater in "The Quarter-deck," Ahab manipulates the crew into joining him in his "dark" purpose to hunt the white whale. The following chapters of this miniplay explore the consequences of this persuasion, closing as the crew, cast as a violent mob, is disturbed in the middle of a brawl by an arriving storm. Reflecting more than just an interest in Shakespearean forms, this miniplay also engages with the contested social content of Shakespearean theater as it emerged in the Riots. Later in the novel, Melville returns to Shakespearean language and forms in a series of encounters between Ahab and two minor characters, Pip and the Carpenter. Far from representing the context of the Astor Place Riots, these later Shakespeareanized exchanges explicitly invoke the Shakespeare of "Hawthorne and His Mosses," articulating the alternately "dark" and "silly" Truth of the "endless sermon" that justified the contradictory professional conjunction of "political equality" and "aristocracy of the brain."

Matthiessen demonstrated the extent of Melville's formal debt to Shakespeare in "The Quarter-deck" when he took a selection and put it into blank verse in his extensive reading in *American Renaissance*.[71] In this chapter, Ahab draws the assembled crew around him and leads them through a series of questions and staged rituals to inspire them to join in his personal hunt for the white whale. As the crew waits for Ahab to speak, the narrator describes them as anxious spectators as they watch "with curious and not wholly unapprehensive faces" for Ahab to begin.[72] Ahab suddenly begins to ask the crew a series of rhetorical questions about whaling: "What do ye do when ye see a whale, men?" "What do ye next, men?" "And what tune is it ye pull to, men?" (36: 141). The crew responds with a "hearty animation into which [Ahab's] unexpected question[s] had so magnetically thrown them" (36: 141). Inexplicably caught up in Ahab's performance, they "gaze curiously at each other, as if marveling how it was that they themselves became so excited at such seemingly purposeless questions" (36: 141–42). While actively responding to Ahab, the crew's responses are slogan answers to "purposeless questions," and it is their "hearty animation" that Ahab will adapt to his cause, turning the general will to hunt whales into the private aim of punishing the white whale.

Ahab's use of questions has a clear source in the hortatory rhetoric of popular antebellum theater. Typically actors operating in the hortatory mode addressed the audience and asked them questions, encouraging the audience members to involve themselves actively in the performance as part of the "democratic" appeal of antebellum theater.[73] While this hortatory mode encouraged an active role on the part of antebellum theatergoers, the rhetoric of popular plays typically shaped audience response, so that the impression of activity was more commonly a form of rhetorical manipulation.[74] It is no coincidence that, during the Astor Place Riots, Edwin Forrest was accused by some antebellum New Yorkers of using the nationalist and democratic exuberance of the popular downtown theater audience to forward his personal revenge against Macready. Like the pro-Forrest rioters at the Astor Place Opera House, the *Pequod*'s crew is manipulated by staged rhetoric into forwarding the private goals of a demagogic individual.

Similarly, Ahab's speech and gestures in "The Quarter-deck" reflect Forrest's intensely emotive and physical acting style. In his speech to the crew, Ahab "shouted with a terrific, loud, animal sob, like that of a heart-stricken moose. . . . 'God bless ye,' he seemed to half sob and half shout" (36: 143). In his diary, Evert Duyckinck described in a comment on his *King Lear* of 1847, how Forrest "tramps and staggers and is convulsed like an ox in the shambles. If a bull could act he would act like Forrest."[75] In the years preceding the Riots, Duyckinck, who had once actively supported Forrest, was increasingly drawn to Macready's more restrained acting style and his unadulterated versions of Shakespeare. As with Forrest's oxlike performances, Ahab's "heart-stricken moose" sobs present a problematic mode of theatrical persuasion and manipulation. Ahab's ponderous pacing of the deck with his prosthetic leg, his moose sobs, and his dramatic rituals to consecrate the crew's vow to search for the white whale: all invoke the "Richard the Third humps and Macbeth daggers" Melville bemoaned in his critique of the popular antebellum staging of Shakespeare in "Hawthorne and His Mosses."[76]

In "The Quarter-deck" scene, Melville stages not only Forrest's emotive and persuasive populist Shakespeareanism, but also the elite perspective on the Astor Place Riots through the intervention of the *Pequod*'s first mate, Starbuck. Like the Whig-oriented representatives of New York City's "upper ten" and their allies during the Riots, Starbuck interrupts Ahab's exhortations, presenting himself as the representative of "good sense and respect for order."[77] Although the Nantucket first mate might seem an odd representative of urban elite cultural politics, the terms of his rebuttal of Ahab fit surprisingly well into the stance of conservative stewardship embraced by the Whiggish supporters of Macready. Countering Ahab's use of theatrical rhetoric to transform the ship's goal to personal revenge, Starbuck invokes the economic principles of market exchange ("thy vengeance . . . will not fetch thee much in our Nantucket market" [36: 143]) and religious order ("To be enraged with a dumb thing, Captain Ahab, seems blasphemous" [36: 144]). Like the elite supporters of Macready during the Riots, Starbuck envisions himself as the steward of an economic and religious status quo threatened by Ahab's manipulation of the crew's populist sentiment.[78] The quarter-deck conflict between Ahab and Starbuck has been at the heart of historicist readings of *Moby-Dick* that see the novel as deeply involved in antebellum political divides, but these readings have, for the most part, neglected the role of Shakespeare in that politics.[79]

Meanwhile, Ahab responds to Starbuck's critique by demonstrating the success of his populist Shakespeareanism. Pointing out that the crew, embodying the popular will, is with him, Ahab brags to Starbuck: "The Pagan leopards—the unrecking and unworshipping things, that live; and seek, and give no reasons for the torrid life they feel! The crew, man, the crew! Are they not one and all with Ahab, in this matter of the whale?" (36: 144). The theme of the crew as animalistic and violent is taken up again later in the "Midnight, Forecastle" chapter that closes out the miniplay of this sequence. In this chapter, the unity of Ahab's purpose quickly gives way to a racial divide between two crew members, and the crew quickly shifts into a mob eager to witness the violence that will ensue. Stopped only by an incoming squall, the young black shipkeeper Pip, comments on the crew: "Jimmini, what a squall! But those chaps there are worse yet—they are your white squalls, they. White squalls? white whale, shirr! shirr!" (40: 154). If this association of the crew with violence, whether meteorological or animal, is an implicit commentary on the antebellum popular theater audience, Melville will make this judgment explicit later in the "The Grand Armada" chapter, in which Ishmael defends the self-destructive behavior of a school of whales being hunted by comparing it to the behavior of the antebellum working-class theater audience:

> Witness, too, all human beings, how when herded together in the sheep-fold of a theatre's pit, they will, at the slightest alarm of fire, rush helter-skelter for the outlets, crowding, trampling, jamming, and remorselessly dashing each other to death. Best, therefore, withhold any amazement at the strangely gallied whales before us, for there is no folly of the beasts of the earth which is not infinitely outdone by the madness of men. (87: 322)

The "theatre's pit," the site of the cheapest seats in the antebellum popular theaters, whose attendees were often called "pittites," was commonly seen by wealthier observers as the most unruly and violent element in the antebellum theater. The pits were typically the place where riots had occurred since the advent of popular theater.[80] Like the whales flailing about while under attack and the antebellum "pit" audience in their "sheep-fold," the *Pequod*'s crew is so unthinkingly susceptible to the magnetism of Ahab's performance that they can only "marvel" at their own reaction and quickly participate in or witness violence.

In the allegorical meditation on antebellum theater culture in the sequence from "The Quarter-deck" to "Midnight, Forecastle," Melville explores the context of the Astor Place Riots and takes a dim view of all the participants in the antebellum American cultural landscape. With the crew as a violent and animalistic popular theater audience eager to be manipulated, Ahab as the self-serving manipulator of populist rhetoric and Starbuck as the ineffectual defender of the status quo, the Shakespearean sequence from "The Quarter-deck" to "Midnight, Forecastle" dramatizes an American cultural landscape in crisis. If these were the only uses of Shakespearean form or language in *Moby-Dick*, one could argue that Shakespeare and theater meant simply "the tricky stage" of antebellum class conflict for Melville.[81] But just as he elaborated the limitations of antebellum elite and popular versions of Shakespeare to put forward his own vision of Shakespearean "Truth" in "Hawthorne and His Mosses," Melville moves beyond his apparent meditation on the Astor Place Riots to present a positive vision of Ahab's Shakespeare in *Moby-Dick*, particularly in a sequence of exchanges between Ahab and secondary characters such as the young black ship-keeper Pip and the mechanically minded ship's Carpenter.

Ahab's exchanges with Pip and the Carpenter explicitly evoke the dynamics and themes of Shakespearean intertexts, particularly that of *King Lear* and *Hamlet*. It is no coincidence that Melville identified Lear and Hamlet as two of Shakespeare's "Truthful" "dark characters" in "Hawthorne and His Mosses." Explicitly associating Ahab with both Lear and Hamlet, Melville's later version of Shakespeare in *Moby-Dick* presents Ahab as the speaker of a subversive "Truth," less a demagogue than a private individual musing on the philosophical consequences of his observations and insights. The Shakespearean "Truth" of Ahab's exchanges with Pip and the Carpenter map out a contradictory social politics, one that very much mirrors the "endless sermon" of Melville's letter to Hawthorne in which he resolved the "inconsistency" of "assert[ing] unconditional democracy in all things, and yet confess[ing] a dislike to all mankind—in the mass." Recasting Ahab as Lear and Hamlet, Melville adapts Shakespeare to validate the paradoxical synthesis of meritocratic and egalitarian cultural politics of antebellum professionalism.

The interactions between Ahab and the young black ship-keeper Pip, widely acknowledged as Shakespearean, elaborate the "democratic" half of the "endless sermon." The Ahab–Pip relationship has been important to critical understandings of *Moby-Dick* since 1937, when Charles Olson drew attention to its overt parallel to Lear's bond with the Fool.[82] Explicitly invoking Shakespeare, Melville recasts the maddened Lear's bond with the crazy–wise Fool through Ahab's relationship to Pip, who is driven mad after being abandoned at sea during a whale hunt. Cast in the role of "holy fool," Pip's madness is described as similar to the "ridiculous" and subversive "Truth" Melville imagined in his letter to Hawthorne: "He saw God's foot upon the treadle of the loom, and spoke it; and therefore his shipmates called him mad. So man's insanity is heaven's sense; and wandering from all mortal reason, man comes at last to that celestial thought, which, to reason, is absurd and frantic" (93: 347). When they meet later in the narrative, Ahab and Pip take up with each other as kindred spirits, both sharing a madness that is constructed around "Truth."

Ahab's recognition of Pip's madness late in the novel in "The Log and Line" leads to the white captain's surprising bond with the black ship-keeper. Ahab sees in Pip another forsaken by the Gods, presented in Shakespearean diction: "Oh, ye frozen heavens! look down here. Ye did beget this luckless child, and have abandoned him, ye creative libertines" (125: 428). Ahab instantly forges an emotional bond with Pip and proclaims the intensity of his identification with him: "Here, boy; Ahab's cabin shall be Pip's home henceforth, while Ahab lives. Thou touchest my inmost centre, boy; thou art tied to me by cords woven of my heart-strings. Come, let's down" (125: 428). Ahab constructs his bond to Pip as a response to "the omniscient gods oblivious of suffering man" and as an assertion of the common bonds of humanity over social hierarchy: "Come! I feel prouder leading thee by thy black hand, than though I grasped an Emperor's!" (125: 428). The old sailor observing this interaction proclaims their shared madness: "There go two daft ones now, . . . [o]ne daft with strength, the other daft with weakness" (125: 428).

This vision of a shared bond of madness clearly invokes the context of *King Lear*. But if the Lear–Fool intertext invokes Melville's "Hawthorne and His Mosses" vision of a Shakespearean "Truth," the bond between Ahab and Pip, explicitly understood as a refutation of the conventions of social hierarchy, also replays the elaboration of Melville's social and political model of "Truth" in his letter to Hawthorne: "[W]hen you see or hear of my ruthless democracy on all sides, you may possibly feel a touch of a shrink, or something of that sort. It is but nature to be shy of a mortal who boldly declares that a thief in jail is as honorable a personage as Gen. George Washington."[83] Melville's political "Truth' of "ruthless democracy" connects Washington, the stereotypical embodiment of American virtue, with "a thief in jail" to produce a vision of egalitarianism. In *Moby-Dick*, however, this vision of "ruth-less democracy" is embodied in Ahab's being "prouder" to grasp Pip's "black hand" than an "Emperor's," reflecting the unseating of the racist hierarchy of white over black[84]

If Ahab's Shakespearean exchanges with Pip seem to model a "ruthless" or "unconditional democracy," Ahab's equally Shakespearean exchanges with the ship's Carpenter portray the other side of his seemingly "inconsistent" social message: the "dislike to mankind—in the mass." Like Pip, the Carpenter becomes significant only late in the novel. If Pip is an other-worldly seer, the Carpenter, however, is notable only for his quotidian mechanical competency. The Carpenter is introduced in the novel in a chapter in which his nature and his connection to his mechanical labors are discussed at length. While not particularly Shakespearean, this chapter begins by explicitly recalling Melville's "endless sermon":

> Seat thyself sultanically among the moons of Saturn, and take high abstracted man alone; and he seems a wonder, a grandeur, and a woe. But from the same point, take *mankind in the mass*, and for the most part, they seem a mob of unnecessary duplicates, both contemporary and hereditary. But most humble though he was, and far from furnishing an example of high, humane abstraction; the Pequod's carpenter was no duplicate; hence, he now comes in person on this stage," (107: 387—*my italics*).

Posed against the divide between the "wonder" of elevated individuality and the "unnecessary duplicat[ion]" of the degraded collectivity, the Carpenter's anomalous status—neither a "duplicate" nor an individualized "abstraction"—is something of a conundrum.[85] Defined wholly by his multiple manual tasks, the Carpenter becomes a man of machinelike parts, the human embodiment of what we now would call a "swiss army knife," but which Melville identified with its British antecedent:

> He was like one of those unreasoning but still highly useful, *multum in parvo*, Sheffield contrivances, assuming the exterior—though a little swelled—of a common pocket knife; . . . So, if his superiors wanted to use the carpenter for a screw-driver, all they had to do was to open that part of him, and the screw was fast; or if for tweezers, take him up by the legs, and there they were. (107: 388–89)

Defined by the "strange uncompromisedness" of his manual labors (107: 388), the Carpenter is an unsettling combination of man and machine, individual and collective. The human embodiment of "*multum in parvo*" (much in little), the Carpenter is literally the individual man as mass. His "certain impersonal stolidity," is seen as "half-horrible," as it embraces as "an all-ramifying heartlessness" (388). His mechanical usefulness reveals "a sort of unintelligence," as he works not "so much by reason or instinct, or simply because he had been tutored to it, . . . but merely by a kind of deaf and dumb, spontaneous literal process" (388). In the Carpenter, mechanical labor reveals its dehumanizing effects: "He was pure manipulator; his brain, if he ever had one, must have early oozed along into the muscles of his fingers" (107:386). While *Moby-Dick* has been cited for its "democratic" validation of labor and the laborer, the scenes between Ahab and the Carpenter are, in fact, some of the few encounters in the novel between manual labor and non-manual labor, and these adapt the "dark" Shakespeare to justify a hierarchical "dislike" of the manual laborer as an embodiment of the "mass."[86]

While Ahab was imagined as Lear in his encounters with Pip, the mad captain is recast as Hamlet in his exchanges with the Carpenter. Embodying another of Shakespeare's prized "dark characters," Ahab's comments are again implicitly linked to a valorized "Truth." While Pip functioned as a reimagined Fool, the Carpenter becomes Ophelia's sexton in a series of explicitly staged and Shakespearean chapters.[87] Speaking to the Carpenter, who is noisily converting Queequeg's now-unnecessary coffin into a life buoy, Ahab explicitly invokes the Shakespearean intertext of their exchanges: Act V, scene 1, of *Hamlet*, when Hamlet comes upon the grave-digger singing as he digs Ophelia's grave. In the novel, Ahab enters the scene, asking, "[T]he grave-digger in the play sings, spade in hand. Dost thou never?" (127: 432). Like Hamlet's exchanges with the grave-digger, Ahab's encounters with the Carpenter in "Ahab and the Carpenter" and "The Deck" revolve around a divide between literal and philosophical understandings of death and the prospects of an afterlife.[88] The exchanges between the two are a source of frustration for Ahab as the Carpenter can only understand his tasks literally. Thus he responds to Ahab's charges against the unthinking hubris of mechanical production of being "as unprincipled as the gods" by asserting, "But I do not mean anything, sir. I do as I do" (127: 432). The Carpenter, whose brain has "oozed along into the muscles of his fingers," is unable to see the possible philosophical ramifications of his mechanical actions, whether making a new leg for Ahab or transforming a coffin into a life buoy. When Ahab questions the meaning of the Carpenter's use of the word "Faith," the mechanical laborer can only explain: "Why, faith, sir, it's only a sort of exclamation-like—that's all, sir" (127: 432). While Ahab's monomaniacal search for Moby-Dick can be understood, as Starbuck asserted in "The Quarter-deck," as blasphemy, the Carpenter is unthinkingly blasphemous, having reduced faith to an exclamation only. For Ahab, the Carpenter is simply an annoyance: "The grey-headed wood-pecker tapping the hollow tree! Blind and dumb might well be envied now" (127: 432). His encounters with the Carpenter inspire Ahab to aver, "Oh! How immaterial are all materials! What things real are there, but imponderable thoughts?" (127: 432–33). The mad captain's "dark" Shakespearean scenes with the Carpenter legitimate the production of thought over any sort of "material" production, validating the work of abstraction, the symbolic mind-work of the nonmanual laborer.[89] In this way, Ahab's Shakespearean embodiment of Melville's dislike of "mankind in the mass" validates the hierarchy of nonmanual over manual labor.

In contrast to the earlier Shakespeareanism of the "Quarter-deck" persuasion, this later Shakespeareanism of Ahab embodies the valorized "Truth" of Shakespeare's tragic heroes as well as the "seeming inconsistency" of Melville's "endless sermon." The "ruthless democracy" of Ahab's bond to Pip is balanced by his "dislike [of] the mass," embodied by the *multum in parvo* Carpenter. These Shakespearean encounters ennoble Ahab, reinforcing his humanity and validating his status within the book without substantially altering its tragic trajectory. For all of its embodiment of "democracy," for example, the bond between Pip and Ahab is still understood as hierarchical, with Pip as the willing vassal of Ahab, calling him "master" and offering up his body to serve Ahab: "[D]o ye but use poor me for your one lost leg; only tread upon me, sir; I ask no more, so I remain a part of ye" (129:436). In this way, Ahab's more "democratic" Shakespeareanized relationship with Pip takes the form of paternalism or patronage, while his relationship with the Carpenter takes the form of contempt. If this cultural modeling of social values does not resolve Melville's "endless sermon," it does model a contradictory version of culture, one that makes gestures to democracy, but more materially bolsters social hierarchy, reflecting the ambivalent social aims of the professional middle class. It is this ambivalent professional model of culture that would be increasingly associated with Shakespeare over the course of the second half of the nineteenth century and beyond into the twentieth.

Moby-Dick *and the Professionalization of Shakespeare*

James Russell Lowell, in an 1887 lecture on "Shakespeare's *Richard III*, commented: "I never open my Shakespeare but I find myself wishing that there might be professorships established for the expounding of his works as there used to be for those of Dante in Italy."[90] To say that Lowell's "wish" has been fulfilled in the American academy is something of an understatement. It is a relatively unusual English department in an American institution of higher education that does not have a professor specializing in Shakespeare or a curriculum that does not require its undergraduates to take a course on Shakespeare to complete the major. A. C. Lipscomb's 1882 prediction that the most common model of Shakespeare in America was "destined to become the Shakespeare of the college and the university" has largely come true.[91] Few people attend Shakespearean performances who have not studied the playwright's work in some academic setting, and it is a very common assumption that to attend without some kind of training or preparation is almost to guarantee confusion or incomprehension. Most Americans who have any investment in the matter at all would agree with F. O. Matthiessen's 1941 assertion that "Shakespeare's language seems to us anything but 'simple'...."[92]

Not coincidentally, Matthiessen's comment arose as he sought to explain the intensity of Melville's response to Shakespeare as a generative source for *Moby-Dick*, Matthiessen saw him following the same logic that inspired Emerson to write in his journal in 1843:

> Do not write modern antiques like Landor's *Pericles* or Goethe's *Iphigenia* . . . or Scott's *Lay of the Last Minstrel.* They are paste jewels. You may well take on an ancient subject where the form is incidental merely, like Shakespeare's plays, and the treatment and dialogue is simple, and most modern. . . . Shakespeare's speeches in *Lear* are the very dialect of 1843.[93]

To accept this version of Shakespearean inspiration for Melville, Matthiessen had to reject the Emerson claim of the simplicity of Shakespeare, because few Americans in 1941 held the view, which Emerson could assert so blithely, that Shakespeare was easily understood and very much of the common culture of America. In making this claim, Emerson was presenting a view held by both "high" and "low" cultural groups in his time. Matthiessen's association of Melville with a Shakespeare not "simple" but difficult, however, is not simply an anachronistic imposition of twentieth-century cultural meanings upon a nineteenth-century text, but rather the fulfillment or recognition of Melville's project of constructing a professionalized Shakespeare.

During the Astor Place Riots and when Melville wrote *Moby-Dick*, the most commonly understood meaning of Shakespeare's plays was represented either by the inclusivity of democratic individualism to a popular audience *or* by the exclusivity of divinely sanctioned hierarchy to an elite audience. From the late-nineteenth-century and into the early decades of the twentieth century, however, the plays have become a bizarre cultural hybrid that represents neither the "high" nor the "low" of its mid-nineteenth-century significances, but has come to symbolize both at once. No longer an elite embodiment of a divinely sanctioned status quo, Shakespeare contains lessons about heroic individualism and selfhood, a meaning very much associated with the "low" or popular antebellum American Shakespeare. However, if this Shakespeare expresses a message of democratic selfhood, he does so through a language that is commonly understood as, to use Matthiessen's term, "anything but 'simple.'" Under this model, Shakespeare is defined by what Janice Radway has described as the professional construction of "literature" and the "literary," embodying a "kind of special opacity produced by complexity, subtlety, and intricacy of verbal organization, an opacity that demanded the hard work of the professionally trained, technically expert critic."[94] This model of Shakespeare establishes a hierarchy, but it is a different one from the antebellum "high" culture that cast hierarchical social relations as part and parcel of the natural order.[95] Now, the status is imbued by the specialized nonmanual labor of education or training that legitimizes one's position in a cultural spectrum. Simultaneously inclusive—offering lessons in individualism reflective of all human experience—and exclusive—unavailable to all who do not have the leisure or capital to invest in education—this professionalized model of literature and culture that Shakespeare so firmly embodies in modern American life is also the model of cultural politics imagined by Melville in his "endless sermon" on Shakespearean "Truth."

Perhaps the best proof for the assertion that our modern professionalized version of Shakespeare is also Melville's version can be found in contemporary response to the novel. For Melville's contemporaries in 1850, his version of Shakespeare in *Moby-Dick* carried none of the sanctifying weight that it has carried for twentieth-century readers such as Matthiessen. William Charvat summarized the antebellum response to Melville's Shakespeareanized depiction of Ahab in this fashion:

> Fewer than half the reviewers even bothered to mention him, and most of those either dismissed him as a crazy bore or condemned his speech as extravagant and bombastic. Clearly, the method of Shakespearean tragedy with which Melville invested the Ahab story . . . [was] generally considered a violation of verbal realism.[96]

Charvat's claim that Melville's contemporaries perceived his Shakespeare-anism as a "violation of verbal realism" seems somehow off-target, especially in light of Emerson's claim to the "simplicity" and "modernity" of Shakespeare—a view commonly shared in the period. The fact is that most of Melville's readers did not even recognize Melville's use of Shakespeare as Shakespearean. Most simply saw the language as wildly excessive. Among the many negative responses to *Moby-Dick*, the reviewer for the *Southern Review Quarterly*, highlighted Ahab's language as "raving" and included Melville along with his characters in calling for "a writ *de lunatico* against all parties."[97] Another reviewer similarly described the style as "maniacal—mad as a March hare—mowing, gibbering, screaming, like an incurable Bedlamite."[98] At least one reviewer recognized the place of Shakespeare in the work, asserting that Melville's "delineation of character is actually Shakespearean."[99] But for the most part, Melville's invocation of Shakespeare was missed by his contemporary readers. Even Evert Duyckinck, his fellow Macready petitioner, described Melville's use of dramatic form as "a bit of German melodrama" and used Shakespeare as a critical contrast: "If we had as much of Hamlet or Macbeth as Mr. Melville gives us of Ahab, we should be tired even of their sublime company."[100] Far from identifying Melville's text with Shakespeare, Duyckinck ironically seems to encourage his friend to model his work more on Shakespeare, understood here as an exemplar of aesthetic restraint and control. For nearly all of his antebellum readers, Melville's version of Shakespeare was not Shakespearean.

Melville scholars have sought to find an explanation for the contrast between the contemporary rejection of *Moby-Dick* and its modern canonization. Historically inclined criticism has rejected the romanticized claim that Melville's early readers could not understand his "genius," replacing it with a range of claims—from Perry Miller's 1950s claim that the politics of the Young America–Knickerbocker debate determined the book's reception to Sheila Post-Lauria's more recent argument that shifts within the literary marketplace and aesthetic preferences among reviewers caused its failure.[101] However, the shift in response to Ahab from "incurable Bedlamite" to Matthiessen's "Shakespearean king" traces a trajectory of cultural meaning that hints at the ideological nature of Shakespeare as a model of cultural politics in American life.

The shift in critical response to *Moby-Dick*'s Shakespeare traces the transformation of Melville's expression of professional, middle-class cultural and social values from marginality into the ideological norm in twentieth-century America. Melville's sense of Shakespeare in *Moby-Dick*, different from either of the two dominant antebellum models of cultural politics, was merely an oddity when he published the novel in 1850. But when the novel was "rediscovered" in the 1920s, Melville's version of Shakespeare reflected what had become more the norm, embodying the traits of "complexity, subtlety, and intricacy of verbal organization" which Janice Radway associated with the professional construction of the literary. Melville's Shakespeare, unlike either Forrest's or Macready's, is our modern professional middle-class version. In some ways, this vision seems to recapitulate the logic under which *Moby-Dick* was recovered in the 1920s as a lost or neglected work of genius. But rather than positing Melville as a "genius" whose "modernity" could not be understood in his own time, this reading understands him within a social or ideological narrative as a writer whose aesthetic model of social practice traveled from nascent or emergent in the antebellum era to dominant in the twentieth century. This transformation of Shakespeare from "simple" to sophisticated and *Moby-Dick*'s canonization through Shakespeare marks the rise to dominance of a professional model of literature and culture, a social transformation in which Melville participated, both through his signature on the Macready petition and his writing of *Moby-Dick*. Both as a public figure and through his writing, Melville modeled a new professional middle-class cultural politics via Shakespeare in antebellum New York City.

This cultural politics is reflected not only in Ahab's Shakespeare, but also in *Moby-Dick*'s other narrative persona, Ishmael. Although both formalist and historicist readings of *Moby-Dick* have opposed the narratives of Ahab and Ishmael, finding meaning in their differences, the next chapter will explore their similarities, situating Ishmael's narrative as another example of Melville's attempt to articulate his professional model of cultural politics. Instead of responding to the Astor Place's divide between "high" and "low," however, the next chapter charts Melville's response to the threat of the emergence of a commercialized "mass" and "middlebrow" culture in antebellum America through Ishmael's narration.

CHAPTER FOUR

Ishmael on the Lecture Circuit
Middlebrow Culture and Professionalism

In the important late chapter, "A Bower in Arsacides," Ishmael, the narrator–sailor of *Moby-Dick*, imagines readerly skepticism of his authority to speak on whale anatomy. In an ironic rejoinder, Ishmael suggests that Stubb, the "happy-go-lucky" mate might have given anatomy lectures to the crew.

> But how now, Ishmael? How is it, that you, a mere oarsman in the fishery, pretend to know aught about the subterranean parts of the whale? Did erudite Stubb, mounted upon your capstan, *deliver lectures on the anatomy of the Cetecea*; and by help of the windlass, hold up your specimen rib for exhibition? Explain thyself, Ishmael. (102:373, *my italics*)

More than a simple joke, Ishmael's ironic invocation of the lecture reflects upon its prominence in the antebellum era. In fact, the lecture and its institution, the lyceum or lecture hall, were at the center of the spread of specialized knowledge in antebellum America. By the 1850s, attendance at public lectures had grown to an estimated half-million people a week in the approximately four thousand lecture societies in cities, small and large, across the nation.[1] Ishmael's reference to the lecture can help us to rethink the meaning of his project of narration in *Moby-Dick*, as it situates his discourse within a social context. The lecture hall conveyed a certain kind of "useful" knowledge to a certain kind of audience in antebellum America, primarily the status-aspiring urban middle class. This is not Ishmael's only citation of the context of the lecture hall: with chapters touching upon many of the popular themes of the lecture circuit and making use of many of its interpretative approaches, Ishmael's narration transforms him from merely a teller of a tale into a purveyor of information, a raconteur of knowledge, and, one could say, our lecturer on all things to do with whaling and the whale.

Ishmael's narration consists primarily of a long series of intermittent chapters that explain and defend whaling, describe the process of hunting, killing, and making use of the whale, and explore cetology, the study of the whale. One consequence of this focus is that the narration is commonly read as a reflection upon knowledge or epistemology, the philosophical study of how we know what we know. Some critics have taken this further, reading Ishmael's narration, and particularly the cetology, as an explicitly pedagogical project, training the reader, as William Charvat suggests, "in imaginative, exploratory thinking."[2] Without negating either the philosophical or pedagogical element in Ishmael's narration, I would like to emphasize its social context, reading it as a commentary on the uses of knowledge in institutions, such as the lyceum and the proprietary museum, that sought to spread knowledge to assuage both the epistemological and social anxieties of the new urban middle class. Mocking the terms under which knowledge is popularized and diffused in the antebellum era, Ishmael's narration is also a canny appropriation of the rhetorical strategies, from bombastic oratory to sophistic argumentation, and of the interpretative approaches, from phrenology to naturalism, used in these institutions. Tracing Ishmael's use of these interpretative approaches and rhetorical strategies of the lyceum and their ilk, I argue that his narration is both an appropriation of and an attack upon what could be called the antebellum "culture industry."

Max Horkheimer and Theodor Adorno introduced the notion of a "culture industry" as a way of thinking through the absorption of the realm of culture into a logic of "standardization and mass production" in the twentieth century.[3] The culture industry is to be distinguished from folk or popular culture, like the Bowery world of working-class cultural rituals, and high culture, like the Astor Place Opera House or, more relevantly to Adorno and Horkheimer, to a modernist avant-garde. Elaborating upon Horkheimer and Adorno's ideas, cultural critics have charted distinctions within the culture industry, most notably the divide between "mass" and "middlebrow" cultures.[4] Mass and middlebrow culture represent a middle range of cultural expression within the spectrum of high and low that embody the culture industry. By antebellum mass culture I mean commercialized institutions or events designed to draw the largest paying audience possible through the careful construction of attractions. Precursors to later, more industrialized versions like Hollywood, antebellum mass culture was a predominantly a Northern urban phenomenon, embodied in such institutions as daguerreotype galleries, proprietary museums and, perhaps most notably, in Jenny Lind's 1850 singing tour of U.S. cities.[5] Mass culture should be distinguished from "popular" or "low" culture by its commercialized appeal to a middle-class sensibility as a "common denominator" that brings culture, as Horkheimer and Adorno famously described, "within the sphere of administration."[6] Closely related to mass culture, "middlebrow"culture is characterized by its controversial commercialization of knowledge and investment in the realm of culture as site for "self-improvement" and status aspiration. Middlebrow culture is most commonly associated with the twentieth-century cultural landscape and institutions such as the Book-of-the-Month Club.[7] Despite its twentieth-century associations, what Jonathan Freedman describes as the conditions necessary for the rise of a middlebrow culture—the appearance of a professional–managerial middle class and "the concomitant rise of a culture increasingly attuned to the ethos of consumption"—were precisely the conditions of antebellum Northern cities like New York City.[8] As the nascent forms of a modern middle class emerged in antebellum Northern cities, this new middle class gravitated to new cultural institutions such as the lyceum circuit and the proprietary museum that offered forms of entertainment that suited their social interests, from "respectable" entertainment to a commercialized culture of self-improvement: in other words, mass and middlebrow cultural institutions and forms.[9] From the rise of institutions like the lyceum and the proprietary urban museums of Barnum and Kimball, to events like Jenny Lind's triumphant, but eminently "respectable" tour of America, the antebellum era shows every sign of being the starting point for the American culture industry.

Just as Ahab's narrative is deeply rooted in the social politics of culture of the antebellum city through its appropriation of Shakespearean forms, Ishmael's narrative is also engaged in the social work of making meaning out of the cultural distinctions of the period. The ambivalence of Ishmael's narration, its simultaneous appropriation of and undermining of claims to authoritative knowledge, has led to critical debates over its seriousness or its irony: a divide embodied in the question of whether Ishmael's narration is an earnestly romantic or slyly deconstructive discursive project. But just as the complications of Ahab's negotiation of Shakespeare speaks to Melville's attempt to articulate his own professionalized model of cultural politics, I would argue that Ishmael's conflicted and contradictory narration represents a professional attack upon what Pierre Bourdieu terms "the cultural allodoxia" of the middlebrow. Bourdieu describes cultural allodoxia, "the heterodoxy experienced as orthodoxy," as "all the mistaken identifications and false recognitions which betray the gap between acknowledgement and knowledge," defining the middlebrow through the insecurity of its place within a world of cultural distinctions.[10] For Bourdieu, culture is a "game" that middlebrows, lost in their allodoxia, do not know how to play, a game in which the terms are established through subtle distinctions by those who set cultural standards.[11] Long read through its "playfulness," Ishmael's narration can be understood within this social frame as a "game of culture," toying with the allodoxia of the middlebrow's relationship to knowledge and culture, a relationship characterized by its "undifferentiated reverence, in which avidity combines with anxiety."[12] Ishmael's playfulness with knowledge, his mocking of the middlebrow's "undifferentiated reverence," defines his authority, his own cultural professionalism, while it also tests his readers' investment in the "game of culture," transforming his narration into a gauge of cultural competency.

This aggression against the culture-industry forms (and readers) should not, however, be read simply as a statement of Melville's confident claim to cultural authority and hierarchical status, but more as a mark of the threat of mass culture and the middlebrow to professional cultural authority. In fact, Melville's deep involvement in the forms of middlebrow culture through Ishmael signals the complex mixture of dependence and antagonism that binds professionalism and middlebrow culture, demonstrating how the middlebrow helped justify professional authority in American life, but also how it threatens professional autonomy by revealing culture's easy absorption into commercialism. A decidedly serious cultural game, Ishmael's narration reflects this broader dilemma of professionalism's relationship to mass culture and the middlebrow, showing the contradictions at the heart of professional visions of cultural authority.

The Antebellum Culture Industry

In the same set of letters written to Evert Duyckinck in 1849 in which he fantasized about Shakespeare promenading on Broadway (cited in the previous chapter), Melville mentioned attending a lecture by Ralph Waldo Emerson in Boston.

> I was very agreeably disappointed in Mr. Emerson. I had heard of him as full of transcendentalism, myths & oracular gibberish; I had only glanced at a book of his once in Putnam's store—*that was all I knew of him, till I heard him lecture.*—To my surprise, I found him quite intelligible, tho' to say truth, they told me that this night he was unusually plain.[13]

Duyckinck was apparently as displeased by Melville's blandly positive comment on Emerson's lecture ("Say what you will, he's a great man") as he had been by the "seeming irreverence" of Melville's association of Shakespeare with the Messiah. That Melville was first truly exposed to Emerson's ideas at a lecture might seem odd to us, but, in fact, the lecture circuit was one of the most common ways that antebellum intellectuals, scientists, historians, and other cultural professionals reached members of their wider audience, the predominantly urban middle class. The lecture circuit or lyceum was one of a number of institutions that consolidated a distinctive middle-class audience in the antebellum era.

The various elements of this new mode of entertainment were defined by their shared commitment to "moral" entertainment, to the spread of educative or "enlarging" information, and to cultural experience as a means of self-improvement. These various institutions were part of what has been called the movement of "self-culture," embodied in a proliferation of discourses in the period—not only lectures, but also advice or conduct manuals—that encouraged "the cultivation of an internalized system of morality."[14] Participation in the institutions of this self-culture was designed to inculcate a "self-reliance," which would help the subjects, most often figured in the antebellum era as young middle-class men in Northern cities, to uphold moral behavior and succeed in the world of business.[15] Defined as entertainment that bolstered middle-class social and moral values, these new institutions of antebellum self-culture were a form of what is now called "middlebrow" culture.

No single institution revealed the middlebrow tendencies of this self-culture movement better than the lecture hall or lyceum. The lecture circuit had its origins in a variety of local organizations such as Mechanics' and Young Men's Institutes as well as Mercantile Libraries that appeared in the North to encourage commercial habits among the young men of the working- and lower-middle classes who were entering the cities in throngs during the Jacksonian era. These early forms, related to the new reformist movement encouraging a tax-supported public education system, were decidedly local, funded by local elites, particularly wealthy merchants, and the lectures were conducted by local authorities.[16] By the late 1840s, however, lyceum halls in cities across the North had broadened their focus from the working- and lower-middle-class youth toward adult men and women of the middle class, and the speakers were more likely to come from a national circuit of famous performers, including Ralph Waldo Emerson, the travel writer and poet Bayard Taylor, the minister Henry Ward Beecher, *Tribune* editor Horace Greeley, phrenologist Orson Fowler, abolitionist Wendell Philips, and minister–physiologist Sylvester Graham. During the 1840s and 1850s, the lyceum became an important element of American "respectable" entertainment, with attendance during the lyceum's weekly winter evening sessions part of the social ritual of urban middle-class identity. One lecturer went so far as to assert that in his experiences on the lyceum circuit in the 1850s he "saw what might be called the middle-class culture in process of formation."[17]

The popularity of the lecture circuit hints at the social meanings of knowledge in the period. Its rise was understood as a response to the widely acknowledged concern that during the 1830s and 40s, as J. G. Holland noted in *The Atlantic Monthly* in 1865, "American life [had become] crowded with facts." Holland explained that the lecture-goer wished for "nothing more than to know how to classify their facts, what to do with them, how to govern them and how far to be governed by them"[18] As Holland implies, the epistemological uncertainty of a new world full of facts produced concerns about authority and status that were about power, agency, and control: was one to "govern" facts or "be governed by them?" At first glance, the lecture circuit might seem simply a symptom of this threatening proliferation of "facts" as the content of the lecture circuit presented what might look to us now like a dizzyingly random assortment of subjects. For example, the 1850 season at the Brooklyn Female Academy included lectures on "Success or Failure in Life" (given by *Tribune* editor Horace Greeley), "Ventilation," "The Literary history of the English Bible," "The capacity of Americans for the cultivation of music," "The Crusades," as well as lectures on "phrenology, Egyptian art, national law, electricity, the European Revolution of 1849, and the microcosmos."[19] But what unified the miscellaneousness of the antebellum lecture was an epistemological purpose. The lecture functioned to assure the audience that they could govern facts, that they could leave a lecture confident that they had secured what was alternately called "useful knowledge," a "comprehensive view," or an "enlarged understanding" that confirmed their privileged place in American society.[20]

While the lyceum helped assuage its audiences' anxieties and assure them of their rightful place within American culture, the institution also benefited those who supplied the information, the lecturers. Ralph Waldo Emerson famously turned to the lyceum after leaving the ministry, resolving a personal crisis by selecting a new vocation as lecturer.[21] Emerson's vocational turn to lecturing in the mid-1830s was perhaps prescient: over the course of the next thirty years, the institution of the lyceum would grow from a local New England practice to a national circuit, producing what a variety of contemporary observers called "a new profession" in the lecturer.[22] Emerson would be joined by a variety of people on the lyceum as "professional" lecturers, from aspiring doctors, lawyers, and clergymen who were unable to establish local practices and turned to itinerant lecturing as a kind of "improvised career," to affluent professionals, much like Emerson, who rejected traditional careers as "intellectually confining or spiritually and emotional unsatisfying" and turned to this new profession as a more rewarding alternative, to professionals who retained their standing in traditional professions such as college professors and presidents, yet turned to lecturing.[23] The antebellum lecturer emerged out of the welter of professionalism in the period, traditional and modern, and, as such, the lyceum became an important site for the spread of a populist professional authority. Whether addressing the lyceum public out of economic need or a sense of public service, lecturers were highly visible embodiments of professional cultural authority in the antebellum cities of the North in which they proliferated, spreading their gospel of "useful" knowledge.

That Melville's first real contact with Emerson's ideas, described in his 1849 letter to Duyckinck, came in the lecture hall was reflective of the institution's significance in the period. But Melville's surprised response to Emerson's "intelligibility" is instructive of some of the pitfalls of the lyceum and antebellum middlebrow culture as a whole. Although Emerson had a long and illustrious career on the lyceum, his success was a complex social phenomenon, reflective of the ambivalent relationship between professionalism and middlebrow culture. Surveying his career on the lecture circuit, William Charvat explains:

> [Emerson] was not popular in the ordinary sense: he did not draw the biggest audiences, and he was not offered the highest fees. But for some forty years he

was invited everywhere, and repeatedly invited back, by people who "understood" (in the ordinary sense) little of what he said; who often resented not understanding him; and who frequently were offended by what they did understand.[24]

As Charvat suggests, Emerson's prominence on the lecture circuit was more reflective of his celebrity, his status as "America's philosopher" than his specific philosophical message. Though the content of his lyceum lectures, typically converted later into his essays, was structured around Transcendentalism's antimaterialist, idealist philosophy, his middle-class lyceum audience seemed less interested in the philosophical content than in the experience of having witnessed Emerson lecturing: their incomprehension, resentment, and even offense overwhelmed by the authority or status that Emerson represented.

It would be a mistake simply to see Emerson as speaking over the heads of the greater number of his lyceum audience, with his listeners passive and resentful of their inability to "master" his philosophical message.[25] This seemingly contradictory "popularity" of Emerson might not simply represent a version of Bourdieu's middlebrow "allodoxia," the lyceum-goers' passive misrecognition of the clues in the cultural "game." Emerson's middlebrow audiences seem to have reshaped his message, turning it to their own interests and values. As Mary Kupiec Cayton notes in her survey of contemporary newspaper responses to Emerson's lyceum lectures in Ohio (which often contained summaries and partial excerpts of the lectures), far from being resented for his idealism or his sophistication, he was embraced as "the epitome of the commercial values prized by the audiences who invited him."[26] When newspapers reported on the content of Emerson's lectures, they noted, with pleasure, his basic, "common sense" values. In 1850, the Cincinnati newspapers reported that he was "as unpretending as . . . a good old grandfather over his Bible" and "his most remarkable trait is that of plain old *common sense*."[27] It is certainly also true that Emerson shaped his message to suit the demands of his middlebrow audience. For example, his 1858 lecture series "The Conduct of Life" included individual lectures on "Power," "Wealth," and "Culture."[28] While the lectures were intended to critique the shortcomings of the materialist values of a status-hungry middle class, it is not always so clear that his middlebrow lyceum audience heard anything other than what they wanted to hear.[29] Like Melville himself, Emerson's lyceum audience could report to their friends and neighbors that they "found him quite intelligible, tho' to say truth, they told me that this night he was unusually plain." At the lyceum, the meanings of what was said and what was heard could be startlingly different, a sign of the possibly different social and cultural purposes of the professional lecturers and their middlebrow audiences.

This was the situation for Emerson as a reasonably successful professional lecturer on the middlebrow circuit, but the conditions were hardly less problematic for the more prominent lecturers. Travel writer and poet Bayard Taylor was the most successful lecturer of the antebellum lyceum circuit, earning up to $6,000 a year for his efforts in the 1850s. Taylor would at times appear in costume of the exotic region he described in his lectures, but spoke not only of his travels, but also on more complex subjects such as the "Philosophy of travel," geographical approaches to man, and social criticism of Americans.[30] Carl Bode, however, cites a bit of doggerel written by Taylor that attempted to capture his experience on the lecture circuit:

> Comes a rapping, tapping/At my chamber door,
> But, unlike Poe's raven/ Crying 'Evermore!'
> 'Tis the new Committee/ Any one can tell,
> Come to see the lecturer: /'Hope you're very well!'. . .
>
> Thicker than the deluge/ Pouring out-of-doors
> Comes a rain of questions/ From the crowd of bores;
> . . . Oh, I want to be/Where for information,
> No one comes to me./I'd be a bloody whaler
> A tearing, swearing sailor/Among the Kurile Isles,
> Whom the Captain riles,/Anything but Taylor
> Lecturing in Niles![31]

Taylor presents lecturing in Niles, Michigan, as subjection to a "crowd of bores," a situation less favorable than being a common sailor aboard a whaling ship (a condition that Melville will ironically select for his narrator in *Moby-Dick*). Here, Taylor's comic verse plays up the complicated costs of constructing one's professional authority through the middlebrow institution of the lecture circuit. Although it bestows profit and authority, these gains come at a high cost—both in terms of the message that can be conveyed to the public and to its effect upon the professional's autonomy.

For many cultural entrepreneurs of the period, the investment in a new cultural mode carried no such problematic consequences, because they had no investment in anything other than profit. For P. T. Barnum, one of the primary architects of a commercialized realm of mass culture in the antebellum era, the combination of morality and entertainment was the fulfillment of his marketing dreams and was directly embodied in his proprietary museum, The American Museum, in New York City. The proprietary museums—so called because they were directly associated with their proprietors (Mose Kimball with Kimball's Museum in Boston is another prominent example) marked a significantly popular moment in American museum history between the earlier eighteenth-century museums—typically miscellaneous naturalist collections established by elite patricians and guided by a sense of cultural stewardship—and the new museums established after the Civil War—again founded by elites, but at that time established as exclusive and sacralized.[32] During the 1840s and 1850s, Barnum's American Museum occupied the ideal space for a middlebrow institution, at the intersection of Broadway and the Bowery, the streets associated, respectively, with "respectable" and "popular" entertainment in the city.[33] If the external location of Barnum's Museum struck a balance in the divided social geography of New York City, the internal space of the museum was constructed to achieve a similar balance. Barnum set it up so that the whole spectrum of the urban population could be both entertained and enlightened by its range of different displays from waxworks and "freak shows," often presented as displays of naturalism or ethnology, to mechanical and scientific demonstrations, to "moral dramas," plays that blended reformist concerns with sensationalist sensibilities.

When Barnum expanded his American Museum in the early 1840s, he sought to profit from the vogue for lectures and other forms of "respectable" entertainment: though he built a performance space in which he planned to show theatrical pieces, he called his new space a "Lecture Room" to distance himself from "Theatres," which still carried the taint of immorality to many Americans.[34] By 1850, his "Lecture Room" seated nearly three thousand museum-goers, who would first visit the exhibits and then go to the performance. Barnum's "Lecture Room" was famous for its long running "moral dramas." During the 1850s, Barnum emphasized the temperance movement in plays like *The Drunkard* or an adaptation of the popular T. S. Arthur work, *Ten Nights in a Bar-Room.* By the 1860s, the Lecture Room ran H. J. Conway's dramatically revised version of *Uncle Tom's Cabin,* tapping into the increased middle-class urban Northern antagonism to the institution of slavery. Barnum's moral dramas were careful to avoid controversy, though, so visitors to his Lecture Room's dramatic version of the Stowe novel would see Uncle Tom restored to the Shelby family rather than martyred to Simon Legree, with the antislavery whites heroized and the black characters reduced to docile, minstrel stereotypes.[35] Like the lyceum hall, Barnum's "moral dramas" reassured its audiences of their own secure and "respectable" place in a potentially frightening world where social, political, and even epistemological order seemed threatened.

While the lyceum and the proprietary museum were signs of the rise of new related realms of commercialized mass and middlebrow culture in the antebellum era, no one event embodied the commercial possibilities of culture more than Jenny Lind's 1850–51 tour of America. Elaborately orchestrated by Barnum, the Norwegian singer's tour carefully balanced the competing cultural politics of the period to astounding financial success. Lind's performances consisted of a judicious mixture of arias from foreign-language opera, associated with American elite culture, and homely folk songs, such as "Home Sweet Home" and "The Bird's Song," with their more popular associations. Meanwhile, Barnum's promotions highlighted Lind's "respectable" and "artless" domestic femininity: the close of her performance was typically followed by an announcement of the local charities to which Lind would be donating the proceeds. Though Lind assiduously donated sums to local fire companies, a traditional site of working-class male socializing, the bulk of her charitable attention was turned to the concerns of the urban middle class, who constituted the majority of her audience simply because more of them could afford her expensive tickets.[36]

Despite the obvious disparity in the social make-up of her audiences, many observers emphasized the "democracy" of Lind's tour. N. P. Willis would position Lind as a cultural symbol against the Astor Place Opera House (an embodiment of elite culture even before the Riots, but now even more so) to imagine the singer's "universal" appeal:

> While the Astor Place Opera House will hold all who constitute the fashion, it would take the Park and all the squares of the city to hold those who constitute the rage for Jenny Lind. No! Let the city be as thick and the taste for the meretricious and artificial be as apparently uppermost—the lovers of goodness are many, the supporters and seekers of what is pure and disinterested are the substantial bulk of the people.[37]

Although Willis, Barnum, and others proclaimed Lind's audience as "the substantial bulk of the people," in fact, the Norwegian singer's tour became an important site for what Bluford Adams terms "the emergence of U.S. middle-class as a cultural and commercial force."[38] The avidity with which the urban middle class purchased tickets to Lind's tour led commentators to note their new social prominence as supporters of culture, as when the New York *Herald* commented on the social make-up of Lind's audience at a particular concert: "The audience consisted for the most part of the middle classes, who are the support of concerts and theatres, and public amusements of every kind."[39] With the rowdier working-class audiences kept outside the theaters, Lind's predominantly middle-class audience and its commentators could look around and see themselves as *the* collective embodiment of American cultural values.[40]

Listening to Jenny Lind sing, or watching "The Drunkard" at the Lecture Room, or listening to Emerson lecture at the lyceum hall, the antebellum urban middle class could see their values performed on stage and their collective identity embodied by their fellow audience members, reassuring them of their prominence in American life; for a number of cultural historians of the period, these antebellum versions of mass culture and the middlebrow came to stand in as *the* model of the American public.[41] That the middle-class audience of mass culture and the middlebrow could stand in as the embodiment of the American public, despite its occasional revision of the cultural content directed at them and its self-serving exclusion of other social interests, speaks to middle-class promise and power in antebellum America.

Call Me Ishmael: Oratory, Rhetoric, and the Lyceum

In the mid- to late-1830s, Herman Melville himself, then a teenaged clerk, joined the Albany Young Men's Association for Mutual Improvement and participated in a related debating society. In fact, his first published writings were letters to a local newspaper, the Albany *Microscope* (itself a penny paper aimed primarily at young clerks) in an exchange over management of the debating club, the Philo Logos Society:

> We ask no higher testimony in favor of its advantages, than the recorded opinions of all great men. Burke, the English Orator and Statesman acknowledged that the first spring which moved him on in a career of fame and honor was the fostering encouraging effect of a literary club. . . . The learned are as one man, in their opinion of the importance of the debating societies in developing the mind, and prompting to greater and higher efforts.[42]

The nineteen-year-old Melville's defense of the literary society or debating club speaks to the classic logic of antebellum middlebrow culture, highlighting the club's role in the self-culture project of "developing" the mind, but also forwarding social ambitions. As a young man entering the lower rungs of the Northern urban middle-class work force after a somewhat limited education, Melville was the ideal target of this middlebrow self-culture.

And it was this early experience with the lyceum and debating society, Hershel Parker suggests, that led to "the essayistic chapters of *Moby-Dick*," those most associated with Ishmael's narration.[43] Certainly, the chapters of Ishmael's narration show signs of influence from the lyceum and the debating society. These chapters frequently take on distinctive and narrowly framed topics, indulge in elaborate rhetoric and overtly oratorical forms, and even take on the pose of debates. Parker suggests that this early experience emerges in *Moby-Dick* as "the sheer delight in championing a position eloquently," but I would argue that Ishmael's appropriation of Melville's own adolescent middlebrow experience has a more pointed and critical purpose: simultaneously appropriating the cultural authority bestowed upon these forms and mocking and undermining their values. In this way, Melville uses Ishmael's narration to unpack the logic of the middlebrow, exposing its flaws and limitations, while still claiming its cultural power.

From its earliest beginnings, the lecture was part of an educational system that interpellated lecturer and audience into a set of ideological attitudes and behavior.[44] When local mercantile leaders helped fund the Young Men's and Mechanic's Institutes and Mercantile Libraries in the 1820s and 1830s, they encouraged their clerks and other workers to advance their education, read improving literature and, perhaps most important, develop their public-speaking skills, to inculcate commercial values among the young men.[45] In William Ellery Channing's lecture on *Self-Culture* (1838), the importance of speech, or "Utterance," was stressed not only because public speaking could be understood as a way to improve one's intellect, but also because "our social rank too depends a good deal on our power of utterance."[46] Channing emphasized proper speech because "[It] gives a man access to social advantages, on which his improvement very much depends."[47] Both the lectures by the local authorities and the evenings with the local debating societies that were the mainstays of these Jacksonian institutions trained young men to present themselves in speech and behavior in a manner at least well suited to making them better workers, if not aiding in their climb up the economic ladder. The lyceum's emphasis on rhetoric and oratory was part of an ideological project to train the new urban nonmanual workers in the behavior most demanded by their employers.

Although the lyceum hall lost some of its focus on younger workers in the 1840s and 1850s, replacing local authorities as speakers with popular professional lecturers who toured the nation, the emphasis on oratory and rhetoric remained, as did the overarching ideological purpose of encouraging discipline and commercial behavior. For example, the New York lawyer and writer Park Benjamin experienced great success on the circuit declaiming long satires in verse on such subjects as "Fashion," "Hard Times," "Modern Society," "True Independence," and "The Age of Gold." In the last, an 1849 satire on the California Gold Rush, Benjamin closed by praising the diligent worker who remained in his place:

> He, whose firm souls resists Temptation's wile,
> Sees every firmament above him smile . . .
> He need not seek for treasure-teeming mines,
> Beneath his feet more precious metal shines.
> In a conscience clear, in duty, virtue bold,
> Here is his placer, *now* his Age of Gold.[48]

The rhetorical conceit of Benjamin's 800 lines of heroic couplets found favor with audiences who identified with and were flattered by the praise for their resisting the "Temptation" to hunt for gold. The minister Henry Ward Beecher, who Carl Bode claimed was famous on the circuit for his "theatrical effects, his humor, and his general flamboyance," preached a similar adherence to commercialized, self-disciplining virtue in his lectures specifically addressed to young men on such topics as "Industry and Idleness," "Twelve Causes of Dishonesty," "Six Warnings," "The Strange Woman," and "Popular Amusements."[49] In "Strange Women," Beecher warned young men against adultery, prostitution, and female seduction: "But ah! every one of you who are dancing with the covered paces of death, . . . let me break your spell; . . . Look!—Listen!—Witness your own end, unless you take quickly a warning! . . . Oh! That the young might see the *end* of vice before they see the beginning!"[50] Beecher's emphatic rhetoric hails the audience into identifying themselves both with the tempted young men and the people who would advise them. Like Benjamin's poetic praise for the virtuous workers who remain to do their duty, Beecher's lecture encourages an internalized, self-disciplining commercial subjectivity. Both the rhetoric and content of the antebellum lecture had a normative content, modeling a certain kind of self-disciplining behavior and interpellating the audience into that same behavior and identity.

In *Moby-Dick*, the narrator Ishmael uses elaborate rhetoric and oratorical strategies to establish exactly the kind of relationship with his readers upon which the antebellum popular lecturers depended. From his famous self-introduction, "Call Me Ishmael" (1: 12) onward, Ishmael hails a present audience, using direct address and rhetorical questions to situate his readers–

listeners in a particular relation to his ideas. In the first chapter "Loomings," Ishmael uses the lecture circuit's rhetorical hailing to transform his poverty-driven decision to sign on with a whaling ship into a universal metaphysical need:

> Circumnambulate the city of a dreamy Sabbath afternoon. Go from Corlears Hook to Coenties Slip, and from thence, by Whitehall, northward. What do you see?—Posted like silent sentinels all around the town, stand thousands upon thousands of mortal men fixed in ocean reveries. . . . How then is this? Are the green fields gone? What do they here?
>
> But look! Here come more crowds, pacing straight for the water, and seemingly bound for a dive. Strange. . . . Tell me, does the magnetic virtue in the needles of all those ships attract them hither?
>
> Once more. Say, you are in the country; in some high land of lakes. Take almost any path you please, and ten to one it carries you down in a dale, and leaves you there by a pool in the stream. There is magic in it. (1: 12–3)

Ishmael identifies his fellow "silent sentinels" as precisely the urban, primarily entry-level nonmanual workers hailed by the lecture: "all landsmen; of week days pent up in lath and plaster—tied to counters, nailed to benches, clinched to desks" (1: 12–3). In this passage, Ishmael's various hailings ("What do you see?," "But look," "Tell me," "Say, you are in the country") follow the lecture mode by interpellating his readers, enlisting them, however, into a mindset of contemplation, reverie, or metaphysics. While rhetorically this mode follows the discourse of the lecture, its message goes completely against the lecture's middlebrow project of self-culture and self-discipline. Henry Ward Beecher would attack precisely this mindset of reverie and contemplation in his lecture "Industry and Idleness" in his popular *Addresses to Young Men* series:

> Men may walk much, and read much, and talk much, and pass the day without an unoccupied moment, and yet be substantially idle; because Industry requires, at least, the intention of usefulness. But gadding, gazing, lounging, mere pleasure-mongering, reading for the relief of *ennui*,—these are as useless as sleeping, or dozing, or the stupidity of surfeit.[51]

Beecher's lecture seeks to warn his young male audience against "the wiles of idleness," likened to a "mischievous enchantress," by describing the "advantage of Industry."[52] Just as Beecher's lecture on "Industry and Idleness" uses rhetoric to interpellate his audience as "young men" and encourages them to identify with his productive, self-disciplining perspective, Ishmael's rhetoric in "Loomings" hails his readership, but interpellates them into an antithetical normative identity, one in which the "idle" contemplative/metaphysical tendency of mind becomes universal. If Ishmael's narration mirrors the interpellative forms and processes of the antebellum lecture circuit, his content is a dramatically different one, replacing the normative "self-culture" commercial model with an alternative vision of culture that both rejects and benefits from the hierarchies established by the lecture.

Having enlisted the reader through the orator's normative hailing, Ishmael uses his discursive authority to unseat many of the assumptions and values of the self-culture that fueled the antebellum lecture circuit. In the period, the lecture was explicitly understood as a moment for "Improvement" (as the word's appearance in the titles of many of the societies that sponsored lectures demonstrated), an element of the antebellum culture industry's transformation of social aspiration into a leisure pursuit. As a result, the antebellum lecture, implicitly or explicitly, became a lesson on how to move up the economic and social ladder. In "Loomings," however, Ishmael uses his rhetoric to justify a kind of downward mobility, transforming his social marginality as an unemployed city dweller forced to turn to whaling into a model of success, albeit a success that is either counter to or plays on contradictions within middlebrow self-culture.

The middlebrow self-culture of the lyceum sought to achieve a delicate balance of values and impulses within the culture, negotiating between capitalism and Christianity, social aspiration and the maintenance of the social order. As Daniel Lord, one of the founders of the Young Men's Christian Association (YMCA), founded in New York City in 1852, proclaimed in the organization's first annual report:

> The principles of temperance, moderation, industry, and perseverance which flow from religion acted out, seldom fail to lead to influence and fortune. . . . You can turn your eyes to not a few among our merchants and men of wealth who are examples of social virtue and religion. Soon will you stand in their places and from you will be expected those devotions of wealth to purposes of usefullness [*sic*] which make wealth an honor.[53]

Directly addressed to the young men constituting the membership of the YMCA, Lord's speech encourages his audience to embrace virtuous Christian behavior, as this behavior "seldom fail[s] to lead to influence and fortune," seen in the example of present successful men whom the Association members will be replacing in due time. Combining emulation, Christianity, ambition, and respect for the current social order, Lord's address is a characteristic example of the balanced forces of the antebellum self-culture.

Having already hailed the reader into his counternormative metaphysical sailor identity in "Loomings," Ishmael exposes the ideological contradictions of antebellum self-culture by playing its values against itself. Ishmael's justifications of his position as a common sailor on a whaling ship become not a sign of his lack of ambition, but a questioning of worldly ambition and its relation to Christian values:

> What of it, if some hunks of a sea-captain orders me to get a broom and sweep down the decks? What does that indignity amount to, I mean, in the scales of the New Testament? Do you think the archangel Gabriel thinks anything the less of me, because I promptly and respectfully obey that old hunks in that particular instance? Who aint a slave? Tell me that. . . . I have the satisfaction of knowing that it is all right; that everybody else is one way or other served in much the same way—either in the physical or metaphysical point of view. (1: 15)

Exploiting the "New Testament" view that "the last shall be first," Ishmael enlists his audience in questioning class aspiration. The logic of Lord's address to the Young Men's Christian Association (given, admittedly after the writing of *Moby-Dick*, but hardly unique in the period as a whole) places Christian belief and practices in a context that suggests their rewards are wealth and influence, not spiritual gain. Ishmael's narration throws this logic into question.

Ishmael tips the balance here and in a variety of other moments in "Loomings." For example, in defending his necessity-driven decision to go to sea as a sailor, Ishmael contrasts his being paid to sail to the more genteel status of the paying customer: "And there is all the difference in the world between paying and being paid. The act of paying is perhaps the most uncomfortable infliction that the two orchard thieves entailed upon us. But *being paid*,—what will compare with it?" (1: 15). In this, Ishmael playfully invokes the mercantilistic logic of the middlebrow self-culture that emphatically instructed its subjects in the virtues of saving. For example, the popular author T. S. Arthur, most famous for his temperance novel *Ten Nights in a Bar-Room*, introduced his didactic novel *Sparing to Spend* (1853) by explaining:

> Extravagant expenditures—living beyond the means—is the besetting evil of social life in this country. . . . *Sparing to Spend* has for its aim the correction of this evil, in so far as an exhibition of its folly, and the peace, prosperity, and happiness almost certain to flow from an opposite course of life, can effect so desirable an object.[54]

But if Ishmael seems to playfully invoke self-culture's moral valuation of saving, he quickly offsets this by posing it against Christian values once again:

"The urbane activity with which a man receives money is really marvellous, considering that we so earnestly believe money to be the root of all earthly ills, and that on no account can a monied man enter heaven. Ah! how cheerfully we consign ourselves to perdition!" (1: 15). Ishmael's cheerful hailing of his readers in "Loomings" implicates them in the contradictions of the mercantilist Christian values that the antebellum middlebrow self-culture was designed to resolve. In this way, "Loomings" initiates a discursive project for Ishmael that will run the course of the narrative, speaking within the forms and discourses of the antebellum lecture circuit and middlebrow culture, appropriating the authority inherent in those forms and discourses, but turning them against themselves and articulating a position that asserts an alternative cultural authority and hierarchy.[55]

The antebellum lecture circuit was one of the most prominent cultural sites for rhetoric and oratory in a culture that made some of its most famous orators into heroes. The antebellum lecture emphasized rhetoric and oratory in what Donald M. Scott has called a "performance" of "intellectual theatricality," making intellectual life into a newly important part of middle-class entertainment.[56] As an explicitly oral performance, the lecture form made special demands upon the lecturers to convey their ideas and arguments. Many lecturers depended upon vivid language and emotional delivery to captivate an audience whose attention might easily drift. One of the most successful lecturers on the antebellum circuit was John Gough, a former singer and alcoholic turned temperance advocate. Gough was famous for "his dramatic action [and] intense and impassionate earnestness" in his lengthy lectures on the evils of drink.[57] As Gough himself explained, "The public do not expect from me a literary entertainment, an intellectual feast, or a logical argument."[58] While Gough's melodramatic enactments and visions of the suffering alcoholic may have been extreme, many popular lecturers depended upon a dramatic oratorical style. The example already cited from Beecher's lecture "Strange Women" can give one a sense of the oratorical norms—"Oh! That the young might see the *end* of vice before they see the beginning!"—carefully using emphasis and expostulations to draw in the listener. The demand for entertainment as well as "improvement" helped make the lecture hall the site of bombastic oratory and convoluted rhetoric.

Appropriating the rhetorical forms of the lecture from the novel's first moments, Ishmael will continue to use this explicitly oratorical lecture form in chapters on whaling such as "The Advocate" and "The Affadavit." In doing so, Melville ironizes the persuasive logic of the lecture while retaining the cultural authority inherent in the forms of middlebrow culture. In "The Advocate," Ishmael appropriates these oratorical forms to become an advocate not for temperance or sexual self-restraint, but the "honor of whaling": "[T]his business of whaling has somehow come to be regarded among landsmen as a rather unpoetical and disreputable pursuit; therefore, I am all anxiety to convince ye, ye landsmen, of the injustice hereby done to us hunters of whales" (24: 98). Adopting the highest of rhetorical tones, Ishmael's 'advocacy' compares whaling with the military and imperial exploration, making the "butchery" of the whaling industry and its relentless pursuit of profit into an explicitly "noble" endeavor: "How comes all this, if there be not something puissant in whaling?" (24: 99). Playing with the emotionalized oratory of the lecturer's advocacy, Ishmael responds to imagined naysayers with italicized indignation: "*Whaling not respectable?* Whaling is imperial. By old English statutory law, the whale is declared a 'royal fish'" (24: 101). Ishmael even plays with the lecturer's expostulations, exclaiming at one point: "Ah, the world! Oh, the world!" (24: 100). But if Ishmael is mocking the bombastic oratorical forms of the lecture, that does not mean that his advocacy does not work to convince the reader not only of his knowledge and authority, but also of the importance of whaling.

This same process is in action in Ishmael's appropriation of legalistic rhetoric and historical argumentation in "The Affadavit." In the aftermath of the Quarter-deck conversion of the crew to the hunt for Moby-Dick, Ishmael seeks to persuade his audience of the possibility of reencountering a particular whale over the years, but the chapter is also about the ways in which the forms of formal argumentation can bestow authority upon the speaker, even when extreme skepticism is probably the more responsible response. Ishmael intimates this very view in his introduction, but hides behind the circumlocution of the language: "I care not to perform this part of my task methodically; but shall be content to produce the desired impression by separate citations of items, practically or reliably known to me as a whaleman; and from these citations, I take it—the conclusion aimed at will naturally follow of itself" (45: 175).

If many antebellum lecturers depended upon dramatic and emotional speech to persuade their audiences, others recognized, like Ishmael, that other rhetorical methods, such as the careful exposition of numbered arguments and the citation of recognized authorities, would naturally produce organization and bestow authority upon them. Ishmael's production of enumerated points in "The Affadavit," however, imposes an arbitrary structure upon a confusing argument, where numbers are forwarded as proof and withdrawn as speculation or dim memory with equal aplomb. Describing an instance where "three years intervened between the flinging of two harpoons" at the same whale, Ishmael hints at two other similar instances, then admits of the other one, "I say three years, but I am pretty sure it was more than that" (45: 176). The proliferation of numbered arguments and increasingly distant evidence culminates in Ishmael's conclusion in the example of an event described by the sixth-century Roman historian Procopius, who, Ishmael suggests, was considered "by the best authorities . . . a most trustworthy and unexaggerating historian, except in one or two particulars, not at all affecting the matter presently to be mentioned" (45: 182). Narrating Procopius's story of a "great sea monster" who attacked vessels in the Sea of Marmora for over fifty years, Ishmael emphasizes the authority of historical discourse: "A fact thus set down in substantial history cannot be easily gainsayed. Nor is there any reason it should be" (45: 182). Speculating from the vague evidence of Procopius, Ishmael concludes decisively: "If, then, you properly put these statements together, and reason upon them a bit, you will clearly perceive that, according to all human reasoning, Procopius's seamonster, that for half a century stove the ships of a Roman Emperor, must in all probability have been a sperm whale" (45: 182).

Ishmael's theatricalized rhetoric in "The Affadavit" dramatizes the contradictions of the lyceum circuit. On the one hand, Ishmael bestows authority upon the information he presents, encouraging his audience not to "gainsay" or question the knowledge they are being given. On the other hand, he presents this information as a series of facts that the audience can "put . . . together, and reason upon them a bit." Can it be both authoritative and subject to the audience's testing at the same time? Or does the lecturer simply benefit from a gesture toward democracy, while still retaining authority through rhetoric? By any logical reckoning, Ishmael's congery of speculative evidence should persuade no one: his personal evidence undercuts its own logic, his research-based evidence is a flimsy veil of legend, and his method is haphazard. To "put [this] together, and reason upon them a bit" should convince the reader of its falsity. But Melville/Ishmael also understands that such a task is actually a difficult one and that few readers would do so. In fact, the reviewer for New York's *Spirit of the Times*, America's first sporting journal, found a "disposition to be critical" of Moby-Dick's "admissability as an actor into dramatic action," but proclaimed,

"'The Affadavit [chapter], disarms us; all improbability or incongruity disappears, and 'Moby Dick' becomes a living fact. . . ."[59] Appropriating the forms of the antebellum lecture circuit and the complacent epistemology of the culture industry, Ishmael both asks his audience to question how they know what they know and benefits from the authority he garners by their willingness to accept his narration without question. Ishmael's rhetorical voice appropriates the forms of the middlebrow lecture, but also points his readers toward an alternate way of listening–reading, one that demands critical judgments and subtle distinctions, one that could be associated with a model of professionalism in literature.

Cetology: "Enlarged" Understandings vs. "Subtle" Critiques

Moby-Dick is, by all accounts, a famous book in American culture. But no element of *Moby-Dick* is more famous, or perhaps more infamous, than the "cetology" section. The word "cetology" is defined as the study of the whale, and the middle section of *Moby-Dick* enacts an episodic study of the whale, moving from an examination of its surface to its internal structure and even its fossil history. The cetological project of *Moby-Dick* is introduced in chapter 32 (entitled "Cetology") and comes to a close in chapter 105, but critics have haggled over what precisely constitutes cetology in the book.[60] Rather than engaging in debates over textual inclusion or exclusion, I want to focus instead on how Ishmael's attempt to interpret the whale throughout *Moby-Dick* is deeply enmeshed in the forms of cultural or social inclusion and exclusion through its appropriation of antebellum middlebrow culture and its production of knowledge in the period. In the cetology chapters, Ishmael repeatedly enacts an epistemological project akin to the lecture, leading his readers through a sequence of observations, facts, and episodes that seem to be headed toward the "useful knowledge" or "enlarged understanding" that the lecture demanded. Ishmael even turns to many of the specific interpretative approaches or disciplines popular on the lecture circuit, apparently with a view toward what one commentator on the lecture circuit described as its characteristic gesture: "draw[ing] from [the facts] their nutritive and universal good."[61] But Ishmael's cetology project repeatedly forecloses on the completion of the lecture's middlebrow epistemological goal, rejecting "enlarged" or "comprehensive" or even "useful" knowledge for "subtle" distinctions and uncertainty. Appropriating the interpretative approaches of the antebellum lecture circuit,

Ishmael's cetology constructs what we can read as a professional response to the possibilities and threats of middlebrow culture. In the process of producing the cetology, Melville absorbs the various scientific and analytic discourses of the lecture circuit and constructs his literary text as a discourse of cultural authority in its own right.

Although Ishmael's "lecture series" on the whale follows the erratic course of the antebellum lecture circuit's production of knowledge, *Moby-Dick* displays a dramatically different attitude toward the philosophical and social consequences of this knowledge. Throughout *Moby-Dick*, Ishmael applies different interpretative methodologies to the whale and whaling, ostensibly to produce a systematic understanding of the subjects. In "Cetology," Ishmael asserts: "My object here is simply to project the draught of a systematization of cetology" (32:118). But "system" and "order" are precisely what Ishmael is unable, or unwilling, to supply in a satisfactory manner. Mocking the consoling empiricism of Linnaean naturalist categorizing, Ishmael's first attempt in "Cetology" produces a "Bibliographical system" to classify the whales, turning to the whale's external size, or "volume," as the "only [system] that can possibly succeed," and then linking the measurement of volume to the bibliographic system of organizing books by size as "volumes" (32: 123). Self-evidently arbitrary and incomplete, Ishmael's cetology raises questions about the possibilities of the organization of knowledge. If the antebellum lecture offered a vital service to its audience by allowing them to understand where to situate themselves amid the world of "facts" (governing them or being governed by them), Ishmael's analyses and classifications undermine the reassuring effect of the lecture by throwing all claims to "system" and "classification" into doubt.[62]

Throughout the novel, Ishmael will turn to a variety of different interpretative discourses to forward his analysis, all reflecting popular genres on the antebellum lecture circuit. More important, though, these lecture genres were popular precisely because they offered reassurance to the lecture-going audience members about their place within American social life. By turning to them in his narration, however, Ishmael submits their reassuring effect to a kind of critical and/or ironic deflation. For example, in the companion chapters "The Prairie" and "The Nut," Ishmael assays physiognomical and phrenological "readings" of the whale's face and head. Phrenology, the "science" of analyzing the shape of the head to understand an individual's character, was introduced to America by the Austrians Franz Joseph Gall and Josef Spurzheim in 1832, and was most promoted in America by the brothers Lorenzo and Orson

Fowler, who established a "Phrenological Cabinet" on Broadway in 1837, exhibiting the phrenological traits of prominent people and offering to do phrenological readings of individuals, for a price.[63] Orson Fowler further promoted phrenology through his lectures, becoming one of the more prominent figures on the lecture circuit in the 1840s and 1850s.[64] Physiognomy, the "scientific" study of the face had been introduced by the Swiss Johann Caspar Lavater in the eighteenth century, but became a subject of popular interest in the antebellum era. Both phrenology and physiognomy became remarkably popular during the antebellum era, in part because they so clearly filled the social and epistemological needs of the new urban middle class.[65]

Tapping into the conjunction of social uncertainty and status aspiration among the middle class in Northern cities, phrenology and physiognomy were embraced as "science[s] for the people." Phrenology and physiognomy provided important interpretative tools with which the urban middle classes armed themselves for the threatening alienation of the new life in cities, where their livelihoods frequently depended upon the interdependence of exchanges, both social and economic, with strangers.[66] Each discourse promised insight into understanding one's own character as well as those of others, available upon having one's head or face examined, reading a manual, or attending a lecture. Thus, when Dr. J. W. Redfield lectured at the New York City General Society of Mechanics and Tradesmen in 1850, he entitled his talk "Physiognomy: On the Signs of the Selfish and Social Faculties."[67] If physiognomy promised to help one identify selfishness in others by interpreting facial expressions, phrenology assured readers, "Your head is the type for your mentality," as the Fowler brothers proclaimed in the first epigraph on the title page of their *Illustrated Self-Instructor in Phrenology and Physiology* (1852).[68] Both interpretative "sciences" became commonplaces in the advice literature of the period, with chapters on the subjects appearing in such works as popular children's author Peter Parley [Samuel G. Goodrich]'s *What to Do, and How to Do It* (1844) and William Alcott's *Familiar Letter to Young Men* (1849).[69] Both physiognomy and phrenology became tools in the preservation of social order, offering their adherents, whether through advice manuals or lectures, a solution to the problem of assessing the character of others, reassuring the primarily middle-class readers and listeners that they could find comfort and stability in their new urbanized world.[70] Lydia Maria Child proclaimed phrenology "the democracy of metaphysics," making it a perfect embodiment of the middlebrow ethos of ambition and accessibility.[71]

The overall ethos of Ishmael's cetology project is often characterized by his assertion of an experimental ethos in the physiognomical chapter, "The Prairie," "I try all things; I achieve what I can" (79:291). "The Prairie" and its companion phrenological chapter, "The Nut," come at the end of a sequence of chapters investigating the whale's head. "The Prairie" and "The Nut" and Ishmael's "application of these two semi-sciences to the whale" (79:291), however, can also be read as examples of Melville's engagement with the lecture and middlebrow culture.

Ishmael's attempts at phrenological and physiognomical readings seem alternately serious and comical, but the overall effect is that of a critique of the drive for reassuring knowledge embodied by these interpretative "sciences."[72] Ishmael ends his physiognomical reading, "The Prairie," by challenging his readers' middlebrow demand for reassuring knowledge presented by an authoritative specialist:

> Champollion deciphered the wrinkled granite hieroglyphics. But there is no Champollion to decipher the Egypt of every man's and every being's face. Physiognomy, like every other human science, is but a passing fable. If then, Sir William Jones, who read in thirty languages, could not read the simplest peasant's face in its profounder and more subtle meanings, how may unlettered Ishmael hope to read the awful Chaldee of the Sperm Whale's brow? I put that brow before you. Read it if you can. (79: 292–93)

Ishmael's invocation of Jean-François Champollion overdetermines the context for popular meanings of knowledge in the period. Champollion deciphered the Rosetta Stone in the 1820s, an interpretative feat that led to an American mania for Egyptian art and culture in the 1830s and 1840s. Champollion's reading was thus a reassuring intellectual accomplishment, described by Edward Everett, a noted politician, orator, and vice-president of the National Lyceum, as "throw[ing] ... a flood light on a chapter in the history of mankind, hitherto almost a blank."[73] Citing both Champollion and Sir William Jones, an expert on Asian languages in the period, Ishmael both acknowledges the expertise of these linguists and draws the limits of their authoritative "reading" to unseat physiognomy's claim to a reassuring understanding of others via their faces, upending the epistemological project of the middlebrow lyceum. In "The Prairie," Melville seems to play with the demand for authoritative and reassuring knowledge on the lecture circuit, turning the "democratic" interpretative practice of phrenology and physiognomy into a challenge to his readers to become more active participants in the construction of knowledge rather than simply passive consumers: "I put that brow before you. Read it if you can."

This challenge to his readership to take up a more active role in interpretation finds a model in an earlier chapter in this same cetological
sequence on the whale's head. In the chapter "The Sperm Whale's Head—
Contrasted View," Ishmael studies the eyes and ears of the whale and pro-
poses a counter-epistemology to the middlebrow ethos:

> Is it not curious, that so vast a being as the whale should see the world through
> so small an eye, and hear the thunder through an ear which is smaller than a
> hare's? But if his eyes were broad as the lens of Herschel's great telescope; and
> his ears capacious as the porches of cathedrals; would that make him any longer
> of sight, or sharper of hearing? Not at all.—Why then do you try to "enlarge"
> your mind? Subtilize it. (74:280)

Like the challenge to members of his audience to interpret the whale's face
themselves, Ishmael's analysis questions his readers' relationship to knowledge. Putting "enlarge" into quotation marks, Ishmael cites its conventional
association with the middlebrow vision of knowledge as "self-improvement."
Questioning the middlebrow impulse to "enlarge" their understanding, Ishmael demands instead that his readers "subtilize" their minds.

Ironically, by drawing a broader lesson for his readers from the specific
example of the whale's sensory organs, Ishmael replicates the logic of the
lecture—to "draw . . . from [facts] their nutritive and universal good"—but
for a completely different purpose. Far from reassuring his readers, Ishmael's challenge to them to "subtilize" their minds—to "indulge in subtleties"—models a far more active vision of knowledge as sophisticated,
demanding labor.[74] "Subtlety," with its association with "acuteness, sagacity, penetration," encourages readerly investment in "keen perception of fine
distinctions" in contrast to the widening scope of the middlebrow project of
"enlargement."[75] Identifying insight with small-scale perceptions and distinction rather than enlargement, Ishmael's cetology transforms the epistemological impulses or interpretative discourses of the lecture circuit,
appropriating and then twisting middlebrow cultural forms. This process of
challenging readers' epistemological impulses and demanding "subtle"
interpretive work is repeated throughout the cetology. The cetology, in
effect, instructs its readers in the benefits (and pitfalls) of professionalism's
investment in the "subtle" work of cultural distinction.

Leaving the frustrating surface of the whale, Ishmael's cetology ultimately moves to read the depths of the whale, studying its tissues, its bones,
and even its fossil remains. In doing so, Ishmael depends particularly upon
the scientific discourses of naturalism, which branched out into anatomy

and zoology, and geology, especially in relation to the history of fossil animals. These subjects were popular ones on the lecture circuit as well. Some
of America's most prominent scientists, including the Harvard zoologist
Louis Agassiz and Benjamin Silliman, Yale professor and coeditor of the
American Journal of Science (the first U.S. scholarly scientific journal), toured
on the lyceum circuit, giving lectures on these subjects.[76] The Swiss-born
naturalist Louis Agassiz came to the United States to lecture at Boston's
Lowell Institute in 1847 and, at least partially on the basis of his popularity,
a professorship in geology at Harvard was established for him. Agassiz
became a central player in the institutionalization of science in America,
helping to form the American Association for the Advancement of Science
in 1848.[77] Agassiz's lyceum courses in naturalism covered a range of material from taxonomy of the forms of life to fossil life and geological processes.
Agassiz's popular courses in naturalism particularly fit the lyceum's
demand that the lecture take what was called a "comprehensive view" and
produce "enlarged understanding," contextualizing its information in such
a fashion that it situated the listener in a structured "cosmic and moral
order." Agassiz's naturalism certainly served this purpose, presenting a
vision of the world and all its inhabitants as created by a "Deity" for the purpose of mankind. As one biographer of Agassiz explains, "The men and
women who listened to Agassiz [in his lyceum lectures] heard that their
species was not only the highest form of vertebrates but represented the
direction and the purpose to which all creation had moved from the beginning."[78] Moreover, in achieving this understanding of the development of
life and the earth, the naturalist and, presumably, the lecture-goer was
empowered with insight into the divine project. In his lectures, Agassiz proclaimed that "To study . . . the succession of animals in time and their distribution in space, is, therefore, to become acquainted with the ideas of God
himself."[79] Naturalism's anthrocentric, ambitious, and empowering interpretative scope made it the ideal lyceum subject.

It is precisely the reassuring grandiosity of naturalism that Ishmael
attacks in his analysis of the whale's skeleton. Playing on the lecture's impulse
to gravitate toward subjects that would create "enlargement" or "comprehensiveness," Ishmael begins his chapter on "The Fossil Whale" by asserting:
"From his mighty bulk the whale affords a most congenial theme whereon to
enlarge, amplify, and generally expatiate. Would you, you could not compress
him" (104: 378). Ishmael satirizes this middlebrow discursive mode by defining the whale as an appropriate subject simply because it is already so big. Ish-

mael's consideration of the fossil whale leads to a hyperbolic expansion of scope, a mockery of the ways that specific knowledge inevitably led to "enlarged" and "comprehensive" understanding in the lecture:

> For in the mere act of penning my thoughts of this Leviathan, they weary me, and make me faint with their outreaching comprehensiveness of sweep, as if to include the whole circle of the sciences, and all generations of whales, and men, and mastodons, past, present, and to come, with all the revolving panoramas of empire on earth, and throughout the universe, not excluding its suburbs. Such and so magnifying, is the virtue of a large and liberal theme! (104: 379)

Just as naturalism allows one to see "the ideas of God himself" for Agassiz, the "large and liberal theme" of the whale allows Ishmael to encompass all the sciences and speak to the infinite scope of "the universe" (including "its suburbs," as he ironically points out). This hyperbolic vision reduces the reassuring "enlarged" perspective of the lecture circuit to an absurdity, reflective of no great insight other than a fantasy of "comprehensiveness" and mastery.

Although this moment can (and has) been read as a critique of science, a philosophical critique of the empirical method, it also operates along a social axis, commenting on the social uses of scientific knowledge in the period. Taking up where this discussion began, with Ishmael's defensive joke on the lecture as the source of his knowledge in "A Bower in the Arsacides," the chapter that initiates the final cetological section by reading the whale's internal structure and fossil history, I would like to focus here on how, in introducing this interpretative project, Ishmael uses "A Bower in the Arsacides" to comment more broadly on historical shifts in the social meanings and uses of knowledge, revealing the problematic alternatives for professional authority in antebellum America.

"A Bower in the Arsacides" ostensibly tells the story of Ishmael's attempt to get a measurement of a whale's skeleton, but it would be more apt to say that it is about residual and emergent uses of knowledge, mapping the changing social uses of knowledge in a moment of cultural transition. In this chapter, Ishmael defends his knowledge of the whale's dimensions by first describing his encounter with a skeleton of a whale on the imaginary island of Tranque. The Tranquean whale has been transformed into a temple, the bones "hung with trophies," carved with "Arsacidean annals, in strange hieroglyphics" and issuing smoke from its spout hole (102: 374). Attempting to measure the length of the whale's skeleton, Ishmael is stopped by priests who seek to keep the knowledge to themselves:

From the arrow-slit in the skull, the priests perceived me taking the altitude of the final rib. "How now!" they shouted; "Dar'st thou measure this our god! That's for us." "Aye, priests—well, how long do ye make him, then?" But hereupon a fierce contest rose among them, concerning feet and inches; they cracked each other's sconces with their yard-sticks—the great skull echoed—and seizing that lucky chance, I quickly concluded my own admeasurements. (102: 375)

For Ishmael, the transformation of the whale's skeleton into a temple and its accommodation of priests who comically fight over their arcane monopoly on knowledge of the whale's dimensions depicts an outmoded model of authoritative knowledge. The priests' desire to maintain a monopoly on this knowledge exposes both its arbitrariness and their social investment in the authority that control over knowledge bestows.

Ishmael's mocking and critical attitude toward this priestly obscurantism could be said to reflect the Jacksonian impulse to democratize the bases of knowledge in American life. For most antebellum Americans, as Neil Harris explains, "Secret information and private learning were anathema. All knowledge was meant to be shared."[80] In fact, it was this logic that served as one of main philosophic justifications for the rise of the lecture circuit and middlebrow culture more generally in the antebellum era. For example, Louis Agassiz explained his presence on the lecture circuit in this light:

> If . . . the results of science are of such general interest for the human race, . . . then it is well that all should share in its teachings, and that it should not be kept, like the learning of the Egyptians, for an exclusive priesthood who may expound the oracle according to their own theories, but should make a part of all of our intellectual culture and of our common educational systems.[81]

Like Agassiz's Egyptians, Ishmael's Tranquean priests are an image of an unjust and obsolete authority over knowledge that needs replacement. But if Ishmael's comical depiction of the Tranque priests evokes an archaic dead end for cultural authority, the other description of a whale skeleton in "A Bower in the Arsacides" demonstrates the problems of that cultural model that seemed destined to replace it, the emergent mass-culture construction of knowledge.

From the imaginary temple in Tranque, Ishmael shifts to a description of an actual display of a whale skeleton transformed into a tourist attraction in Yorkshire, one owned by Sir Clifford Constable:

> Sir Clifford's whale has been articulated throughout; so that, like a great chest of drawers, you can open and shut him, in all his bony cavities—spread out his ribs like a gigantic fan—and swing all day upon his lower jaw. Locks are to be

put upon some of his trapdoors and shutters; and a footman will show round future visitors with a bunch of keys at his side. Sir Clifford thinks of charging twopence for a peep at the whispering gallery in the spinal column; threepence to hear the echo in the hollow of his cerebellum; and sixpence for the unrivalled view from his forehead. (102: 376)

In distinction to the Tranquean priestly hermeticism, Sir Clifford opens up the whale, making it available for investigation or even play. As Samuel Otter suggests, Melville plays with the meaning of "articulation" here. Assembling the skeleton, Sir Clifford articulates it, but also makes it articulate—it becomes expressive and meaningful.[82] But this articulation is inextricably linked to a commercial motive, as it allows Sir Clifford to control access, putting "locks" on certain parts and charging admission. Sir Clifford's work of articulation produces distinct, multiply profitable attractions of the parts of the whale.

Sir Clifford's use of the whale is particularly reflective of the cultural logic of mass culture in the antebellum era. In his exhaustive study of the sources of *Moby-Dick*, Howard Vincent explicates this passage as a satire of guidebook language derived from Melville's 1850 visit to St. Paul's Cathedral in London, but it can also be seen to refer more generally to the articulation of mass cultural space, whether in the tourist site or P. T. Barnum's proprietary American Museum.[83] Like Sir Clifford's whale, Barnum's American Museum was carefully "articulated," maximizing access and use—and, of course, profit. In an open letter to the public, Barnum would explain the logic of his Museum in 1850: "My whole aim and effort is to make my museums totally unobjectionable to the religious and moral community, and at the same time combine sufficient amusement with instruction to please all proper tastes and to train the mind of youth to reject as repugnant anything inconsistent with moral and refined taste."[84] Modeling the self-culture logic that joined morality, amusement, and instruction, Barnum demonstrates the complicity of the middlebrow with commercialism. In this overdetermined effort to produce a "respectable" amusement, Barnum turned his museum into what Peter Buckley has called a "proto-department store of entertainment."[85] Under mass-culture logic, the realm of culture becomes, in the words of Horkheimer and Adorno, "a species of commodity . . . , marketable and interchangeable like an industrial product."[86] Like Barnum's Museum, Sir Clifford's whale in "A Bower in Arsacides" represents the expressive possibilities of mass culture's "articulation" as a cultural logic of commercialism and profit.

Caught between obsolete hermeticism and emergent commercialization, "A Bower in Arsacides" presents knowledge and cultural authority in a tricky transitional moment in the antebellum era. On the one hand, specialized authority retained a residual association with obscurantism and the self-interest of elites. On the other hand, the impulse to widen the basis of knowledge in the society was inextricably implicated in commercialization and the profit motive. Representing two different, but equally problematic models for knowledge and cultural authority, "A Bower in the Arsacides" encapsulates the ideological bind faced by the emergent professional class in the antebellum era. In fact, one could argue that Ishmael's cetology, with its balancing of the interpellations of the middlebrow, which seek to widen the cultural basis of knowledge, and its critical, questioning epistemology that demands subtle acts of interpretative distinction, represents Melville's attempt to articulate a new professional cultural authority, one that seeks to respond to the flaws and limitations revealed in the models depicted in "A Bower in the Arsacides." If that new professional cultural practice of authority embodied by Ishmael's cetology, one that mixes cultural "democracy" with dauntingly specialized demands of its readers, seems contradictory, this reflects some of the pressures and tensions within the new construction of professional cultural authority in the antebellum era.

Ishmael, Professionalism and the Middlebrow

In 1836, Ralph Waldo Emerson declared, "My pulpit is the lyceum platform." Oliver Wendell Holmes, offering advice to Melville in 1857, pronounced, "[The lecturer is a] literary strumpet subject for a greater than whore's fee to prostitute himself."[87] Melville himself explicitly addressed the context of the lyceum circuit in the famous satirical "Young America in Literature" chapter in *Pierre* (1852), where his young author–hero deals with invitations from "Lyceums, Young Men's Associations, and other Literary and Scientific Societies" after his premature literary success. One "Chairman of the Committee on Lectures" from a town named "Zadock-prattsville" solicits a lecture, suggesting that the teenaged Pierre speak on "Human Destiny." Melville reports that Pierre "most conscientiously and respectfully declined all polite overtures of this sort."[88] Despite his 1852 satire of the lyceum and ignoring the warning of Holmes, his Berkshires neighbor, Melville did go on the circuit in the winters from 1857 through 1860, with increasingly dismal results. In fact, his failure at this was perhaps the nadir of a literary career filled with low points.[89] Rather than seeing Melville's satire of the lyceum followed by his involvement in it as part of a trajectory of professional failure on Melville's part, however, I would rather consider it for its reflection upon the horizon of opportunities for cultural professionals and the complications of antebellum cultural politics.

The lyceum and the antebellum middlebrow culture more generally had a complex effect on professional authority. On one hand, it "democratized" specialized knowledge, making it available to anyone with a moderate surplus of time and money and a personal investment in learning. On the other hand, with its dependence upon professionals to supply the content, the lyceum circuit could be said to have constituted the first national audience for cultural professionalism and encouraged its expansion by spreading the reputation of individual exponents, which, in turn, led to a more widespread acceptance of professional authority.[90] But if the lyceum and middlebrow culture seemed to promise greater authority for professionals, the professional lecturers also came to recognize their relative lack of autonomy, embodied both by the requirement that they fit their material to middlebrow audience demands and by the lack of control over the message they might have for that audience. Although its public component validated the nobility of their professionalism, the lyceum's complacent interpretative concerns and obvious commercialism also signaled the penetration of capital into the realm of culture and threatened to expose professional authority as simply another commodity. In this way, middlebrow culture simultaneously bolstered professional authority and threatened to reveal the tenuousness of professional claims to its distinctive and privileged position within antebellum culture.

While Emerson and a host of other antebellum writers, intellectuals, and scientists adopted the lecture circuit as a profession, the professionalization of lecturing was short-lived, ending by 1870 in most accounts.[91] This tapering-off reflected professionalism's increasing disenchantment with the middlebrow and its ultimate dilution of professional authority. Donald Scott suggests that, by 1870, lecturing had become more oriented toward entertainment than to "instruction and inspiration."[92] Over the course of the second half of the nineteenth century, intellectuals, writers, and scientists, the core constituency of lecturers, would show increasing ambivalence toward this mode of addressing the public. For example, when a fire damaged the Smithsonian Institution in 1865, Joseph Henry reconstructed the building, pointedly without a lecture hall, having earlier expressed his resentment of members of the audience who "attend as a mere pastime, or assemble in the lecture room as a convenient place of resort. . . ."[93] Increasingly, American cultural professionals, given the choice between drawing away into specialized enclaves and discourses that separated them from the prescriptive demands of the marketplace or embracing a more popularizing role in cultural forums such as the lyceum hall, chose the former. Although the commercial forms of middlebrow culture may have grown only over the course of the nineteenth century, exploding into cultural prominence in the twentieth with institutions like the Book-of-the-Month Club, the antebellum era was not only its birthplace, but the birthplace of professionalism's problematic negotiation of its own cultural authority through it.

Ishmael's cetology chapters reflect that complicated negotiation of professional cultural authority in the antebellum era. Ishmael's cetological project is characterized throughout by the complexity of his subtle register of ironic voicing and the display of knowledge without closure. If, as William Charvat suggests, Ishmael's narratorial role is pedagogical, "training the reader," we must acknowledge how much at variance it is from some of the cultural institutions of knowledge in the period, particularly the lyceum hall. In fact, though Ishmael's narrative voice is often associated with "democracy," it is clear that his pedagogical project is quite distant from knowledge's democratization (and its consequent commercialization) in the antebellum culture industry. While he mocks the logic that endorses certain hierarchical thinking, Ishmael both invokes and rejects the impulse to make his training "practical" or "useful," or to reward his listeners–readers with a reassuring "comprehensiveness." In doing so, Ishmael's "pedagogy" becomes an act of distinction, designed as much to exclude as to educate.

Similarly, the cetology chapters, with their many detours away from the narrative, function structurally within the novel as a test of readers' resolve, of their willingness to defer narrative closure and their ability to derive pleasure from abstruse and often inconclusive erudition. As such, Ishmael's cetological project can be associated with the ethos of antebellum professionalism that sought to train American scholars, scientists, and professionals in more rigorous methodologies, but, in doing so, also established social barriers to authority over knowledge. It is no coincidence that Melville scholars in the twentieth century have spilled so much ink over the meaning of the cetology chapters, while students and other nonprofessional readers either struggle through or skip them altogether, recognizing them as an important (or discouraging) test of their skill and competency. The cetology chapters were written very much as a rejection of the antebellum middlebrow culture's display of democratized and commercialized knowledge and as a valorization of professional investment in discourse as a source of social distinction and authority. As a challenge to readers, the cetology chapters test their investment in a formalized realm of "Culture" and demand a reading aided by editorial apparatuses and formal training: in other words, a professional reading.

It is ultimately the very complications of *Moby-Dick*'s cultural politics that define its professionalism. Although one might easily argue that all cultural politics are based upon subtle distinctions—whether attending the Astor Place Opera House, striding down Broadway, or sauntering in the Bowery—*Moby-Dick* demands of its readers complicated acts of distinction, differentiation, discourse analysis, and interpretation that reflect the complicated cultural forms and social interests of the emergent professional middle class in antebellum America. Posing Ahab and Ishmael as alternative voices, Melville encourages the reader to work through different narrative motives and discursive authorities. In contrast to the common critical move that pits Ahab and Ishmael as antagonists or at least representatives of different philosophical modes, typically identifying Ishmael's survival at the novel's end as symbolic of his "triumph" (itself often representative of a variety of philosophical and social divides), I want to emphasize the common ground that the discourses Ahab and Ishmael share in demanding readerly effort and work. Far from the Cold War–era reading that associates Ishmael with a distinctly American practice of "freedom" and "democracy" and Ahab with a fascistic totalitarianism, we can see that Ahab and Ishmael do share an ambivalent cultural politics—appropriating discourses for establishing their authority, while meditating at length on the consequences of using discursive authority to influence (whether the crew or the reader).[94] In other words, *Moby-Dick* demands professional readers, but also asks professionals to ponder the possibilities, dangers, and limitations of their emergent role in American culture. As a result, it is not surprising that *Moby-Dick* was recovered in the twentieth century by a professoriate invested in recovering an American literary tradition. Ostensibly an "epic" about whaling, *Moby-Dick* is more concretely an epic about American professional-class cultural politics, a veritable lexicon of the distinctions to be made between other available models of cultural politics and the skills needed to construct one's self as a cultural professional.

There is no small irony in the fact that Melville's novel, written in part against the middlebrow cultural values of his period and canonized by a professionalized literary academy in the twentieth century that recognized its own values in his text, now finds itself re-appropriated into middlebrow culture in the twentieth century. Now that *Moby-Dick* has been sanctified as one of the "central" or "important" works of American literature, it has taken on symbolic meaning as a kind of cultural accomplishment and thus regularly appears on offer in the middlebrow book clubs, often illustrated with "fancy woodcuts."[95] This does not mean that *Moby-Dick* or even the cetology sections of the novel are necessarily read: ownership of the book, particularly an "art edition," and its presence in one's library has its own social significance exclusive of reading, comprehension, or mastery. This does, however, draw attention to the fragile boundaries between "high" and "middlebrow" culture (and, correspondingly, between "middle" and "low" culture) in modern American life. The complications of the cultural work of distinction in *Moby-Dick* highlight the difficulties that professionals face in defining their importance to American life.

We can read this cultural history of *Moby-Dick* as a reflection on the problems of professionalism in American culture. *Moby-Dick*'s twentieth-century reabsorption into middlebrow culture illustrates, at the very least, the difficulties professionals face in defining their identity through cultural distinctions and then using their authority to establish and maintain cultural boundaries. Professionalism strives, above all else, to be an autonomous economic, social, and cultural enterprise. But even as it establishes boundaries between itself and other social and cultural values or identities, it can only sustain itself through the marketing of those values. Distinction and autonomy are the essential act and state that professionalism strives for, but they are never truly realizable, as they are always reintegrated into the market as a service.

This is the lesson that Melville himself learned after publishing *Moby-Dick*, receiving some of the worst reviews of his career and experiencing miserable financial returns on his investment of time and effort. In his next work, *Pierre; or The Ambiguities* (1852), Melville would turn his frustration against his readership—producing a subversive and dark narrative posing as a sentimental romance ("a rural bowl of milk" as he would describe it to Sophia Hawthorne)—and his New York literary colleagues—profiling the absurdities of the literary marketplace in Pierre's famous "Young America in Literature" chapter. His frustration, however, would also be turned against the professional ideology that had structured his writing and his sense of the meaning of his labor. Recognizing professional meritocracy as a self-serving social hierarchy and the professional drive for autonomy as simply a self-disciplining internalization of the capitalist social order, Melville depicts professional authorship in *Pierre* as a self-deluding nightmare. In the next chapter, I explore *Pierre* as a savage auto-critique of professional ideology.

CHAPTER FIVE

The Ambiguities of Professionalism
Pierre, *Authorship, and Autonomy*

The narrator of Herman Melville's 1852 novel, *Pierre; or, The Ambiguities*, opens the "Young America in Literature" chapter with this metafictional commentary:

> Among the various conflicting modes of writing history, there would seem to be two grand practical distinctions, under which all the rest must subordinately range. By the one mode, all contemporaneous circumstances, facts, and events must be set down contemporaneously; by the other, they are only to be set down as the general stream of the narrative shall dictate; for matters which are kindred in time, may be very irrelative of themselves. I elect neither of these; I am careless of either; both are well enough in their way; I write precisely as I please.[1]

This chapter is famous (or infamous) for its midnarrative transformation of the novel's protagonist, Pierre Glendinning, from youthful aristocrat to fledgling author. This shift opened up much of the second half of *Pierre* to the most overt and substantial commentary on the New York literary community and the conditions of authorship in Melville's career. Over the course of the novel, Pierre suffers horribly as he struggles to write a novel that "will gospelize the world anew," producing instead a work that captures his own partial understandings and self-torment, a frustration that culminates in his committing murder and then suicide.

Modern critical response to Melville's depiction of Pierre's authorship has varied widely. Many scholars have noted biographical parallels between author and protagonist and identified Pierre as a stand-in for Melville himself.[2] Others have highlighted the narrator's ironic perspective upon Pierre throughout the book, no less present in the later urban authorship section than in the early pastoral and aristocratic setting of the first half, thus making the shift to authorship not so much as a transformation but rather as a continuation of the novel's critical or cynical vision of individualism and romanticism.[3] Certainly it is no coincidence that Melville subtitled his novel "The Ambiguities," thus reflecting not only the mental uncertainty that Pierre experiences, but also the uncertainty of the lesson we as readers are to derive from Pierre's life.

Many critics have pondered Melville's transformation of Pierre into an author. None more so than textual critic and biographer Hershel Parker, who has presented a convincing argument that Melville's launching into the subject of authorship late in the course of writing *Pierre* can be explained as a reaction to the negative reviews of *Moby-Dick* appearing at the time, especially from some of his New York literary colleagues, most notably Evert Duyckinck.[4] Whether or not one accepts Parker's reading, there is little question that the "Young America in Literature" chapter presents an acid satire of the New York literary community and the conventions of the antebellum literary marketplace. But this chapter is a relatively small portion of *Pierre*'s "digression" on literary matters. Far more involved is Melville's meditation upon Pierre's vocational logic. Moving Pierre to New York City allows Melville to explore the shift in Pierre's vision of his own authorship from genteel amateurism to ambitious professionalism, which is described at length in a series of chapters following "Young America in Literature." Although Melville's depiction of Pierre's authorship has long been read through the lens of romanticism (whether as idealization or critique), the terms used to represent Pierre's new vision of his authorial labors are explicitly embodied in a privileged vision of specialized nonmanual authority and autonomy. In other words, Melville's study of Pierre touches not only upon romanticism's vision of the artist, but also the vocational logic that validated the new professional middle-class status more generally. In this, Pierre not only embodies the logic of professionalism, but also exposes the internal contradictions of the professional drive for autonomy, revealing both the self-interest behind the impulse to justify professional status and the punishing self-discipline that legitimizes that supposedly autonomous role. By inserting this exploration of vocational logic, Melville shifts his narrative focus to make Pierre's choice of career increasingly central to his downfall, turning his narrative into more than a critique of the New York literary community or the antebellum literary marketplace, but one of professional ideology more generally.

This critique of professionalism emerges not only within the "Young America in Literature" chapter and Melville's depiction of Pierre's authorship. It is written into the narrative voice of the text, embodied in a narrator who has been seen alternately as earnest or satirical, creating an uncertainty of tone and meaning that unsettles distinctions and meanings, threatening the message of the text with ambiguity. Thus, although Melville's attitude toward professional authorship is framed by the first paragraph of "Young America in Literature," in which the narrator poses literary conventions (the "various conflicting modes of writing") against the authoritative claim of his own authorial autonomy ("I write precisely as I please"), the narrator's later ambiguous exploration of narrative conventions and of the meaning of reading more generally throughout the novel throws such autonomy into doubt; instead, it unsettles both the writer's and the reader's role in relationship to the text. Can the writer really write "precisely as [he] pleases" and would that be such a good thing, if he could? Simultaneously critiquing the institutions that limit literary autonomy and attacking the drive for autonomy, claiming to be writing from a space of professional autonomy while questioning the possibilities and benefits of that autonomy, *Pierre* becomes a deeply ambiguous autocritique of professional ideology.

"Young America in Literature": Pseudo-Professionalism and the New York Literary Community

Given the chapter's title, Melville's bitter satirical portrait of the New York literary community therein has long been read as a critical commentary on his Young American literary associates, particularly Evert Duyckinck. Even a cursory glance at the chapter, however, demonstrates its avoidance of the topics nearest and dearest to the Young Americans: nationality in literature and copyright law.[5] Instead, the story of Pierre's early literary success reveals many of the older practices that the Young Americans most avidly attacked: abusive publishing contracts, "puff" criticism, and the embrace of genteel amateurism in literature more generally. In fact, if Melville intended to critique his Young American literary colleagues in this chapter, he did so by exposing the hypocrisy of their public advocacy of a new professionalism in literature and their private embrace of the residual practices of the genteel amateurs. As a satiric exposé of the New York literary community, "Young America in Literature" depends upon the acceptance of new professional standards of literary subject matter, publishing, and criticism for its comical force. In this way, the chapter highlights the gap between professional ideals and the unprofessional practices of New York writers. In effect, "Young America in Literature" is a satire of the pseudoprofessionalism of the New York literary community.

In "Young America in Literature," Pierre embodies the idealized form of the genteel amateur and Melville's profile of the New York literary community savagely critiques the conventions of literary gentility. Pierre comes to the attention of the New York literary community ("his magnificent and victorious *debut*") through his poem, "that delightful love-sonnet, entitled 'The Tropical Summer'" (244). Satirizing the superficiality of the genteel aesthetic, Melville belittles "the high and mighty Campbell clan of editors of all sorts" who praise Pierre's "surprising command of language," "his euphonious construction of sentences," and the "pervading symmetry of his general style" and, when "transcending even this profound insight...looked infinitely beyond" to "the highly judicious smoothness and genteelness of the sentiments and fancies expressed"(245). Melville also mocks the genteel literary emphasis on morality, with critics and editors giving their highest praise in labeling Pierre "a highly respectable youth" and "blameless in morals, and harmless throughout" (245–46). When an elderly friend of Pierre's comments that responses to his work are "high praise," but notes that he "do[es] not see any criticisms as yet," Pierre exclaims "Criticisms?... why, sir, they are all criticisms! I am the idol of all the critics!" (246).

One of the crucial projects of American literary professionalism was the construction of an authoritative role and ethical standards for the literary critic. The rise of criticism was an important step toward the professionalization of literary pursuits. As Thomas Bender suggests, "With the collapse of the traditional pattern of patrician patronage and its replacement by the market, the critic emerged in literary culture."[6] As the market replaced the intimate local community of patronage, the critic took on increasing importance as an intermediary between author and reader. Appearing in print, an apparent public role, the critic became the authoritative representative of morality and aesthetic standards. Ostensibly an objective mediator between author and publisher and reader, the critic in early- and mid-nineteenth century America, however, was far more commonly a representative of the writer or publisher, and the review was more commonly what was called a "puff," a form of praise or publicity often drafted by the writer or the publishing house and sent to the newspapers or journals.[7] The puff, with its blurring of criticism and publicity, was a trait of the market logic of the antebellum publishing industry. As stalwart New York *litterateur* Charles Briggs exclaimed in an 1848 editorial column in *Holden's Magazine*: "The art of puffing is the art of all arts at the present day, when nothing will sell which is not first puffed into notice."[8]

The Young Americans, with their drive toward professionalizing authorship in the antebellum era, took up literary criticism and "puffery" as one of their main objects of attack. In his short-lived satirical magazine *Yankee Doodle*, the avid Young American Cornelius Mathews profiled the "Puff Critic" as the first in a planned series of "City Characters." Mathews predicted the end of puffery, based upon the ennobling of criticism and literary pursuits more generally:

> The Puff Critic in fine is a poor creature who might have passed all his days as a lying drummer in a jobber's store, or a false clerk over the counter, without being suspected of much more wickedness than falls to a man's trade generally; nay, he might have become rich, kept his gig and been accounted respectable; but he unfortunately blundered into a business where honesty and independence are the standard, and where the demand for false coin is only temporary, —sure to be repudiated in the end.[9]

Recognizing puffery as simply a device in marketing, Mathews opposes the field of literary endeavors, where "the demand for false coin is only temporary," to the world of the market, embodied by the nonmanual workers of the new market economy ("lying drummers" and "false clerks"). In contrast to the market dependence of these workers at the low end of the middle class, Mathews imagined a new vocational standard for literary professional behavior. The "man of letters'" embrace of "honesty and independence" will be rewarded and his rejection of them punished: "As these noble ends are cherished there is no vocation worthier than his; as they are defeated by his own act there is none more contemptible." As we saw in the critical debate over *Mardi*, the new vocational standards of Young American criticism modeled its professionalization of the literary sphere.

Young American literary critic William Jones attacked the conservatism of genteel critics in his 1845 *United States Magazine and Democratic Review* essay, "Amateur Authors and Small Critics," in terms mirrored by Melville in

"Young America in Literature." Like the mocking depiction of Pierre's ador-ing "critics," Jones belittles genteel preferences in criticism: "The small critic is delighted with petty beauties and the minutest details. . . . Originality puts him out; boldness he styles extravagance, and acknowledges none but imita-tive excellence. All inventors, he looks upon as arrogant interlopers. He is dis-trustful of novelty, and apprehends failure in every new scheme."[10] Attacking the superficial formalism and worship of conventionality by the genteel crit-ics, Jones imagined the negative effects of their dominance in American liter-ary criticism: "the mob of readers follow established names and reigning fashions; they follow their chosen leaders with implicit credulity."[11]

In fact, the 1840s saw important developments in the professionalization of literary criticism in New York City, perhaps most notably in Margaret Fuller's 1844 appointment to the New York *Tribune* as the first full-time book reviewer.[12] Despite this, few would argue that the professional stan-dards for literary criticism were upheld in the period, even by the Young Americans themselves. The example of Duyckinck's repeatedly failed attempts to bolster Mathews' career over the course of the 1840s and 1850s alone attests to a gap between professional ideals and the literary critical practice in antebellum New York City.[13] If Melville was criticizing the Young Americans in his "Young America in Literature" chapter, it was for their failure to uphold their own ideals. It is more likely, however, that Melville was generally criticizing the larger literary community for its con-tinued embrace of the most traditional and genteel literary values.

The New York literary scene of "Young America in Literature" marks the anachronism of this genteel model of authorship through its depiction of the commodification of literature and the transformation of the author into a celebrity. In this way, Melville makes overt what was covert in his first book, *Typee:* a critique of the market process within antebellum literary produc-tion. On the basis of his early success, Pierre is contacted by two tailors turned publishers, whose solicitation of his works for a "Library" edition highlights the new role of literature simply as a commodity in antebellum America. The decision of the publishers, named Wonder and Wen, to aban-don the "ignoble pursuit of tailor for the more honorable trade of publisher" is revealed to be simply an "economical" decision, related to converting "the linen and cotton shreds of the cutter's counter" into books through the "action of the paper-mill" (246). The comedy of the publishers' solicitation letter, such as it is, comes from their repeated slippage between literature and clothing as commodities ("Your pantaloons—productions, we mean"), demonstrating literature's easy transmutation into simply another mass-produced object for sale. Under this market logic, the publishers' offer to produce Pierre's "Complete Works," if Pierre will pay the printer's and binder's bills (written as "seamstresses" in the letter) for the possibility of earning "one tenth of the profit (less discount)" of sales exposes the chicanery of the antebellum publishing business.

In any case, this exploration of the market in antebellum literary production leads Melville to the topic of "literary celebrity" (252). On the basis of his literary success, Pierre is swamped by requests for autographs and invitations to lecture. When Pierre encounters a "literary acquaintance—a joint editor of the "Captain Kidd Monthly," he demands a "Daguerreotype" of Pierre for the next issue. Perry Miller notes the similarity of Pierre's rejection of this demand to Melville's own refusal of Duyckinck's request for a daguerreotype for *Holden's Magazine* in the winter of 1851.[14] Given the new ease with which one could get a portrait taken by daguerreotypy, Melville complained to Duyckinck that having one's "mug" in a magazine was not a mark of distinction, but "presumptive evidence" of being "a nobody."[15] In *Pierre*, Melville extended this thinking by explaining that, "when everybody has his portrait published, true distinction lies in not having yours published at all" (254). By naming the magazine "The Captain Kidd Monthly," with its association with "piracy"—a term for the editorial practice of republishing uncopyrighted British and American writings without recompensing authors—Melville was perhaps trying to avoid any association with Duyckinck: the Young Americans were strongly antagonistic to piracy.[16] In any case, Melville/Pierre's response is not so much a rejection of Young American literary principles, but a reflection of his attempt to bolster his professional status as author. Although the penetration of the market opened up possibilities for literary profit, it also commodified and devalued the traditional authority of the status of author. The Young Americans, like the modern movement of professionalism more generally, had sought to balance market demands and status, finding a way to establish "distinction" for its practitioners while still profiting from the new readership.[17] Again, Melville's response to the New York literary community in "Young America in Literature" was not a rejection of Young American's values per se, but a critique of their failure to embody them in a literary practice.

In "Young America in Literature," Melville critiques the double bind of antebellum authorship, pulled backward by the persistence of the anachronistic values of elite, amateur literary gentility and forward into the corrosive pool of the urban–industrial capitalist marketplace that threatened to reduce everything to a commodity. In doing so, he recapitulated the problem he faced in writing *Typee*, his text marked by his struggles with the limiting definitions of authorship in the period. In his own career, Melville attempted to negotiate this bind with *Mardi*, and in the process constructed a new model of professional authorship that was readily embraced by his Young American colleagues, if not by many others. *Pierre* follows this trajectory, shifting to Pierre's decision to pursue a new model of authorship in chapters such as "Pierre as Juvenile Author, Reconsidered" and "The Flower-Curtain Lifted." In this process, Melville shifts the object of his critique from both the residual genteel ethos and the industrialization of the antebellum literary field to the ideological response to both: professionalism.

Pierre's Authorship: Professionalism and Autonomy

Hershel Parker's critique of the introduction of Pierre's authorship into the narrative is that it is an arbitrary shift and out of context with the rest of the narrative. Parker's "Kraken" experiment of simply removing any reference to Pierre's authorship was designed to restore Melville's "original intent" and, with it, reveal a more coherent and consistent work of art.

> For readers of *Pierre* as originally published but not as originally completed, the aesthetic lesson of my evidence is that it is folly to look for ways of seeing the Pierre-as-author theme as unified with the rest of the book. To find unity in the mixed product of ecstatic confidence and reckless defiance after failure is to trivialize Melville's aspiration, his achievement, and his wrecking of that achievement—to dehumanize Melville as man and artist.[18]

However, an examination of the secondary characters of the novel reveals that the turn toward authorship was not simply a fugitive whim on Melville's part: nearly every living male character profiled in *Pierre* (the only notable exception is Pierre's cousin, Glen Stanly) is involved in some manner with authorship, from the Reverend Falsgrave to Charlie Millthorpe, from Pierre himself to Plotinus Plinlimmon. More than just a poison-pen letter to his former colleagues among the New York City literati, Melville's meditation on authorship in *Pierre* transforms writing into a typology for middle-class professional labor that allows him to explore a spectrum of vocational attitudes. Presenting a range of characters who write and exploring the nature of their labors, *Pierre* carefully charts the ability of the author–workers to set the terms of their own work, a kind of autonomy that is perhaps the most crucial justifying trait of professional status within the vocational hierarchy in modern American life. In this process, Melville rather methodically explores the consequences of the professional middle-class investment in the notion of work as an ennobled and privileged calling or vocation. Plotting out the self-destructive consequences of Pierre's seemingly arbitrary selection of the literary vocation, Melville critiques professional ideology, from the specious logic that valorizes nonmanual over manual labor to the problematic results of professional investment in autonomy. Whether one wants to argue for the unity of *Pierre* or not, Melville's meditation on authorship, both before and after Pierre's decision to write professionally, functions as a surprisingly consistent commentary on authorship in relation to trends in antebellum discourses of labor and professionalism.

Profiles of two characters from Saddle Meadows, both involved with authorship, frame the "Young America in Literature" revelation of Pierre's authorship: the Reverend Falsgrave and Charlie Millthorpe. Despite the apparent differences between the characters, both are from the rural working class and improve their social standing by entering a profession—Falsgrave through the ministry and Millthorpe as a lawyer. As such, both characters signal the new democratic possibilities of the professions in the antebellum era, breaking the traditional association of the professions with elites. Falsgrave is described as "[t]he child of a poor northern farmer who had wedded a pretty sempstress" and thus "had no heraldic line of ancestry to show, as warrant and explanation of his handsome person and gentle manners" (98). Charlie Millthorpe, the son of a noble-faced but failed tenant farmer of the Glendinnings at Saddle Meadows, abandoned the country for the city, where he took up the business of law and "had really advanced his fortunes in a degree" (279).[19] Both Falsgrave and Millthorpe have improved their status through entrance into the professions, but Melville's interest in them seems not simply to present the expanded opportunities within the antebellum professions, but to explore the ideological range of professionalism and its relationship to authorship.

Given Melville's supposedly arbitrary interest in exploring Pierre's vocational choice of authorship, it is certainly no coincidence that both Falsgrave and Millthorpe are also writers. The traditional professions—ministry, law, and medicine—had long been the mainstays of American literary production in both its genteel origins and in its nascent professionalism. As the minister of Saddle Meadows, Falsgrave embodies the most traditional and conservative of professional roles, and his authorship reflects the residual model of literary production as the product of gentlemanly leisure and aestheticized amateurism:

> Besides [Falsgrave's] eloquent persuasiveness in the pulpit, various fugitive papers upon subjects of nature, art, and literature, attested not only his refined affinity to all beautiful things, visible or invisible; but likewise that he possessed a genius for celebrating such things, which in a less indolent and more ambitious nature, would have been sure to have gained a fair poet's name ere now. (98)

With his literary efforts those of a dilettante, Falsgrave's vision of his authorship is simply another social attainment in his quest for gentlemanly status.[20] By contrast, Millthorpe approaches his authorship more seriously. In addition to his legal practice, Millthorpe "pursu[ed] some crude, transcendental Philosophy, for both a contributory means of support, as well as for his complete intellectual ailment" (280). The Transcendental lawyer plans to "displace some of [his] briefs for [his] metaphysical treatises" and to lecture: "Stump[ing] the State on the Kantian Philosophy! A dollar a head, my boy! Pass round your beaver, and you'll get it!" (281). Millthorpe's vision of "stumping the state" for Kant seems to mock the paradoxical materialist antimaterialism that shaped Emerson's lyceum career. For Millthorpe, an entrepreneurial idealism seems no paradox or contradiction, but a perfectly viable model of literary professionalism.

Later, Millthorpe will slight Pierre's concentrated literary effort in favor of his own literary productivity, claiming to have produced:

> Ten metaphysical treatises; argued five cases before the court; attended all our society's meetings; accompanied our great Professor, Monsieur Volvoon, the lecturer, through his circuit in the philosophical saloons, sharing all the honors of his illustrious triumph; and by the way, let me tell you, Volvoon secretly gives me even more credit than is my due; for 'pon my soul, I did not write more than one half, at most, of his lectures; edited—anonymously, though, a learned, scientific work on "The Precise Cause of the Modifications in the Undulatory Motion in Waves," a posthumous work of a poor fellow—fine lad he was, too— a friend of mine. Yes, I have been doing all this, while you still are hammering away at that one poor plaguy Inferno! (317)

Far from Falsgrave's genteel "papers" on "nature, art, and literature," Millthorpe's literary pursuits become a kind of intellectual industrial production, pursuing literary activities in a variety of different arenas and valuing quantitative productivity as its own virtue. In this way, the literary work of Falsgrave and Millthorpe models a spectrum of authorship within professional vocations, ranging from leisured amateurism to a kind of entrepreneurial market production.

Both Falsgrave and Millthorpe function to highlight the limitations on the professions in the antebellum era that called modern professionalism into being. Reflecting that era's increasing skepticism toward the older genteel vision of the professions, Reverend Falsgrave, with his pseudo-gentlemanly manners and his dilettantish literary dabblings, is exposed as powerless. Revealing the effects of the older professionalism's dependence upon elite patronage, the narrator points out that Mrs. Glendinning was the "untiring patroness of [Falsgrave's] beautiful little marble church," as well as "the same untiring benefactress, from whose purse, he could not help suspecting, came a great part of his salary, nominally supplied by the rental of pews" (97). It is this dependence that exposes Falsgrave's lack of autonomy when faced with the moral quandary of what to do about Delly Ulver's out-of-wedlock pregnancy. Forced to choose between Pierre's call for mercy and Mrs. Glendinning's indignant wrath toward the farm girl, Falsgrave completely repudiates his professional authority. He explains:

> It is one of the social disadvantages which we of the pulpit labor under, that we are supposed to know more of the moral obligations of humanity than other people. And it is a still more serious disadvantage to the world, that our unconsidered, conversational opinions on the most complex problems of ethics, are too apt to be considered authoritative, as indirectly proceeding from the church itself. Now, nothing can be more erroneous than such notions; and nothing so embarrasses me, and deprives me of that entire serenity, which is indispensable to the delivery of a careful opinion on moral subjects, than when sudden questions of this sort are put to me in company. (102)

Although Falsgrave's refusal to follow his own apparent sympathy with Pierre's mercy is a form of hypocrisy, the novel presents, not so much a critique of Christianity per se, but of the dependent condition of the rural ministry as a holdover of the older patronage model of professionalism. At the close of his final encounter with Falsgrave, in which the minister again avoids taking a stand against Mrs. Glendinning's wishes, Pierre exclaims:

> I once cherished some slight hope that thou wouldst have been able, in thy Christian character, to sincerely and honestly counsel me. But a hint from heaven assures me now, that thou hast no earnest and world-disdaining counsel for me.... I do not blame thee; I think I begin to see how thy profession is unavoidably entangled by all fleshly alliances, and can not move with godly freedom in a world of benefices. I am more sorry than indignant. (164)

Falsgrave's ministerial authority is inevitably limited by its dependence upon patronage, thus making Falsgrave's weakness less an individual character flaw than an "unavoidable" consequence of the economic and social conditions of the "profession."

If the portrait of Falsgrave highlights the limitations upon the autonomous practice of the older model of professionalism, the novel's depiction of Millthorpe highlights the dangers of an open, market-oriented professionalism. Far from a model of wisdom and dependable authority, Millthorpe is defined by his ill-informed and contradictory pronouncements. In fact, the narrator notes that his professional success seems to be derived primarily from a "certain harmless presumption and innocent egotism" (279). Millthorpe's professional prosperity, modest as it is, is likened to "the glory of the bladder that nothing can sink" (280): derived entirely from its lack of substance or weightiness rather than from any essential authority. From the dependence of the genteel model of the professions, with its patronal curbs to autonomy and authority, to the new, democratic, and open model of professionalism, with its unsubstantiated presumption and egotism, *Pierre* portrays the limitations of professional identity in the antebellum era.

In the novel, Pierre's decision to launch himself on the career of professional author is situated between the profiles of Falsgrave and Millthorpe, these two problematic representatives of the poles of professional identity in the period, and could be said to respond to their problems by articulating the new model of professional ideology that sought to escape patronage, address the market, and establish legitimizing standards of professional authority all at once. In this way, Pierre seems to present a potential new model of a legitimate literary professional authority. Despite the seemingly negative models that Pierre's authorship seems designed to supersede, however, Melville's depiction of Pierre's professionalism does not justify this new vocational standard, but rather exposes its deep problems and, in the process, undermines the ideological project of modern professionalism.

Arriving in New York City after his disinheritance, Pierre turns to writing, apparently for lack of any better option: "For what else could he do? He knew no profession, no trade" (260). But if this decision seems arbitrary in relation to the first half of the novel, Pierre's authorship reflects a distinctly professional vision of the writer's life in antebellum America. Once an "indifferent and supercilious amateur" (263), Pierre rejects Falsgrave's and his own earlier genteel and unambitious approach to writing. In contrast to his intentionally minor and occasional sentimental poetical earlier works, such as "The Tear," "The Tropical Summer: A Sonnet," or "The Weather: A

Thought," Pierre's decision to make authorship a career transforms his vision of his work into a serious endeavor with deep responsibilities and moral overtones: "Isabel, I will write such things—I will gospelize the world anew, and show them deeper secrets than the Apocalypse!—I will write it, I will write it!" (273). If Pierre rejected Falsgrave's genteel piety and amateur authorship for religious doubt and greater seriousness of effort, he also sought to distinguish himself from Millthorpe's industrial literary work. Like Millthorpe with his family to support and his Transcendental ideals to spread, Pierre would write for a double purpose: "the burning desire to deliver what he thought to be new, or at least miserably neglected Truth to the world; and the prospective menace of being absolutely penniless. . . ." (283). While Millthorpe wrote to advocate his Transcendentalist schemes and to earn money, he did so by producing a seemingly endless flood of ephemeral pamphlets and lectures. By contrast, Pierre invests all of his energy in "a comprehensive compacted work" (283), following his belief that "the most grand productions of the best human intellects" are unitary works that "digestively includ[e] the whole range of all that can be known or dreamed; Pierre was resolved to give the world a book, which the world should hail with surprise and delight" (283). Rejecting Millthorpe's market-oriented model of industrialized literary production, Pierre wants to produce one profound text. Rejecting genteel amateurism but also seeking to control the terms of his entrance into the marketplace as an authoritative individual, Pierre's authorship reflects the professional model that Melville had seemingly articulated for himself in the preceding years.

As Melville discusses Pierre's new vision of his literary labors, in "Pierre as Juvenile Author, Reconsidered," Pierre's professionalism becomes an avenue not just for Melville's autobiographical musings on his own work, but also for a consideration of the social meanings of work in antebellum America. That era was a period in which definitions and understandings of work underwent significant revision. In Puritan America, an individual's work was characterized by the Protestant notion of a "calling," defined by the Puritan minister William Perkins as "a certain kind of life, ordained and imposed on man by God for the common good."[21] The sense of the calling glorified all work done in the interest of the public good and vitiated the hierarchy between worldly and spiritual activity, finding spiritual meaning in ascetic worldly success.[22] This Puritan vocational notion retained significance well into the nineteenth century. In his 1837 lecture "Trades and Professions," Ralph Waldo Emerson suggests that the "heroism of a calling" is "to prefer the work to its reward."[23] In a fairly conventional invocation of the legitimating force of the calling, Emerson spoke of the calling as "foreordained" and asserted, "If today you should release by an act of law all men from their contracts and all apprentices from their indentures and pay all labor with equal wages, —tomorrow you should find the same contracts and indentures redrawn. . . ."[24] Asserting the "dignity of labor," Emerson imagined the reward of the worker pursuing his calling was an "increase of power in his craft and the manifold benefits flowing out of it," so that the worker "comes to love his work for its own sake." [25]

Emerson's blithe assertions aside, this concept of the calling became increasingly anachronistic in the antebellum era, particularly in urban areas such as New York City. The rise of industrialization in the Northern cities of the period largely undermined the artisan system and, in the process, degraded the skills of many members of the working class and reduced their income, allowing relatively few to experience the rewards of a calling as Emerson imagined them.[26] In this context, the notion of a calling seemed to have class-interested, quietist tendencies, encouraging members of the working class to accept their new lot as divinely determined. Rejecting this model, many of the working class and their advocates responded to industrialization by invoking a republican discourse of work that privileged artisan and agrarian labor and a labor theory of value.[27] Derived from Adam Smith, the labor theory of value, described by Sean Wilentz as "the doctrine that all wealth is derived from labor," could be a particularly elastic concept depending upon how one defined work, but in antebellum cities the theory became associated with an attack on economic inequality. [28] As Edward Pessen observes, this privileged, but abused notion of labor was particularly associated with "those who worked with their hands for wages."[29] John Commerford, a mechanic who became an important figure in the New York Working Man's Party, an early labor organization, argued in an 1835 speech that the worker was the "real producer of all wealth and luxury possessed by the rich and powerful."[30] In its extreme stance, such as that espoused by Orestes Brownson, the labor theory of value called into question the distinction between wage labor and slavery and found a solution to inequality only in an end to private property. For most advocates of "free labor," however, more moderate reforms were encouraged. Rejecting the disempowering and anachronistic logic of the calling, industrialized urban laborers embraced a political economy and the vocational identity of the "manual" laborer to fight their disenfranchisement in antebellum America.

While the "manual" labor theory of value attacked social injustice in ante-bellum America, others in the society, particularly those of the middle and upper classes turned to an alternate model that valorized "nonmanual" pro-ductivity, reflecting the replacement of the unified vocational vision of the calling with the hierarchical distinction between men who "worked with their heads" and men who "worked with their hands," a model that increasingly defined the world of work in nineteenth-century American life.[31] Refuting the "manual"-oriented labor theory of value in his *Political Economy* (1841), Alonzo Potter claimed "that by far the most productive labour of all is that of the *mind*, which is not susceptible of compulsion."[32] For Potter, only mind labor was free labor, not the constrained experience of the manual worker. For the many professional middle- and upper-class politicians, reformers, and social theorists who addressed the topic, the manual–nonmanual divide established a hierarchy by associating nonmanual labor with "mind" and "soul," in contrast to manual labor's "body" or "matter."[33] As William Ellery Channing asserted in his "Lecture on the Elevation of the Laboring Classes"(1831): "Matter was made for spirit, body for mind. The mind, the spirit, is the end of this living organization of flesh and bones, of nerves and muscles."[34] Even for those who intended to support workers' interests, as did Channing, this Christianized hierarchy fed back into an inevitable social hier-archy. The new valorization of nonmanual labor could retain the spiritual quality of the calling, but only at the expense of excluding the working class whose manual labor would come to take on an uncertain meaning and value in American life.[35]

In *Pierre*, Melville directly explores this manual–nonmanual labor split by unpacking the contradictions within the problematic social attitudes that emerge out of Pierre's own investment in the hierarchy of professionalized nonmanual labor. In the chapter "Pierre as Juvenile Author," Melville describes the result of Pierre's first money-earning writing, a realization that "he could live on himself" (261). Continuing, the narrator comments: "Oh, twice-blessed now, in the feeling of practical capacity, was Pierre" (261). To explain why Pierre is "twice-blessed" for his ability to profit from his writing, Melville launches into an elaborate discussion that begins by invoking the conventional middle-class logic on the limitations of manual labor, but also reveals the troubling consequences of embracing the "soul/body" hierarchy of nonmanual labor: "The mechanic, the day-laborer, has but one way to live; his body must provide for his body. But not only could Pierre in some sort, do that; he could do the other; and letting his body stay lazily at home, send off his soul to labor, and his soul would come back faithfully and pay his body her wages" (261). Like Alonzo Potter, Pierre understands his nonmanual labor as a kind of freedom, a lack of the constraint or necessity experienced by the "day-laborer" who "has but one way to live." But Melville explores the consequence of this model by extending the trope. Under the logic of this manual–body/nonmanual–soul division, the nonmanual laborer "send[s] off his soul to labor," while letting the "body stay lazily at home." Is this really a better arrangement? The soul, configured as feminine ("her wages"), becomes subject to the will of the body. Far from seeming a beneficial work scheme, the ostensibly "higher" spiritual element seems to become the slave to the "lower" bodily element as Melville further extends this trope: "So, some unprofessional gentlemen of the aristocratic South, who happen to own slaves, give those slaves liberty to go and seek work, and every night return with their wages, which constitute those idle gentlemen's income" (261). Here, the hierarchy of Pierre's non-manual labor is ironically likened to the labor of "idle" southern slave owners who work neither with their "minds" nor "souls" nor their "bodies." Starting as a justification of vocational hierarchy, Pierre's vision of labor becomes instead a revelation of self-serving hypocrisy and false consciousness. [36]

In this, Melville mocks the broader ideological project of the hierarchy of nonmanual labor. This hierarchy of labor could feed into a totalizing model of society that justified the social and economic status quo, as suggested by Theodore Sedgwick in his *Public and Private Economy* (1836):

> The more ideas, the more mind a man has, the better for him; all agree on that; so, also, the more a man *labours* with his mind, which is mental labour, the higher he is in the scale of labourers: all must agree to that whether they will or no. This is a real distinction in nature, and can no more be got rid of by laws, customs, and form of government, than the complexion of the face, or color of the eyes. . . . It is upon this ground, that there ever have been, and ever will be, high and low, rich and poor, masters and servants.[37]

For Sedgwick, the hierarchy of mind over body labor was a natural distinction, like "complexion," which justified a stratified social order. In this way, the discourse of the hierarchy of nonmanual over manual labor fed into other notions of the "natural hierarchy" in the period.

What Sedgwick makes implicit in his manual–nonmanual divide, others would make explicit: advocates and apologists of slavery would defend its practices by using the same Christianized hierarchy of labor, identifying the African slaves with "body" and the Christian slaveholders with "spirit." As one Southern editor proclaimed in 1860, "The sons of Ham are particularly fitted for menial service and the heavier duties of the field. . . ."[38] The Southern association of manual labor with slavery could lead to disdainful comments upon white farmers "who make Negroes of themselves."[39] The "natural" hierarchies of race and labor formed a complex justification of slavery in antebellum Southern discourse. On the other hand, Northern abolitionist discourse attacked white Southerners for their "dissipation" and "indolence," exposing their embrace of a hierarchical logic not as political economy, but as self-interest. In 1861, Wendell Philips suggested that between the inefficient, coerced labor of the slaves and its "idler" slave-owner population, it was as if only "one quarter of the population" of South Carolina was "actually at work."[40] Even Southern apologist and editor J. G. B. De Bow complained that "it is the great fault of Southern people that they are *too proud to work*."[41] Ironically, the abolitionist movement, despite its critique of slavery's model of hierarchy, was itself largely characterized by its embrace of a hierarchical model of labor and social life.[42] Thus, while the abolitionists could critique the logic of the Southern racial/economic hierarchy, they were endorsing the same vocational hierarchy themselves. Melville's satire of Pierre's vision of his nonmanual "practical capacity" highlights the similarities between professional middle-class vocational hierarchy and the deeply "unprofessional" practices of aristocratic Southern gentlemen.

Many critics have observed that Pierre's "pride" expresses itself in a vision of individualism, but it is notable that this individualism finds fulfillment through a specific kind of work experience.[43] Melville ascribes Pierre's choice of vocation to "pride," an expression of a drive for autonomous selfhood:

> Pierre was proud; and a proud man . . . ever holds lightly those things, however beneficent, which he did not procure for himself. . . . A proud man likes to feel himself in himself, and not by reflection in others. He likes to be not only his own Alpha and Omega, but to be distinctly all the intermediate gradations, and then to slope off on his own spine either way, into the endless impalpable ether. (260–61)

This vision of autonomous selfhood embodied through work was a new creation in American life, one central to the new ethos of professionalism. As Burton Bledstein suggests, "The [nineteenth-century] professional person strove to achieve a level of autonomous individualism, a position of unchallenged authority heretofore unknown in American life."[44] Autonomy was absolutely essential to the project of modern middle-class professionalization, as John and Barbara Ehrenreich suggest: "[T]he role the PMC [professional managerial or middle class] was entering and carving out for itself—as technical innovators, social mediators, culture producers, etc.—required a high degree of autonomy, if only for the sake of legitimation."[45] It was this work autonomy that defined professionalism in distinction from working-class labor, as Eliot Freidson explains, "typically, professional autonomy is the antithesis of proletarianization."[46] In the face of the emergent industrialization of labor, the discretion and responsibility of the professional worker became a crucial marker of hierarchical social status. The autonomy of professional labor justified a vision of individualism that distinguished among the classes. Whether this "precious autonomy" legitimated "a life and a career around noble aims and purposes" or simply social self-interest, autonomy was a crucial trait of professionalism. [47]

In "Pierre as Juvenile Author, Reconsidered," Melville's elaboration of Pierre's privileged vision of his work explores the contradictions within this notion of autonomous professional nonmanual labor and selfhood, as he continues his discussion of Pierre's "twice-blessed" capacity:

> Both ambidexter and quadruple-armed is that man, who in a day-laborer's body, possesses a day-laboring soul. Yet let not such an one be over-confident. Our God is a jealous God; He wills not that any man should permanently possess the least shadow of His own self-sufficient attributes. Yoke the body to the soul, and put both to the plough, and the one or the other must in the end assuredly drop in the furrow. Keep, then, thy body effeminate for labor, and thy soul laboriously robust; or else thy soul effeminate for labor and thy body laboriously robust. Elect! The two will not lastingly abide in one yoke. (261)

Extending his exploration of the soul–body and nonmanual–manual labor trope, Melville presents the "twice-blessed" nonmanual laborer as "both ambidexter and quadruple-armed" in his productive ability, so much so that his "self-sufficient" autonomy takes on a Godlike quality. But unlike those "idle gentlemen" of the South who appropriate the labor of their slaves, the nonmanual laborer can only appropriate himself or at least some part of himself, so that the autonomous attempt to make both body and soul productive can only bring about personal destruction, the failure of either the body or the soul. Melville suggests, then, that one must make a choice: keep the body "effeminate for labor" and the soul "laboriously robust" or vice versa.

The gendered language of this distinction—"effeminate" or " robust"— plays into overdetermined masculine anxieties about labor in this period. The association of nonmanual labor with mind or spirit led to concerns about the overemphasis of mind over body, which might lead to "weakness" or "effeminacy" in the middle and upper classes.[48] In turn, the increased dependence upon wage labor among the working classes limited their independence, sometimes described in association with the woman's dependence upon the man in the economic logic of the divided-spheres model.[49] As Horace Greeley explained in an 1843 commencement lecture at Hamilton College: "The division of the race into two unequal, contrasted classes—the few Thinkers, the many Workers—has been and is the source of many sore evils, including the loss of the fitting and manly independence of each." [50] Given the impossibility of "yoking" the productive forces of the soul and body together and the choice of emphasizing one aspect of the self to maximize its productivity at the expense of the other, Melville exposes the divide of manual and nonmanual labor as an arbitrary and destructive binary logic.

Closing out the characteristically elaborate discussion in *Pierre*, Melville attacks the discourse of labor hierarchy, mocking the pretense of transcendence in nonmanual-labor discourse by exclaiming: "Thus over the most vigorous and soaring conceits, doth the cloud of Truth come stealing" (261). If the "cloud of Truth" seems an unlikely agent of enlightenment, speaking more to obscuring and obfuscation, Melville continues by suggesting that the earth's gravitational pull places an inevitable curb on the elevated and spiritual ambitions of professionalized nonmanual labor: "[T]hus doth the shot, even of a sixty-two-pounder pointed upward, light at last on the earth; for strive we how we may, we can not overshoot the earth's orbit, to receive the attractions of other planets; Earth's law of gravitation extends far beyond her own atmosphere" (261). Playing out the consequences of Pierre's "twice-blessed" valorization of his nonmanual labor, Melville suggests that, no matter how elevated, spiritual, and otherwise transcendent terms are used, professional labor will always ultimately depend upon "earthly" effort. Even the "most soaring . . . conceits" must crash to earth like a cannonball—and a cannonball pointed straight upward will most likely harm the individual who fired it off.

Certainly, this will be the course of Pierre's literary career. After the "Young America in Literature" chapter, Pierre's investment in the legitimating discourse of nonmanual labor becomes a predetermining factor in his inevitable fall. Pierre chooses professional authorship as a vocation because of its possibilities for autonomy, but Melville reveals that vision of nonmanual autonomy as not only a specious social hierarchy, but also a deeply problematic practice of selfhood. In fact, Melville demonstrates how the practice of professionalism transforms Pierre into the "most unwilling states-prisoner of letters" (340).

Professionalism's autonomous individualism was a two-edged sword. If professionalism offered unprecedented authority, it was counterbalanced by a moral demand for self-examination. As Burton Bledstein argues, the authority of the professional could not be defended "in the name of an irrational egotism but [only] in the name of a special grasp of the universe and a special place in it."[51] Professionals could only justify their "precious autonomy" and the status and authority it entailed by structuring "a life and a career around noble aims and purposes, including the ideal of moral obligation."[52] And Melville is careful to demonstrate Pierre's commitment to such noble purposes through his avid desire to "gospelize the world anew" and "deliver . . . [a] new, or at least miserably neglected Truth to the world" through his writing. But because autonomous professionals were the only qualified people to judge their actions, the professional became, above all else, "a *self-governing* individual exercising his trained judgment in an open society."[53] Self-governance as a whole took on new importance, as professionals sought to remake the culture in their image.

Looking at both social problems and themselves, nineteenth-century professionals "threw responsibility pitilessly inward."[54] This "inward" turn toward self-regulation was both empowering and disempowering at the same time. Ralph Waldo Emerson addressed this doubleness of professionalism's new self-governance, when he tried to characterize the rise of the New England intelligentsia from the 1820s through the 1840s in his essay "Life and Letters in New England": "It is the age of severance, of dissociation, of freedom, of analysis, of detachment. Every man for himself. . . . The young men were born with knives in their brains, a tendency to introversion, self-dissection, anatomizing of motives."[55] Emerson notes that the freedom and authority associated with the new generation, one that could be associated with the rise of professionalism (though he does not make this association himself), comes with a constant demand to self-analyze, to regulate and evaluate oneself. To be born with "knives in [one's] brains" must seem like a problematic honor: in fact, it is, in many ways, a dubious trait. And perhaps there is no clearer comment on its dubiousness than in Melville's depiction of Pierre's authorship, where the professional vision of self-governance is transmogrified into a brutal self-denial and self-imprisonment.

In *Pierre*, Pierre turns to authorship to express his autonomy, yet his experience of writing his novel is ultimately one of deprivation and pain. Living among the Transcendentalists in New York City at the converted church, the Apostles, Pierre adopts the "Flesh-Brush Philosophy" of idealist self-discipline while writing (300). Melville's discussion of Transcendentalist "aspirations" to strive after "heavenly ideals" through bodily disciplines highlights their "inevitable perverse ridiculousness" (299), but also links to his critique of professional visions of autonomy. John Carlos Rowe proclaims Melville's discussion of Pierre's privileged vision of artistic labor a critique of Transcendentalist idealism.[56] Melville, however, demonstrates the ways in which "utilitarianism" and other "incomprehensible worldly maxims," such as the hierarchy of nonmanual labor, are far more dangerous than Transcendentalism, precisely because they enacted their supposed "common-sense notions" in the world:

> The so-called Transcendentalists are not the only people who deal in Transcendentals. On the contrary, we seem to see that the Utilitarians—the every-day world's people themselves, far transcend those inferior Transcendentalists by their own incomprehensible worldly maxims. And—what is vastly more—with the one party, their Transcendentals are but theoretic and inactive, and therefore harmless; whereas with the other, they are actually clothed in living deeds. (262)

The Transcendentalist obsession with diet and denial of physical pleasures simply takes the spirit–body hierarchy of professional discourse to its theoretical extreme. Utilitarianism, supposedly the opposite of Transcendentalism, depends upon equally problematic idealist logic, but inflicts more damage upon the world through its "living deeds."

Later, studying Pierre working at his "twice-blessed" chosen trade, Melville exposes the fallacy of the idealism of this professionalized vocational ideology:

> Pierre is young; heaven gave him the divinest, freshest form of a man; . . . Now, look around in that most miserable room, and at that most miserable of all the pursuits of a man, *and say if here be the place, and this be the trade, that God intended him for.* . . . Oh, I hear the leap of the Texas Camanche, as at this moment he goes crashing like a wild deer through the green underbrush; I hear his glorious whoop of savage and untamable health; and then I look in at Pierre. If physical, practical unreason make the savage, which is he? Civilization, Philosophy, Ideal Virtue! Behold your victim. (302, *my italics*)

Melville implicitly asks if bodies were created to be denied, throwing doubt on the Christianized logic of nonmanual hierarchy. Thus, in romanticized terms, the intensely physical experience of the lower "Camanche" is placed against the physical self-denial of Pierre's elevated labor of writing to question the notion of the calling (Is "this . . . the trade, that God intended [Pierre] for"?). The supposed autonomy of authorship is rapidly transformed into a painful sort of self-imprisonment. Pierre himself understands his own status, describing his novel's author–hero, Vivia, in these very terms: "Cast thy eye in there on Vivia; tell me why those four limbs should be clapt in a dismal jail—day out, day in—week out, week in—month out, month in, and himself the voluntary jailer!" (303). Even Pierre understands that it is precisely the hierarchical logic of his nonmanual labor that imprisons him: "This is the larger, and spiritual life? This your boasted empyrean?" (303). Contrary to Pierre's initial belief that he is superior to "day-laborers," the constraint of his professional labor teaches Pierre that, in fact, "he has no power over his condition" (303). Through the process of working, Pierre discovers the "twice-blessed" autonomy of professionalism as an impossible ideological bind. The "freedom" to determine the kind of work professionals do transforms them into their own "voluntary jailers" through the self-disciplining drive for an elevated vocational and social status. In his drive to define himself as a writer, Pierre becomes inextricably bound up in the torturous autonomy of professional ideology.

Despite Parker's claims to the contrary, we cannot separate Pierre's authorship from the structure of the second half of the book, not starting with "Young America in Literature," but even earlier, with "The Journey and the Pamphlet" chapter, in which Pierre encounters the work of the philosopher Plotinus Plinlimmon. Plinlimmon is yet another author–figure worked into the structure of the novel and he, too, functions to comment on the nature of work and professional ideology. Both in his modeling of authorial labor and his effect upon Pierre, Plinlimmon becomes a subversive exemplar of professionalism in the novel, an ironic fulfillment of professional nonmanual labor and authority.

We encounter Plotinus Plinlimmon first in *Pierre* as the author of the fragmentary pamphlet "Chronometricals and Horologicals," which Pierre reads in the carriage ride from Saddle Meadows to New York City. Melville includes the "very fanciful and mystical, rather than philosophical Lecture" (210) in the novel, so that we readers are placed in the same situation as Pierre, seeking to interpret Plinlimmon's meditations on morality.[57] Plinlimmon's musings on a relative versus a strict adherence to Christian doctrine seem particularly relevant to Pierre's response to the appearance of Isabel in the first half of the novel, but Plinlimmon will become even more important to the second half as he becomes a model of literary authority for Pierre as he writes his novel. After settling in New York City and announcing his plan to pursue a career in authorship, Pierre discovers that Plinlimmon is a fellow resident at the Apostles, but is unable to find his copy of the pamphlet, unaware that it had slipped through a hole in his pocket, becoming part of the padding of his coat. This absorption of Plinlimmon's ideas into Pierre's everyday clothing is a metaphor for his adoption of Plinlimmon as an internalized authority, an imagined judge of his personal and professional activity.

Pierre first sees Plinlimmon as "a steady observant blue-eyed countenance at one of the loftiest windows" of a tower across from Pierre's writing chamber (291). Pierre never exchanges a word with Plinlimmon, yet he takes on enormous significance as an embodiment of the autonomy and self-sufficiency that Pierre dreams of attaining through writing:

> [Plinlimmon] was never known to work with his hands (he would not even write a letter); he never was known to open a book. There were no books in his chamber. Nevertheless, some day or other he must have read books, but that time seemed gone now; as for the sleazy works that went under his name, they were nothing more than his verbal things, taken down at random, and bunglingly methodized by his young disciples. (290)

In contrast to the taxing physical demands that Pierre suffers to produce his book, Plinlimmon has liberated himself entirely from any ostensible signs of physical labor, even those that might be put in service of such nonmanual work as writing. Plinlimmon's bookless chamber stands as a challenge to Pierre, whose plan for his book is derived from and highly dependent upon his "varied scope of reading": "He would climb Parnassus with a pile of folios on his back" (283). Plinlimmon is also apparently free from any anxiety about the association of his name and identity with his published works, seeing them as simple commodities, "his verbal things." Plinlimmon's dismissal of his published writings speaks to his liberation from the marketplace, the most intractable threat to professional autonomy. Plinlimmon's blithe unconcern about his "verbal things" stands in stark contrast to Pierre's authorship, profoundly afflicted by an awareness of the market and his insecure place within it:

> Meantime, Pierre was still going on with his book; every moment becoming still the more sensible of the intensely inauspicious circumstances of all sorts under which that labor was proceeding. . . . [I]n the hour of his most clamorous pennilessness, he was additionally goaded into an enterprise long and

protracted in the execution, and of all things least calculated for pecuniary profit in the end. . . . Oh, who shall reveal the horrors of poverty in authorship that is high? (338)

The "inauspicious circumstances" of Pierre's authorship are a marked contrast to Plinlimmon's, not so much because he models the life of a commercially and critically successful author (pointedly, there are no such models in *Pierre*), but because he embodies the independence that Pierre believes professional authorship will allow him.

In the first half of the novel, Pierre was dominated by the image of his father in his "official" portrait as an embodiment of righteousness and masculinity (and haunted by prospect that the earlier "chair" portrait undermined those ideals). The family portrait of his father functioned as a guide and a corrective, as a challenge for Pierre to act in a manner befitting his family heritage. Upon departing Saddle Meadows, Pierre burns the chair portrait and proclaims "Henceforth, cast-out Pierre hath no paternity; . . . therefore, twice-disinherited Pierre stands untrammeledly his ever-present self!—free to do his own self-will and present fancy to whatever end!" (199). In the second half of the novel, however, Pierre finds the face of Plinlimmon a force equally potent as that of his father, this time particularly commenting on his efforts as a writer. A direct counterpart to the portrait hanging in the family hall, Plinlimmon's face looms over Pierre. Melville describes how Plinlimmon's "blue-eyed, mystic-mild face. . . began to domineer in a very remarkable manner upon Pierre" (292). Plinlimmon's face appears only when Pierre feels "depression and despair" and "dark doubts," and particularly "when a thought of the vanity of his deep book would glidingly intrude" (292). The effect of this gaze, Melville suggests, cannot "be adequately detailed in any possible words," but he assays it anyway: "Vain! vain! vain! said the face to him. Fool! fool! fool! said the face to him. Quit! quit! quit! said the face to him. But when he mentally interrogated the face as to why it thrice said Vain! Fool! Quit! to him; here there was no response" (293).

Of course, Pierre cannot expect an answer from Plinlimmon's gaze because Plinlimmon is probably not even looking at him. Plinlimmon's self-contained gaze is nothing more than a mirror held up to Pierre's desire for autonomy as an author. Tellingly, Melville describes this interaction not near the end of Pierre's efforts, but at their very beginning. Plinlimmon's imagined accusations do not close down Pierre's efforts to write, but inaugurate them. But if Pierre requires the imagined authority of Plinlimmon to write, this also suggests that any dream of professional autonomy is merely that, a dream; one, moreover, that is necessarily haunted by internal demands for discipline that will always negate any autonomy derived from hierarchical claims to professional status.

Wai Chee Dimock suggests that "Plinlimmon describes the seer as overseer," reflecting the rise of new technologies of supervision and discipline in nineteenth-century American culture.[58] But while the antebellum factories, prisons, and asylums began to articulate new modes of discipline for the working class, it was the producers of those new disciplines, the professional middle class, who themselves made these disciplines part of their family life and essential to their social reproduction.[59] The professionals who sought to streamline the new factories and construct new, more humane sites for incarceration in antebellum America, used their own families and schools to train their children to discipline themselves, so that they would not have to be disciplined in prisons or factories. Although the factory workers publicly protested the new disciplines of their training and labor, the antebellum middle class understood that their own future depended upon this new discipline. The vocational autonomy that defined professional middle-class status required Emerson's "tendency to introversion, self-dissection, anatomizing of motives."

In *Pierre*, however, Melville demonstrates not only the painful consequences of this new self-discipline through Pierre's authorship, but also the hypocrisy of professional autonomy, which is not actually autonomy, but, instead, the internalization of some imagined disciplinary authority like Plinlimmon. Is autonomy really autonomy if it is contingent upon the internalization of discipline? In *Pierre*, professional autonomy is exposed as a myth, one that is damaging to all. Melville's *Pierre* undermines the hierarchical logic of antebellum labor, using the life of Pierre Glendinning to echo Thoreau in the opening chapter on "Economy" in *Walden*, "It is hard to have a southern overseer; it is worse to have a northern one; but worst of all when you are the slave-driver yourself."[60]

Ironically, but not coincidentally, Pierre ends in a prison after murdering his cousin, an impulsive act that symbolically ends his family line. Receiving a letter of rejection from his publishers ("Steel, Flint & Asbestos," in a return to the satire of "Young America in Literature") and an insulting letter from Glen Stanly and Lucy's brother, Frederick Tartan, Pierre goes forth and shoots his cousin on Broadway, a sign of his impotence. In a way, Pierre's shooting of Glen is a bitter commentary on publication, a reenvisioning of a far more heroic vision of authorship mentioned in an episode in *White-Jacket*, his final fact-based adventure narrative published in 1850. In the chapter "Publishing Poetry in a Man-of-War," one of Melville's fellow sailors, Lemsford, "the gun-deck bard," leaves his manuscript in a cannon that is fired off in a training exercise.[61] Jack Chase, the heroic "First Captain of the Top" (13) proclaims this the ideal mode of publishing, addressing Melville's stand-in, White-Jacket: "That's the way to publish, White-Jacket, . . . fire it right into 'em; every canto a twenty-four-pound shot; *hull* the blockheads, whether they will or no" (192). This episode portrays a vision of authorial aggression against a readership, but also a kind of optimism. In a foreshadowing of *Pierre*, the poet Lemsford describes the response to his publication on land, from the gouging publishers to the disdainful critics to the "sheepish" friends, but, in a classic formulation of romanticism, imagines an audience for his writing in the "people," a democratic social and political entity, while disdaining "the public," a commercial definition of his audience.[62] Issuing from the community of the foretop in *White-Jacket*, publication as cannonade appears as a kind of literary democratic autonomy. Only two years later, however, in *Pierre*, this vision of authorial violence, far from the jaunty tone of Jack Chase, has become a bleak vision of authorial impotence and self-destruction, neither finding—nor from the evidence supplied by the book—deserving a readership.

In *Pierre*, Melville constitutes the hierarchical claims of professional nonmanual labor as a lived contradiction, a paradox that promises freedom, autonomy, and authority only through the internalization of discipline and constraint. William Charvat describes *Pierre* as "Melville's professional self-destruction," suggesting that Melville writes himself out of literary professionalism by presenting Pierre's failed authorship, but I would argue that his response is more complicated, depicting the destructive and self-destructive elements within professionalism itself.[63] It is thus, in *Pierre*, that Melville writes himself out of literary professionalism and into an ambiguous aesthetic and social realm that interrogates the very status that he himself had sought from the time he began his literary career with the publication of *Typee*.

Melville and the Ambiguities of Pierre

"Here, then, is the untimely, timely end;—Life's last chapter well stitched into the middle! Nor book, nor author of the book, hath any sequel, though each hath its last lettering! It is ambiguous still" (360). It is certainly no coincidence that "ambiguity" plays such a crucial role in *Pierre*. Not only does it appear in the subtitle, but the word also reappears throughout the narrative and carries multiple meanings that reflect its importance to Melville's narrative. Tensions within the word itself encompass complexities of both authorial intention and readers' responses to Melville's novel. Ambiguity could be said to refer to Pierre Glendinning's mental condition, a state of "hesitation, doubt or uncertainty" about his choices and decisions that was thought to constitute a mental disorder in the nineteenth century.[64] But, reflecting the word's alternate usage as "capability of being understood in two or more ways; double or dubious signification," ambiguity could also refer to Melville's narration, his use of a discursive, perhaps even hyperbolic, narrative persona that seems to obscure rather than clarify the terms under which we see the characters. [65] The semantic ambiguity of "ambiguity," to fall into tautology, is at the heart of critical responses to *Pierre*: Is *Pierre* an earnest failure, the product of the author's own uncertainty, or is it a careful satire of contradictions within the culture?

Melville's contemporaries largely attacked *Pierre*, with some even going so far as to locate the perceived problems of the novel as a sign of the author's derangement, as did the reviewer for the New York *Herald*, who claimed to emulate Melville's narrative mode in *Pierre* to attack the novel:

> Ambiguities indeed! One long brain-muddling, soul bewildering ambiguity (to borrow Mr. Melville's style), like Melchisedeck, without beginning or end—a labyrinth without a clue—an Irish bog without so much as a Jack o' th'-lantern to guide the wanderer's footsteps—the dream of a distempered stomach, disordered by a hasty supper on half-cooked pork chops.[66]

Although modern critics have been less likely to proclaim Melville's mind "disordered" in response to *Pierre*, many still see the text as an earnest reflection of his views and ideas, reflecting either his misguided attempt to find a popular readership, his serious exploration of the psyche, or his heartfelt expression of an ethos of individualism.[67] Other modern readers, however, have seen the novel as satiric, critical, or deconstructive, undermining all the values it explores through its narrative voice.[68] The critical divide is so stark, in fact, that it is fair to suggest that few books could be made to embody such contradictory meanings as *Pierre*. Like Pierre himself, examining the course of his life from prison, readers are left to exclaim of his eponymous novel: "It is ambiguous still" (360).

This overdetermined narrative ambiguity can be seen as a response to the conditions of professional authorship depicted by the novel itself. Faced with the market and literary-community conditions that limit or constrain authorial autonomy in "Young America in Literature" and the ideological contradictions that reveal the drive for authorial autonomy to be both self-interested and self-destructive at the same time in "Pierre as Juvenile Author, Reconsidered" and elsewhere, Melville depicts the conditions of professional authorship as an impossible bind. Melville finds in ambiguity a response to this bind, a response that alters both the author's place in the narrative and the reader's relationship to the text. Melville initially considered anonymous or pseudonymous publication for *Pierre*, at one point offering up "By a Vermonter" or "By Guy Winthrop" as possible options to his skeptical British publisher, Richard Bentley.[69] This would have been a radical change from his earlier work, which very much depended upon the appeal of his associations within the literary marketplace. Although this seems like a desperate attempt to distance himself from the failure of *Moby-Dick*, Gillian Brown has seen this flirtation with anonymous authorship as an expression of a desire for individual freedom.[70] Meanwhile, Meredith McGill has complicated our understanding of the meanings of anonymous authorship in the antebellum era, seeing it neither as a return to the anachronistic association of authorship with genteel status and publication nor as simply an escape into freedom, but rather as a canny use of the possibilities of the marketplace.[71] Ultimately, Melville chose not to publish *Pierre* anonymously (Bentley refused to publish *Pierre* under favorable terms no matter how the author was identified), but the choice of narrative ambiguity in *Pierre* responds to the concerns broached by this critical debate: particularly the dangers of asserting or being identified with publication, whether in its archaic sense as ungenteel or in its more modern sense as an impulse to authoritative status. Ambiguity also transforms the literary-professional text's relationship to readers, offering not the "subtle" distinctions that reward investment in literature, but an uncertainty that frustrates. In this way, *Pierre*'s ambiguous narration unsettles the cultural project of professional literary authority.

Melville's embrace of narrative ambiguity in *Pierre* is a radical undermining of his earlier literary professional project. We can see this particularly in comparison with his previous novel, *Moby-Dick*, which sought to interpellate readers into an epistemological project of "subtilizing," or "indulging in subtleties."[72] Subtlety, with its association with "acuteness, sagacity, penetration," encourages readerly investment in "keen perception of fine distinctions" by rewarding the reader with authority.[73] By rewarding investment in the work of cultural distinction with authority, *Moby-Dick* modeled the professional investment in discourse, information, and social codes that helped reinforce the distinction between the middle and working classes in the new, industrializing economy of antebellum urban areas. In *Pierre*, however, Melville's embrace of "ambiguity" discourages such readerly investment in the text, by producing not authority but uncertainty. With its multiple metaliterary narrative asides, *Pierre* seems to deconstruct narration, to encourage readers to take up critical attitudes toward narrative acts.[74] But instead of the proliferating distinctions and open-ended meanings of *Moby-Dick*'s "subtlety," ambiguity in *Pierre* falls inevitably into equivocation: it is either earnest or satirical. This equivocation frustrates and thwarts what the previous chapter delineated as the professional middle-class reader's desire for authoritative meaning, transforming the reader's interpretation into an arbitrary choice of two stark options, perhaps nothing more than a simple reflection of the reader's own inclinations and propensities (as the vastly different critical readings suggest).

Melville thematizes this ambiguity in discussions of the act of reading within the novel itself. A notably difficult text to read and interpret, *Pierre* repeatedly stages scenes of reading that throw its benefits into doubt. As Edgar A. Dryden suggests, *Pierre* is "the story of a reader who attempts to become a writer."[75] But Pierre's attempt to become a writer is openly doomed because of his investment in his status as reader, as the narrator explains: "to a mind bent on producing some thoughtful thing of absolute Truth, all mere reading is apt to prove but an obstacle hard to overcome; and not an accelerator helpingly pushing him along" (283). But even before the "problematic" conversion of Pierre into author, Melville staged problematic acts of reading within the novel.

Reading Dante and Shakespeare during his crisis with Isabel, Pierre's actions are shaped by his potentially problematic interpretations of the texts. From Dante's *Inferno*, Pierre, in his unsettled state, realizes the consequences of damnation, "which would forever bar the vast bulk of mankind from all solacement in the worlds to come" (169). Here, the narrator points out that, while "the Dilletante in Literature" misses this conclusion, for "earnest and youthful piercers into truth and reality" like Pierre, this realization of "the horrible allegorical meanings of the Inferno . . . infuse their poison into a spot previously unprovided with that sovereign antidote of a sense of uncapitulatable security, which is only the possession of the furthest advanced and profoundest souls" (169). Pierre's partial understanding of

Dante encourages "Gloom and Grief," as does *Hamlet*, from which he had earlier read, but misunderstood, both the "hopeless gloom of its interior meaning" and "those superficial and purely incidental lessons, wherein the painstaking moralist so complacently expatiates," namely the conclusion that "[A]ll meditation is worthless, unless it prompt to action; that it is not for man to stand shilly-shallying amid the conflicting invasions of surrounding impulses; that in the earliest instant of conviction, the roused man must strike, and, if possible, with the precision and force of the lightning-bolt" (169).

Thus, Pierre's reading impels him to perceive the "hopeless gloom" of his situation and to take decisive action, to "marry" Isabel, ultimately precipitating the death of every major character in the novel. If Pierre's reading assures him of his actions in Saddle Meadows, while in prison in New York City, Pierre can only look over the life to which his reading committed him and describe it as a thwarted book, "Life's last chapter well stitched into the middle!" and, concluding of his life decisions, "It is ambiguous still" (360). Even just after Pierre's initial response to Dante and Shakespeare, the narrator concludes by questioning his interpretation, suggesting that, although the insights derived from these texts "reveal the depths, they do, sometimes, also reveal—though by no means so distinctly—some answering heights" (169). In *Pierre*, reading "sometimes" rewards readers, but it is more likely to produce more problematic consequences.

In fact, Melville will go on to suggest that one never really learns anything from reading, as he describes Pierre's frustrating experience of reading Plinlimmon's truncated "Chronometricals and Horologicals" pamphlet on the carriage ride to New York City from Saddle Meadows in a classically, frustratingly long-winded and circuitous discursive fashion.

> If a man be in any vague latent doubt about the intrinsic correctness and excellence of his general life-theory and practical course of life; then, if that man chance to light on any other man, or any little treatise, or sermon, which unintendingly, as it were, yet very palpably illustrates to him the intrinsic incorrectness and non-excellence of both the theory and the practice of his life; then that man will—more or less unconsciously—try hard to hold himself back from the self-admitted comprehension of a matter which thus condemns him. For in this case, to comprehend, is himself to condemn himself, which is always highly inconvenient and uncomfortable to a man. Again. If a man be told a thing wholly new, then—during the time of its first announcement to him—it is entirely impossible for him to comprehend it. For—absurd as it may seem—men are only made to comprehend things which they comprehended before (though but in the embryo, as it were). Things new it is impossible to make them compre-

THE AMBIGUITIES OF PROFESSIONALISM ⋐ 177

hend, by merely talking to them about it. . . . Possibly, they may afterward come, of themselves, to inhale this new idea from the circumambient air, and so come to comprehend it; but not otherwise at all. It will be observed, that neither points of the above speculations do we, in set terms, attribute to Pierre in connection with the rag pamphlet. Possibly both might be applicable; possibly neither. (209)

Ostensibly offering possible explanations for Pierre's failure to comprehend Plinlimmon's pamphlet, this commentary, as Edgar Dryden describes, has "the effect of seriously limiting the dimensions of reading as an activity."[76] Whether a reader rejects insight from reading because it condemns "the theory and practice of [his] life" or because "men are only made to comprehend things which they comprehended before," reading is invalidated as a viable pedagogical or instructive tool; this judgment presumably includes even Melville's own text. Yet even as it threatens to foreclose on the meaningfulness of reading, including a kind of autocritique, Melville's discussion embraces an ambiguity ("Possibly both might be applicable; possibly neither") that unsettles the authoritative ground upon which we might apply the insights. If we cannot learn from reading, then perhaps we cannot even learn from Melville's dismissal of reading. Or perhaps we can. Melville's embrace of narrative ambiguity undermines the model of reading established in *Moby-Dick*, transforming the professionalized drive for subtlety and distinction into a fun-house mirror of ambiguity that subverts investment in the cultural accomplishment of reading.

There is no small irony in that, as Melville sought to unpack the nascent professionalized vision of the literary through his use of "ambiguity," in that the very same term would become a hallmark of the professionalization of literary criticism in the twentieth-century American academy. Although Melville's mid-nineteenth-century readers understood *Pierre*'s ambiguity as an attack on literature (though most believed that it was simply an unintentional reflection of Melville's own disordered "ambiguous" mind), one of the most important critical movements of the twentieth-century Anglo-American professionalized literary academy, New Criticism, embraced ambiguity as a crucial trait of the privileged form of literature. In 1930, William Empson published *Seven Types of Ambiguity*, in which he sought to replace the negative connotations of ambiguity with a more positive one: "An ambiguity, in ordinary speech, means something very pronounced, and as a rule witty and deceitful. I propose to use the word in an extended sense, and shall think relevant to my subject any verbal nuance, however slight, which gives room for alternative reactions to the same piece of language."[77] Although some etymological or semantic haggling of the negative connotation of the term continued over the years, "ambiguity" became a crucial tool of the New Criticism's interpretative discourse, reflecting a vision of literature as writing that offered the reader the possibility of multiple interpretations, rewarded the act of interpretation, and became "richer" as a result.

The New Critical project of "close reading," searching for ambiguity, as well as irony and paradox in literature, came to dominate literary study in American universities in the 1940s and 1950s, becoming a reading protocol that reflected professional ideology. In the face of the multiple approaches (primarily historical and bibliographic) that had shaped academic literary discourse before, David Shumway suggests that "[The New Criticism's vision of literature] as an autonomous object and the practice of showing how the object worked as an organic whole made criticism look like a kind of science. That is, it became a form of knowledge production that could fit the disciplinary model of the university."[78] This model of criticism rewarded the specialization of university professors. As John Crowe Ransome, a notable advocate of New Criticism, would explain: "the university teacher of literature . . . should be the very professional we need to take charge of the critical activity."[79] The New Criticism imagined literary analysis and judgment of literary value as a set of skills and distinctions that marked the difference between the trained reader, the skilled appreciator of literature, and the untrained, unskilled reader. These skills and distinctions were readily transferable to the college classroom, which became the home of "professional" literary critics and the place where nascent members of the professional middle class acquired their cultural training in the new American university's "liberal arts" curriculum. [80]

While New Criticism focused primarily on poetry and paid little attention to contextual issues such as national literary traditions, the first generation of American scholars who focused upon the "literary" nature of American literature from the 1940s onward adapted New Critical readings to a narrative of American cultural distinctiveness.[81] This synthesis was most apparent in the work of F. O. Matthiessen, who tied the organic wholeness of his "American Renaissance" literary texts to an organic vision of American "democracy."[82] Although Melville was canonized (albeit relatively recently) before the 1941 issue of *American Renaissance*, it was Matthiessen's text that first envisioned Melville's work through the aestheticized lens of New Criticism as a unified and organic whole. It is no coincidence, however, that when

Melville was canonized as suitable for professionalized New Critical literary analysis by Matthiessen, it was not through *Pierre*, but *Moby-Dick*. Though New Critics ostensibly embraced ambiguity, their model fit Melville's vision of "subtlety" in *Moby-Dick* that rewarded the interpretative production of distinctions, rather than *Pierre*'s "ambiguity," a closed circuit of uncertain interpretation that exposed professionalism as both a false and unjust logic of social hierarchy and a self-imposed subjection to an oppressive system of authority and power. Because of its "ambiguity," *Pierre* was long an anomalous text, assessed primarily outside the literary critical terms that validated *Moby-Dick*. In the more poststructuralist-inflected and politicized American literary academy since the 1980s, with the turn away from New Criticism, even in its diluted form in American literary studies, *Pierre* has become an increasingly important text. At first, it was important as a problematic expression of the ideology of individualism and, later, as a critique of that ideology, in some ways even coming to challenge *Moby-Dick* in critical importance. This, I would suggest, is not simply about the vagaries of literary taste, but reflective of shifts in the ideological project of professionalism, through which Melville's literary career was initially constructed and has been recapitulated in the politics of canonization in the twentieth-century American literary academy.

It is to this subject that an epilogue to this project will turn. Looking at Melville's short story "Bartleby, the Scrivener" and critical responses to it over the course of the twentieth century, the Epilogue will explore the politics of professionalism in the contemporary American literary academy. "Bartleby," the 1853 story published in *Putnam's Magazine*, depicts the relationship between a professional, the lawyer–narrator, and his lower-middle-class employees, particularly one recalcitrant employee, and it is told from the lawyer's perspective. Explicitly a narrative of class relations and the nature of social authority and responsibility, "Bartleby" poses an ethical dilemma, one that interrogates professional ideology. In the Epilogue, "Bartleby" is read in its context, in the antebellum New York world of work and culture, but along with that reading, twentieth-century criticism of the story becomes a litmus test of academic and scholarly critical investment in professional ideology.

"Bartleby," Professional Agency, and the Literary Academy

One of the primary claims of this book is that Herman Melville's work has been central to the canonization of American literature because it thematizes issues that have been crucial to modern professionalized understandings of American life, such as resistance to the inscriptive demands of the market, the legitimation of vocational autonomy and nonmanual labor, and the importance of cultural capital. Modern American critics and scholars who have written about and taught Melville's work as a means of defining literary merit and national identity have, in the process, used Melville to legitimate a version of their own professional authority. This epilogue takes up Melville's story "Bartleby, the Scrivener," first published in the November–December 1853 issues of *Putnam's Magazine,* as a crucial example of the way modern critics, particularly the modern professionalized academics of English departments, have made Melville's work an embodiment of their own values, even though the text might offer scant evidence to support such claims. In embracing "Bartleby," critics have validated Melville's importance to American literature, and, in the process, their own importance to American life.

In a departure from the characteristic approach of this study, this epilogue is not so much a reading of "Bartleby" as a window on Melville's career, or the class landscape of antebellum New York City, as a reading of modern criticism. This is particularly appropriate for "Bartleby," as the story has received more consistent critical attention than any of Melville's work other than *Moby-Dick* since the "Melville Revival" of the 1920s.[1] Early scholars identified the story of the "pallidly neat, pitiably respectable, incurably forlorn" law copyist who first works but then refuses (famously claiming to "prefer not to") as an important site for understanding Melville's sense of his work and his literary career, reading it in an autobiographical context as Melville's self-conscious commentary upon his own labor of writing.[2] While retaining the critical emphasis on the story as a site of particular importance to Melville's work, more contemporary critical readings of "Bartleby" have also explored the place of Christian allegory and existential philosophy in, and Marxist social commentary upon, the story. Focusing primarily on these contemporary trends in reading "Bartleby," this epilogue explores the way Melville's story has become a crucial touchstone for the professional values of English professors.

Reading "Bartleby" as a touchstone for those values may seem surprising. It is, after all, quite easy to read "Bartleby" as a story that attacks professionalism by exposing its complicity with an oppressive social system and emphasizing its self-serving manipulation of legitimizing discourses through the narration of Bartleby's employer, a lawyer.[3] But it is also possible to see how twentieth-century American literary scholars use "Bartleby" to justify their own distinct version of professionalism by valorizing personal autonomy over economic rewards and by emphasizing the importance of reading as a socially significant act of cultural resistance. In this way, the dominant strands of modern readings of "Bartleby, the Scrivener"—particularly the heroizing of Bartleby and the discourse analysis of the lawyer's narration—have reflected the professional values (and anxieties) of the twentieth-century literary academy. Melville's story, in all its ambiguities, has been a surface upon which an American literary professoriate has traced and retraced its self-conception.

One of the crucial critical gestures of modern criticism of "Bartleby" has been to portray the character of Bartleby as a heroic figure. Starting in the 1960s, readings of Bartleby emphasized his role as a Christ figure or as the embodiment of Christlike characteristics.[4] For this critical slant, Bartleby is "intended to be the representative of Christ on earth," and the story dramatizes Peter's denial of Christ in the narrator's triple denial of Bartleby.[5] In these Christianized readings, Bartleby embodies Christianity as a rejection of the worldly and compromising values of the lawyer, representing a pure

Christianity against the "pragmatic Christianity" of nineteenth-century America.[6] In the 1960s and 1970s, heroic readings of Bartleby also took on an existential tone.[7] From this approach, the story presents "a sardonic existential comedy in which [Bartleby's] rebellious negation is Melville's affirmation."[8] For many scholars since the 1970s (but more prominently in the 1980s and 1990s), Bartleby has also been seen as a figure for class struggle, an embodiment of the worker under the oppressive force of industrial capitalism.[9] One can, of course, read these multiple meanings for the figure of Bartleby as a sign of the arbitrariness of academic interpretations or as merely reflecting the shifting sands of "fashionable" literary approaches, but my interest here is in the persistence of critical investment in Bartleby as a heroic figure of resistance to the mainstream culture embodied by the lawyer–narrator, who is seen as capitalistic, providential, and compromising. Bartleby's "preference" not to work under the conditions set by the lawyer has come to signify the rejection of marketplace values for a personal autonomy based upon ideals counter to those of marketplace.

This investment in Bartleby as heroic—whatever philosophical or cultural approach he embodies—is less a reflection of Melville and his vision of the artist than a commentary upon modern American humanities scholars' vision of their vocational values. As Cornelia Vismann has observed, Bartleby has become the "preferred identification object of intellectuals."[10] This does not mean, of course, that English professors envision themselves as Christlike, or as existential heroes or alienated proletariat, but that the canonization of "Bartleby," with its critical emphasis on Bartleby's autonomy and on the political significance of his resistance, reflects the terms under which modern American humanities scholars have understood their vocational choices and the purpose of their labors.

For example, Wayne Booth described his decision to become an English major in his 1982 Presidential Address to the Modern Language Association in these terms:

> "All right, then," I intone, pounding my points out on the roof of an old Ford, "I'll *be* an English major, even though it does mean that I'll always be poor. Let's go over it again: I want to work at something that I enjoy doing, something that will contribute to my continuing to grow (Oh, yes, we talked like that, back then). So that means I should be a teacher. . . . If I teach English . . . I can learn to read and write and think."[11]

Booth's gently self-mocking vision pits vocational autonomy against market values, acknowledging what Pierre Bourdieu describes as the inverse relation between the degree of autonomy of intellectual labor and the significance of that work to the process of production (and the resulting economic reward).[12] The English professor trades economic capital ("I'll always be poor") for autonomy ("I can learn to read and write and think"). Just as critics ennoble Bartleby's opting for autonomy, which they tie to his claim of "preference" against the lawyer's vision of the market's conventions of "common usage and common sense" (22), Booth's vision of the vocational choice of the profession of English is ennobled even as he pokes fun at his younger self. The autonomy of English professors is understood not as an avoidance of market-oriented productive labor, but as an active choice to reject the values of the market and to endorse the promise of autonomy offered by the vocation. In this light, it is not surprising that English scholars and students might define Bartleby's acts as noble or heroic. Bartleby's quixotic claim of preference against the market's conventions represents a dramatic recapitulation of the logic with which many twentieth-century humanities scholars envisioned their own vocational choice.

The bond between Bartleby and English professors was constructed in criticism at about the same time that the traditional authority of English professors came into question in American society. Although critics have long been drawn to Bartleby as a powerful symbolic figure, it was primarily in the 1960s that his actions began to take on significantly heroic stature in criticism, imparting a new political resonance to his choice of autonomy. In the late 1980s, it became common to note the "politicization" of humanities scholars, most particularly of English professors, but the reasons for this may have existed earlier.[13] John Guillory points out that, since the 1960s, humanities scholars have faced a long-term crisis that has threatened their position within the university and the society as a whole: "namely the declining value of the cultural capital embodied in their knowledge-products in relation to the cultural capital produced and reproduced in the legal, technical, and managerial disciplines."[14] As the humanities and its cultural distinctions have played a decreasing role in determining the American status hierarchy over the course of the twentieth century, the cultural capital of humanities scholars has diminished. Still largely autonomous but significantly disempowered, many humanities professors have sought to define their work—whether in the classroom or in publication—as a kind of politicized act of cultural resistance to dominant ideologies of capitalist productivity and market individualism.[15] In this light, the politicization of the character of Bartleby since the 1960s could be seen as a striking image of the modern American English professoriate's vocational stance and cultural position. Making Bartleby's stance in the story heroic, scholars have sought to explain or justify the importance of their own stance of autonomous resistance.

This critical gesture, however, is hardly without problems. As constructed by Melville, Bartleby is a highly ambiguous character, one whose claim to autonomy resides within a gesture of resistance that is largely unintelligible to those around him and whose effect upon others is problematic at best. Bartleby's maddening "passive resistance" (20) may indeed highlight the capitalist logic of rigid hierarchy and compulsory productivity behind the veneer of the lawyer's "good natural arrangement" in his office (18) and, with it, the middle-class workplace more generally. But Bartleby's refusal to explain his reasons for stopping work makes his actions as resistant to readers' attempts to arrive at a definitive meaning as it is to the lawyer's: Bartleby's "indifferent" and ambiguous reply of "Do you not see the reason for yourself" (32) to the lawyer's query has generated an incredible range of critical explanations, none any less arbitrary than the lawyer's explanation that Bartleby's vision must be impaired. In fact, no critical reading of the story can offer any insight into Bartleby's condition that isn't highly speculative or present a single view of the story's solution to the questions raised about the workplace or, more broadly, about the antebellum urban social landscape. This is not because the critics have somehow failed, but rather because Melville's story radically forecloses on the possibility of finding that kind of meaning. In "Bartleby, The Scrivener" any attempt to understand Bartleby's resistance fully is limited, because we can never know more than the lawyer who tells the story, making the copyist's motivations inevitably obscure and unintelligible. Moreover, in constructing Bartleby as heroic stand-in, modern American scholars have cast themselves in a role that is hardly encouraging as a justification of their professionalism. In fact, Bartleby's unexplained stance of resistance is shown to be singularly unsuccessful (if any kind of political or moral action is to be its result) and could be said to reflect a bleak vision of the professionalism of the humanities scholar as a kind of hopeless and self-destructive resistance to the powers that be. Although Bartleby's literal starvation is a stark vision of the consequences of choosing autonomy over market demands, there is a counterpart in stereotypes of the suffering English doctoral candidate and the ever-growing army of nonregular faculty in English whose working conditions often achieve Bartlebyean levels of immiseration. Under these conditions, the choice to study English and pursue it as a career could easily be seen as perverse and self-destructive, as the lawyer considers Bartleby's actions to be.[16] To embrace this ambiguous martyrdom is hardly a strong defense of the professionalized values of humanities scholars.

A less ambiguous, if no less problematic defense of these values is articulated in the other dominant strand of criticism of the story: the extensive attack upon the lawyer-narrator and his act of narration. Modern critics have drawn attention to the way the lawyer reveals himself through his narration from his initial description of himself as an "eminently *safe* man" (14), to his justification of generous behavior toward Bartleby as "cheaply purchas[ing] a delicious self-approval" (23), to his moral equivocations in which charity becomes "a vastly wise and prudent principle," as it stops him from murdering Bartleby in a rage of resentful frustration (36), and finally to the postscript "rumor" of Bartleby's previous employment as "a subordinate clerk in the Dead Letter Office at Washington" (45), which the lawyer seems to believe absolves him of any responsibility for Bartleby's death in prison. Scholars from Ann Douglas to Hershel Parker have identified the lawyer as the main object of Melville's interest, making the crucial element not Bartleby's resistance, but the narrator's inability or willed refusal to recognize Bartleby's challenge to his worldview.[17] The narrator is so consistently seen as an embodiment of "bad faith" that one of the most distinctive contemporary studies of the story, Dan McCall's book-length work, *The Silence of Bartleby* (1989), is notable primarily for its defense of the lawyer.[18] Drawing attention to the one-sidedness of contemporary critical attitudes toward the story, McCall's critique offers some checks to what may seem to be unconsidered truisms of "Bartleby" criticism. Although McCall is somewhat at a loss to explain this bias against the lawyer, it might be illuminated by considering these views in the context of academic or scholarly understandings of the professional work of reading.

Just as the critics arguing for Bartleby's heroism reflected humanities scholars' investment in autonomy, this other mode of interpretation of the story, which is oriented around discourse analysis of the lawyer–narrator, is no less reflective of the vocational and cultural interests of a professionalized humanities academe. The emphasis on the narrator's discourse and its political and social ramifications reflects the ways that "critical reading" became an important tool of the modern professionalization of English. In his study, *Work Time: English Departments and the Circulation of Cultural Value* (1989), Evan Watkins traces the modern history of American understandings of academic work in English, demonstrating how English professors legitimated themselves not only by conferring cultural capital, but also by constructing reading as a productive act.[19] While one element of the professionalization of scholarship was tied to an increasing importance of "publishing"—the production of critical analysis of the literary text in journal or book form—the teaching of reading was also a crucial element of the justification of the importance of English professors. Under this construction, English teachers were responsible for teaching students not only what constituted "good literature," but also how to consume all kinds of reading materials properly, whether literary or commercial. Broadening the purview of English pedagogy, the vision of reading as a productive labor made the classroom the site of the important cultural project of teaching students to read critically and to produce analysis. In his 1985 book, *Textual Power: Literary Theory and the Teaching of English*, Robert Scholes articulates this pedagogical project: "What students need from us . . . is the kind of knowledge and skill that will enable them to make sense of their worlds, to determine their own interests, both individual and collective, to see through the manipulations of all sorts of texts in all sorts of media, and to express themselves in some appropriate manner."[20] Scholes's vision of the telos of English pedagogy reflects the way this field could address the potential disempowerment of its association with "literature." No longer just focused on distinguishing between "good" and "bad" literature, the English classroom is the site where students learn to "see through" the deceptive surface of texts of "all sorts" and to stand above the manipulation to which "all sorts of media" subjects them. Scholes constructs the English professor as "professional liberationist," to use Watkins' term, a role that has been an important part of the modern construction of professionalism in the academic field of English.[21] In the face of the declining importance of English departments to the transmission of cultural distinctions, the productivity of critical reading relegitimizes English professors' place in the modern American university and society.

As the subject of critical articles and as canonized for classroom analysis, "Bartleby" offers a case study of the need to "unpack" discourse, to read skeptically, to search for the ideological justifications that lie beneath the surface of discourse. The critical emphasis on the duplicity or contradictions of the lawyer's narrative of the story represents a classic example of the professional legitimation of English professors' need for stories that require critical reading skills. For these scholars, what is important about the story is the process of reading, as evidenced by this comment from Hershel Parker:

> The narrator never suspects that his readers will analyze more deeply than he does and interpret his prudence, his utilitarianism, and even his final sentimen-

tal solemnity in ways quite different from what he intends. Yet our ultimate opinion of him, the product less of what he means to tell than what he unknowingly divulges, is not contempt so much as bleak astonishment at his secure blindness.[22]

When critics argue that the story encourages readers to perceive what the lawyer "unknowingly divulges" and to "analyze more deeply than he does," they convert the story into a political justification of modern professional English practice. This mode of criticism emphasizes the skills needed to be a reader of the story, identifying the importance of the story in its testing of the reader's ability to see beneath the surface of the lawyer's narration not only as a means of cultural distinction, but as an important political act. Implicitly and explicitly, it depicts both narration and reading as acts of power: understanding the lawyer's narration as a gesture of domination over Bartleby and the critical reading of that narration as a counter to domination, an analysis that works to unpack and undermine the lawyer's complacent authority. In fact, this criticism legitimates the labor of English professors by making reading and the skills required to read "critically" a central feature of the story, transforming the criteria of literary merit from cultural to political distinction. Discourse analysis of the lawyer relegitimates the work of English professors, turning Melville into a defender of the need for professional readers and, in turn, constructing professionalized acts of reading as a form of social resistance.

It is no mere coincidence that the object of this critical reading is a lawyer. In their emphasis on critical reading of the lawyer's legal discourse, modern English critics have sought to clarify distinctions between their own professional practice and those of the legal profession, a vocation at once related to and radically different from theirs. Lawyers occupy a structurally symmetrical position to humanities scholars in John Guillory's Bourdieu-inspired schema of modern American intellectual life. Depending upon similar skills, lawyers and humanities scholars embody the category of traditional intellectual laborers. Although lawyers are more directly tied to means of production and the most heteronomous professionals, being both subject to domination and in positions of domination in relation to production, humanities scholars are more disconnected from the means of production and autonomous, neither subject to domination nor in positions of domination.[23] In the context of modern professional discourse, the lawyer of "Bartleby," with his lucrative, but largely repetitive and mechanical Chancery practice (low autonomy/high economic reward), represents the vocational antithesis of English professors (high autonomy/low economic reward) and thus becomes a perfect object of the professional labor of reading. Reading the lawyer's narration and exposing his "hidden assumptions" and "sadistic pity" validates the vocational choices of humanities scholars.[24] Whether the lawyer is a bad man or a good man placed in an impossible situation is to a certain degree irrelevant: his choice of the legal vocation makes him both subject to domination by his clients and in a position of domination over his employees, including Bartleby. In this light, the choice of the vocation of the humanities professor—neither dominated nor dominating— becomes a position of moral superiority over the lawyer. If the scholarly identification with the character of Bartleby speaks to an investment in and anxiety about the autonomy of academic professionalism, the critical attack on the lawyer offers a legitimation of professionalized academic skills and a consistent justification for the humanities professor's choice of autonomy.

Although Melville's work has been crucial to an ideological critical project that has justified the importance of professionalized social hierarchy in modern American life, this study has also sought to demonstrate the way that his writings can also be used to question that project. This examination traces the course of Melville's engagement with a modern professional ethos, from his youthful concern with the market conditions that commodified character as the defining trait of a new middle-class identity in *Typee*, to his deepening investment in professional specialization as a tool for personal and social authority in *Mardi*, to his increasing rejection of social concerns for a greater investment in aesthetic and cultural distinctions in *Moby-Dick*, and finally to a deep cynicism about the personal and public effects of professional ideals in *Pierre*. For professional scholars and teachers of literature to ask ourselves why we read and teach the texts we do should not be a purely rhetorical question, nor should we content ourselves with conventional pieties: the trajectory of Melville's career and tensions within his work have taught me this.

For example, I both teach and write on Herman Melville's famous novel *Moby-Dick* from a now-obsolete Norton Critical Edition I used in graduate school, being unwilling to part with my many "generations" of marginal notes in it. My copy was secondhand, and so my underlinings mingle with the many discoveries of Christian allegory by the previous owner, an undergraduate. Most notable about this copy of the book, however, is its annotated table of contents, where the previous reader has studiously marked several sequences of chapters from the middle part of the book—the cetology chapters—with the terse but conclusive judgment, "Skip." This student's response is hardly idiosyncratic. In an article on *Moby-Dick* and canonicity, Paul Lauter describes his current students' resentment of and frustration with the novel, a reaction with which those of us who teach *Moby-Dick* may be familiar. While Lauter argues that this reaction can be tied to *Moby-Dick*'s association with modernism and masculinity, I would argue that it is more specifically tied to the changing class-meaning of the university experience and the dilution of the cultural hierarchy as a signifier of class experience.[25] As American universities have opened their gates wider, and the American economy's demand for credentialing has expanded, the majority of American college students are less likely to identify with the same professional project of *Moby-Dick*'s canonical heyday, particularly the investment in cultural distinctions and hierarchy. Lauter's students' resentment toward *Moby-Dick* could be explained as the failure of the text to initiate or hail them into a professional identity. Or, rather, that they are being hailed into an anachronistic professional identity, one that does not fit with a newer version that they sought in going to university, one in which these kinds of cultural distinctions no longer play a significant role.

Whether this is something to praise or decry is perhaps a question we all need to answer for ourselves, both as scholars and teachers. I still teach *Moby-Dick* to my undergraduates, but along with discussing the text, we spend time discussing models of cultural identity and authority—the text's, theirs, and mine—tracing where and how we are drawn in and pushed away by the narrative. I believe that if we frame the texts we teach as social and cultural experiences, we can help our students not only to interpret literature, but also to interpret their experience as college students. *Moby-Dick* and Melville's work as a whole thematize these concerns and can become an important critical and pedagogical site for engaging with the forms of professional ideology.

This self-consciousness about reading and its connection to cultural hierarchy, however, should be distinguished from the "politicization" of literature, which transforms professors into "professional liberationists" and invests the act of reading with a kind of social authority. Again, Melville's work can be illuminating. Since its beginnings, modern professionalism has been pulled in contradictory directions: one, outward to reform, and the other, inward to specialization. In *Mardi*, Melville turned, alternately, to political and social reform and aestheticized specialization as part of his search for a new professional authority, revealing each as a deeply ambiguous part of the antebellum effort to establish an authoritative role for a new professional middle class. In light of this, we might well do to reflect upon how much the contemporary scholarly and pedagogical investment in the professional politicization of literature reflects a search very much like Melville's for a legitimating role in the face of the declining significance of cultural hierarchy. This political impulse may, in fact, reflect a turn away from the specialization that established professional authority, but what is the professoriate's real investment in reform? Is it, as Melville's text hints, primarily a means of social legitimation, meaningful only to the point that it does not challenge middle-class status? What kind of political work does "critical reading" produce? What is the actual commitment of the humanities professoriate to political or social change? There cannot be any easy single answer to these questions, but Melville can help us to interrogate the meanings of professionalism as both a personal experience of vocation and a class identity in the present moment.

NOTES

PREFACE

    1. Herman Melville, *Correspondence* (Chicago: Northwestern University Press–Newberry Library, 1993), 138.

    2. The literature on the social politics of antebellum entertainment is extensive. For some of the influential formulations, see David Grimsted, *Melodrama Unveiled: American Theater and Culture, 1800–1850* (Chicago: University of Chicago Press, 1968); Paul Dimaggio, "Cultural Entrepreneurship in Nineteenth-Century Boston: The Creation of an Organizational Base for High Culture in America," *Media, Culture and Society* 4 (1982): 33–50, 303–22; and Lawrence Levine, *Highbrow/Lowbrow: The Emergence of Cultural Hierarchy in America* (Cambridge: Harvard University Press, 1988). Most significant for my project has been Peter Buckley's "To the Opera House: Culture and Society in New York City, 1820–1860" (Ph.D. diss., SUNY–Stony Brook, 1984). Buckley's combination of localism and cultural scope has been both an inspiration and a challenge to me, especially as my notion of antebellum New York cultural politics differs from his in some notable particulars.

    3. The effect of the rise of a marketplace has been a central concern of historically oriented criticism of antebellum literature since Michael T. Gilmore's *American Romanticism and the Marketplace* (Chicago: University of Chicago Press, 1985). It should be noted, however, that Gilmore's vision of the romantic artists' "ambivalent" response to the market is presented within an undifferentiated social setting, not taking account of the relatively narrow setting for the market within Northern cities and the varied reactions of different classes to the market's rise.

    4. Historians who have traced this emergent divide include Daniel T. Rodgers, *The Work Ethic in Industrial America, 1850–1920* (Chicago: University of Chicago Press,

1978); Sean Wilentz, *Chants Democratic: New York City and the Rise of the American Working Class, 1788–1850* (New York: Oxford University Press, 1984); and Stuart Blumin, *The Emergence of the Middle Class: Social Experience in the American City, 1760–1900* (New York: Cambridge University Press, 1989).

INTRODUCTION

1. Augusta Melville, in an 1857 letter to his uncle Peter Gansevoort, cited in Perry Miller, *The Raven and the Whale: The War of Words and Wits in the Era of Poe and Melville* (New York: Harcourt, Brace & World, 1956), 337.

2. Allan Pred, *Urban Growth and City-Systems in the United States, 1840–1860* (Cambridge: Harvard University Press, 1980), 4, 11.

3. Sean Wilentz, *Chants Democratic: New York City and the Rise of the American Working Class, 1788–1850* (New York: Oxford University Press, 1984), 109.

4. Pred, *Urban Growth*, 30.

5. Wilentz, *Chants Democratic*, 112–5.

6. Pred, *Urban Growth*, 169.

7. In *The Emergence of the Middle Class: Social Experience in the American City, 1760–1900* (New York: Cambridge University Press, 1989), Stuart Blumin directly builds upon Sean Wilentz's argument about the rise of an American working class to describe the simultaneity of class formation: "The process that creates one class includes the creation of others" (67).

8. Blumin, *Emergence of the Middle Class*, 66–107.

9. Georg Lukács, "Reification and the Consciousness of the Proletariat" (1922), in *History and Class Consciousness*, trans. Rodney Livingstone (Cambridge: MIT Press, 1971), 87.

10. Blumin, *Emergence of the Middle Class*, 68–78.

11. Magali S. Larson, *The Rise of Professionalism: A Sociological Analysis* (Berkeley: University of California Press, 1977), 105–13.

12. On the Jacksonian and antebellum threats to the traditional forms of the professions, see Daniel H. Calhoun, *Professional Lives in America: Structure and Aspiration, 1750–1850* (Cambridge: Harvard University Press, 1965). On the particular threats to medicine, see Paul Starr, *The Social Transformation of American Medicine* (New York: Basic Books, 1982), 30–78.

13. Noting this antebellum shift from traditional to modern professionalism, Thomas Bender takes the year 1850 as a crucial turning point in the movement from what he terms "civic professionalism," associated with local urban professional communities, to "disciplinary professionalism." See Bender, *Intellect and Public Life: Essays on the Social History of Academic Intellectuals in the United States* (Baltimore: Johns Hopkins University Press, 1993), 3–14. Bender's work on intellectual culture and professionalism is laudably balanced, recognizing that the traditional model of American professionalism, although genteel and elitist, was also "civic" and public in its orientation (even if its public aims were patrician), and noting as well that the new disciplinary form of modern professionalism attained greater rigor, but also privatized itself.

14. "Prospects of the Legal Profession in America," *United States Magazine and Democratic Review* 18 (January 1846): 28. This opinion, coming from a magazine openly affiliated with the Democratic Party, demonstrates that such views were not simply expressions of "Whig" conservatism.

15. "Woman and the 'Woman's Movement,'" *Putnam's Magazine* 1:3 (March 1853): 279. It should be noted that women's involvement in "traditional" professional activity, particularly that of medicine, was a notable threat in the period. See Barbara Ehrenreich and Deidre English, *For Her Own Good: 150 Years of the Experts' Advice to Women* (New York: Anchor Books, 1978), 44–61.

16. For example, see Samuel Haber, *The Quest for Authority and Honor in the American Professions, 1750–1900* (Chicago: University of Chicago Press, 1991), 91–116, and Daniel H. Calhoun, *Professional Lives in America: Structure and Aspiration, 1750–1850* (Cambridge: Harvard University Press, 1965), 178–97.

17. See, for example, John and Barbara Ehrenreich, "The Professional Managerial Class," in *Between Labor and Capital*, ed. Pat Walker (Montreal: Black Rose Press, 1976); Alvin Gouldner, *The Future of Intellectuals and the Rise of the New Class* (New York: Seabury Press, 1979); and Olivier Zunz, *Making America Corporate, 1870–1920* (Chicago: University of Chicago Press, 1990).

18. Business historian Alfred Chandler Jr. locates the first appearance of managers and a legitimating logic for their importance with the development of the railroads, an event inextricably associated with the antebellum era: "A very brief period, specifically from 1849 to 1855 can be identified as the time when modern business administration appeared in the United States." Cited in Burton J. Bledstein, *The Culture of Professionalism: The Middle Class and the Development of Higher Education in America* (New York: Norton, 1976), 195. For the antebellum origins of professional associations, see, 178–96.

19. Larson, *Rise of Professionalism*, 105.

20. Although some of the earliest scholars of professionalism, sociologists associated with the functionalist "Chicago School" such as Talcott Parsons and Everett Hughes, focused on the role professionals played within an increasingly sophisticated society (their "function"), scholarship on professionalism since the 1970s has taken what is called a more "interactionist" bent, exploring how professionals have intervened in modern society. Examples of this interactionist study of professionalism include the work of Eliot Friedson and Magali S. Larson.

21. Larson, *Rise of Professionalism*, xvi.

22. It is notable that this article was published in the same year as the despondent comments about the effects of democracy on the professions. "The Medical Profession," *Putnam's Magazine* 2:9 (September 1853): 315–16.

23. Magali S. Larson, "Expertise and Expert Power," in *The Authority of Experts: Studies in History and Theory*, ed. Thomas Haskell (Bloomington: University of Indiana Press, 1984), 36.

24. "Cultural capital" is a central concept in Bourdieu's work, from his early anthropological fieldwork in Algeria in *Outline of a Theory of Practice* (1972; trans. Richard Nice. New York: Cambridge University Press, 1977), to his study of French cultural life, *Distinction: A Social Critique of the Judgment of Taste*, 1979; trans. Richard Nice (Cambridge: Harvard University Press, 1984), to his study of the fields of French literary and art markets in *The Rules of Art: Genesis and Structure of the Literary Field* (1992), trans. Susan Emanuel (Stanford: Stanford University Press, 1996).

25. Alvin Gouldner, *The Future of Intellectuals and the Rise of the New Class* (New York: Seabury Press, 1979), 27.

26. Gouldner, *Future of Intellectuals*, 21.

27. Larson, "Expertise and Expert Power," 36.

28. Larson, "Expertise and Expert Power," 36.

29. This same conjunction of literary professionalism and the broader ideology of professionalism has been told for different periods as well, particularly for the Progressive era and Modernist writers. See Christopher Wilson, *The Labor of Words: Literary Professionalism in the Progressive Era* (Athens: University of Georgia Press, 1985), and Thomas Strychacz, *Modernism, Mass Culture and Professionalism* (New York: Cambridge University Press, 1993).

30. William Charvat, *The Profession of Authorship in America, 1800–1870*, ed. Matthew J. Bruccoli (1968; New York: Columbia University Press, 1992), 3.

31. Charvat, *Profession of Authorship in America*, 292.

32. Examples of studies that re-envisioned canonical authors and the marketplace include Michael Davitt Bell, *The Development of American Romance: The Sacrifice of Relation* (Chicago: University of Chicago Press, 1980), and Michael T. Gilmore, *American Romanticism and the Marketplace* (Chicago: University of Chicago Press, 1985). For examples of scholarship on antebellum women professional authors and the marketplace, see Susan Coultrap-McQuin, *Doing Literary Business: American Women Writers in the Nineteenth-Century* (Chapel Hill: University of North Carolina Press, 1990), and Patricia Okker, *Our Sister Editors: Sarah J. Hale and the Tradition of Nineteenth-Century American Women Editors* (Athens: University of Georgia Press, 1995).

33. David S. Reynolds, *Beneath the American Renaissance: The Subversive Imagination in the Age of Emerson and Melville* (New York: Knopf, 1988).

34. There are notable exceptions here, and my project owes a debt to works that have begun to explore the class meaning of American literary production. Both Nicholas Bromell's *By the Sweat of the Brow: Literature and Labor in Antebellum America* (Chicago: University of Chicago Press, 1993) and Michael Newbury's *Figuring Authorship in Antebellum America* (Stanford: Stanford University Press, 1997) have sought to move beyond the simple ascription of "middle class" to antebellum authorship and explore the ways the labor of authorship came to function in the dynamic reorganization of social hierarchy in the period. Their efforts are rare; even those literary studies that ostensibly engage with class, often do so in a fashion that negates class as a structure of relation and hierarchy. See, for example, Michael T. Gilmore, "Hawthorne and the Making of the Middle Class," in *Rethinking Class: Literary Studies and Social Formations*, ed. Wai Chee Dimock and Michael T. Gilmore (New York: Columbia University Press, 1994), 215–38, and Walter T. Herbert Jr, *Dearest Beloved: The Hawthornes and the Making of the Middle-Class Family* (Berkeley: University of California Press, 1993), which engage with and define "middle-classness" by the absence of social reference, rather than its construction of hierarchy or engagement with other social positions in American life.

35. As James Callow explains, "Between 1820 and 1852 [New York] city could boast of its 345 publishers. . . . Only Philadelphia had even half this number of publishers," in *Kindred Spirits: Knickerbocker Writers and American Artists* (Chapel Hill: University of North Carolina Press, 1967), 6.

36. Cited in Edward L. Widmer, *Young America: The Flowering of Democracy in New York City* (New York: Oxford University Press, 1999), 101.

37. On the culture of reprinting and its effect upon authorship, see Meredith McGill, *American Literature and the Culture of Reprinting, 1834–1853* (Philadelphia: University of Pennsylvania Press, 2003). On the distinction between "residual" and "emergent" forms of ideology, see Raymond Williams, *Marxism and Literature* (Oxford: Oxford University Press, 1977), 121–27. For a typology of artists in relationship to the marketplace, see his *Sociology of Culture* (1981: Chicago: University of Chicago Press, 1995), 44–52.

38. The principal history of the literary Young America has been told by Perry Miller, *The Raven and the Whale*. Edward Widmer's *Young America* is a more recent study that seeks to restore its political heritage by separating its nationalism from the jingoistic imperialism of "Manifest Destiny" with which Young America has become associated.

39. Evert Duyckinck, "Prospectus," *Literary World* 1:1 (February 6, 1847): 5.

40. William A. Jones, "Amateur Authors and Small Critics," *The United States Magazine and Democratic Review* 17 (July 1845): 62.

41. Bledstein, *Culture of Professionalism*, 31.

42. Jones, "Amateur Authors," 62.

43. Jones, "Amateur Authors," 63.

44. Jones, "Amateur Authors," 64.

45. Jones, "Amateur Authors," 65.

46. Thomas Haskell, *Emergence of Professional Social Science; The American Social Science Association and the Nineteenth-Century Crisis of Authority* (Urbana: University of Illinois Press, 1977), 18.

47. See Bledstein, *Culture of Professionalism*, 178–96.

48. Cited in Haskell, *Emergence of Professional Social Science*, 66.

49. See "The American Authors' Union," *Broadway Journal* 10 (1845), 233–34 and 250–51.

50. Certainly, there are few other literary figures whom one could imagine having an entire critical study devoted to his literary feuds. See Sidney P. Moss, *Poe's Literary Battles: The Critic in the Context of His Literary Milieu* (Durham, N.C.: Duke University Press, 1963). Meredith McGill deflates some of the legendary afflatus surrounding Poe's critical isolation in *American Literature and the Culture of Reprinting, 1834–1853* (Philadelphia: University of Pennsylvania Press, 2003), 187–217.

51. On Poe's drive for a literary career that joined economic, social, and cultural authority, see Terence Whalen, *Edgar Allan Poe and the Masses: The Political Economy of Literature in Antebellum America* (Princeton: Princeton University Press, 1999). McGill's study of Poe's embrace of the market potential within the anonymous "culture of reprinting," in *American Literature*, gives us a very different picture of the relation of the literary artist to the market.

52. Edgar Allan Poe, "The Literati of New York City" (1846), in *Essays and Reviews*, ed G. R. Thompson (New York: Library of America, 1984), 1120.

53. Poe, "Literati of New York City," 1120.

54. Poe, "Literati of New York City," 1118–9.

55, Poe, "Literati of New York City," 1120.

56. On the transformation of attitudes toward vocational terms, see Bledstein, *Culture of Professionalism*, 171–78.

57. Bledstein, 111–12, *Culture of Professionalism, my italics.*

58. On the antebellum origins of Hawthorne's literary status as exemplary American author, see Richard Brodhead, *The School of Hawthorne* (New York: Oxford University Press, 1986), 48–66. In *The Profession of Authorship*, William Charvat makes a case for Longfellow's significance as literary professional, based upon his earnings. Terence Whalen's *Edgar Allan Poe and the Masses* argues for Poe's consistent, if flawed, attempt to establish an authoritative position for himself as a professional author. Both Ezra Greenspan and David S. Reynolds discuss Whitman's construction of an authoritative voice within the literary and broader cultural realm. See Ezra Greenspan's *Walt Whitman and the American Reader* (New York: Cambridge University Press, 1990), and

David S. Reynolds' *Walt Whitman's America: A Cultural Biography* (New York: Knopf, 1995).

59. In this way, I differentiate my sense of authorship from Michael Davitt Bell's vision of the author as marginally "deviant" (a more sophisticated, sociologically inflected take on the romantic notion of the artist as outsider) and the New Historicist vision of the author as unconscious reflector of ideology. With Melville, the most cogent example of this approach is Wai Chee Dimock's *Empire for Liberty: Melville and the Poetics of Individualism* (Princeton: Princeton University Press, 1989). For Bell's vision of authorship, see *Culture, Genre, and Literary Vocation: Selected Essays on American Literature* (Chicago: University of Chicago Press, 2001), 1–12.

60. "In presuming to speak on behalf of the individual, they not only locate the source of writing in themselves, they also imply that writing came from a much larger speech community. In writing his or her 'mind,' in other words, the author always speaks on behalf of such a community. He or she 'represents' the members of that community and acquires authority by his or her exemplary status in this respect as much as they do." From Nancy Armstrong and Leonard Tennenhouse, *The Imaginary Puritan: Literature, Intellectual Labor and the Origins of Personal Life* (Berkeley: University of California Press, 1992), 17.

61. Benedict Anderson speaks to the role of print, both in newspapers and novels, in helping to forge the "imagined community" of the nation. Michael Warner's influential discussion of print culture in late-eighteenth-century America has demonstrated the political and social stakes in transforming the embodied culture of democratic dissent of the Revolution into the disembodiment of national identity into print with the Constitution. Mary Ryan has followed this through the nineteenth century, tracing the process of disenfranchising political and social public gatherings in American life. Each study speaks to the increasingly important role that print could have while standing in for "community" or "public" experience in American life. See Benedict Anderson, *Imagined Communities* (1983; New York: Verso, 1991); Michael Warner, *The Letters of the Republic: Publication and the Public Sphere in Eighteenth-Century America* (Cambridge: Harvard University Press, 1990); and Mary Ryan, *Civic Wars: Democracy and Public Life in the American City During the Nineteenth Century* (Berkeley: University of California Press, 1997).

62. F. O. Matthiessen, *American Renaissance: Art and Expression in the Age of Emerson and Whitman* (New York: Oxford University Press, 1941). On the canonizing role of Matthiessen's work, see Giles Gunn, *F. O. Matthiessen: The Critical Achievement* (Seattle: University of Washington Press, 1975), 69, and Jonathan Arac, "F. O. Matthiessen: Authorizing an American Renaissance," in *American Renaissance Reconsidered*, ed. Walter Benn Michaels and Donald E. Pease (Baltimore: Johns Hopkins University Press, 1985), 90–112. On the importance of *Moby-Dick* to Matthiessen's critical task, see William E. Cain, *F. O. Matthiessen and the Politics of Criticism* (Madison: University of Wisconsin Press, 1988), 176–79.

63. The only reasonable competitor here would be Hawthorne, who was established in his lifetime and has remained a canonical author ever since. On the history of Hawthorne's canonicity, see Richard Brodhead, *The School of Hawthorne* (New York: Oxford University Press, 1986), 48–66, and Jane Tompkins, "Masterpiece Theater," *Sensational Designs: The Cultural Work of American Fiction, 1790–1860* (New York: Oxford University Press, 1985), 3–39.

64. On professionalism and the American literary academy, see Michael Warner, "Professionalism and the Rewards of Literature, 1875–1900," *Criticism* 27 (Winter

1985): 1–28; Gerald Graff, *Professing Literature: An Institutional History* (Chicago: University of Chicago Press, 1987); David Shumway, *Creating American Civilization: A Genealogy of American Literature as an Academic Discipline* (Minneapolis: University of Minnesota Press, 1994); and John Guillory, "Literary Critics as Intellectuals: Class Analysis and the Crisis of the Humanities," in *Rethinking Class: Literary Studies and Social Formations*, ed. Wai Chee Dimock and Michael T. Gilmore (New York: Columbia University Press, 1994), 107–49. Although Hawthorne's writing certainly has fit the professional demand for critical expertise or sophistication (see Brodhead, *School of Hawthorne*, 5), his work does not thematize or explore the same kinds of issues—particularly the nature of work and cultural distinctions—that have structured modern professional experience.

65. Jonathan Arac has observed the odd absence of explicitly "national" issues from *Moby-Dick*, *The Scarlet Letter*, and *The Adventures of Huckleberry Finn*—the most canonical works of nineteenth-century American literature (he has characterized them as "hypercanonical"). See Arac, "Nationalism, Hypercanonization and *Huckleberry Finn*," *Boundary 2* 19:1 (Spring 1992): 14–33.

66. Louis Althusser, "Ideology and Ideological State Apparatuses (Notes Towards an Investigation)," in *Lenin and Philosophy and Other Essays*, trans. Ben Brewster (New York: Monthly Review Press, 1971), 162.

67. On the utopian element of ideology, see Fredric Jameson, "The Dialectic of Utopia and Ideology," in *The Political Unconscious: Narrative as a Socially Symbolic Art* (Ithaca: Cornell University Press, 1981), 281–99.

68. Mary Poovey, *Uneven Developments: The Ideological Work of Gender in Mid-Victorian England* (Chicago: University of Chicago Press, 1988), 3.

CHAPTER ONE

1. Cited in Hershel Parker, *Herman Melville: A Biography, 1819–1851*, vol. 1 (Baltimore: Johns Hopkins University Press, 1996), 354.

2. Reader's report cited in *The Melville Log: A Documentary Life of Herman Melville, 1819–1891*, ed. Jay Leyda (New York: Harcourt, Brace: 1951), 1: 196.

3. Cited in Parker, *Herman Melville*, 11.

4. On this shift to a free-market system, see Karl Polanyi, *The Great Transformation* (1944; Boston: Beacon Press, 1957). For a general overview of this process in an American context, see Charles Sellers, *The Market Revolution: Jacksonian America, 1815–1846* (New York: Oxford University Press, 1991).

5. Robert G. Albion, *The Rise of the New York Port, 1815–1860* (New York: Scribner's, 1939), 12–13.

6. Cited in Parker, *Herman Melville*, 15.

7. Stuart Blumin, *The Emergence of the Middle Class: Social Experience in the American City, 1760–1900* (New York: Cambridge University Press, 1989), 66–107.

8. In *Confidence Men and Painted Women: A Study of Middle-Class Culture in America, 1830–1870* (New Haven: Yale University Press, 1982), Karen Halttunen explores antebellum middle-class anxieties about the young men entering the workforce in cities as a response to the breakdown of older patterns without new models in their place (11–13).

9. Halttunen, *Confidence Men and Painted Women*, 29.

10. Edward Pessen has been most closely identified with this project of debunking the myth of Jacksonian democracy. See his *Jacksonian America: Society, Personality, and Politics*

(Homewood, Ill.: Dorsey Press, 1969), 38–58, as well as his *Riches, Class and Power before the Civil War* (Lexington, Mass.: D.C. Heath, 1973).

11. On downward mobility among the middle class in the period, see Stephan Thernstrom, *Poverty and Progress: Social Mobility in a Nineteenth-Century City* (Cambridge: Harvard University Press, 1964).

12. Cited in Leon Howard, *Herman Melville: A Biography* (Berkeley: University of California Press, 1951), 30.

13. Parker, *Herman Melville*, 355.

14. Melville would actively pursue government work in the first years of his authorship (1846–48) and renew his quest later, finally receiving an appointment to the New York Custom House in 1866. William Charvat estimated that "from 1800 to 1870, from 60 to 75 percent of all American male authors who even approached professionalism either held office or tried to get it." See *The Profession of Authorship in America, 1800–1870; The Papers of William Charvat*, ed. Matthew J. Bruccoli (1968; New York: Columbia University Press, 1992), 294–95.

15. On the restrictions that the limited transportation infrastructure placed upon the publishing industry, see Charvat, *Profession of Authorship*, 28–48, and Ronald J. Zboray, *A Fictive People: Antebellum Economic Development and the American Reading Public* (New York: Oxford University Press, 1993), 37–68.

16. Zboray, *A Fictive People*, xviii.

17. Cited in Zboray, *A Fictive People*, 60.

18. Cited in Ezra Greenspan, *Walt Whitman and the American Reader* (New York: Cambridge University Press, 1990), 34.

19. Cited in *The Melville Log*, 1:196.

20. William Charvat, *Literary Publishing in America, 1790–1850* (Philadelphia: University of Pennsylvania Press, 1959), 75.

21. Charles Roberts Anderson, *Melville in the South Seas* (1939; New York; Columbia University Press, 1967), 67–195.

22. For a representative survey of the range of modern criticism of *Typee*, see *Critical Essays on Herman Melville's 'Typee'*, ed. Milton R. Stern (Boston: G.K. Hall, 1982).

23. See, for example, John Carlos Rowe, "Melville's *Typee*: U.S. Imperialism at Home and Abroad," in *National Identities and Post-Americanist Narratives*, ed. Donald E. Pease (Durham, N.C.: Duke University Press, 1994), 255–78, and Geoffrey Sanborn, *The Sign of the Cannibal: Melville and the Making of a Postcolonial Reader* (Durham, N.C.: Duke University Press, 1998), 75–118.

24. Cited in John Samson, *White Lies: Melville's Narratives of Facts* (Ithaca: Cornell University Press, 1989), 30.

25. Hershel Parker, "Evidences for 'Late Insertions' in Melville's Works," *Studies in the Novel* 7 (1975): 413.

26. Anderson, *Melville in the South Seas*, 191.

27. It is a matter of varying critical opinion whether it is the threat of tattooing or Tommo's discovery of cannibalism among the Typees that propels him back to civilization. See Stern's *Critical Essays on Herman Melville's 'Typee'*.

28. Neil Harris, *Humbug: The Art of P. T. Barnum* (Boston: Little, Brown, 1973), 78.

29. Cited in Harris, *Humbug*, 65.

30. In *Arts of Deception: Playing with Fraud in the Age of Barnum* (Cambridge: Harvard University Press, 2001), James W. Cook addresses the role that Barnum's frauds had in constructing a consumer culture.

31. Neil Harris locates Melville's work—from the descriptions of exotic South Pacific life in *Typee* and *Omoo* to the descriptions of whaling in *Moby-Dick*—as particularly relevant to the context of the operational aesthetic. See his *Humbug*, 76.

32. Herman Melville, *Typee* (Chicago: Northwestern University Press–Newberry Library, 1968), xiv. All further references are to this edition and will be cited, with chapter and page numbers, in the text.

33. Elizabeth Renker emphasizes the "anxiety" here, reading this as an expression of fear of discovery. See her *Strike through the Mask: Herman Melville and the Scene of Writing* (Baltimore: Johns Hopkins University Press, 1996), 4.

34. Parker, *Herman Melville*, 441.

35. Other critics have seen Melville's engagement with taboo as a far more serious and authentic attempt to understand Marquesan culture. See, for example, T. Walter Herbert Jr., *Marquesan Encounters: Melville and the Meaning of Civilization* (Cambridge: Harvard University Press, 1980), and John Samson, *White Lies*, and Alex Calder, "'The Thrice Mysterious Taboo': Melville's *Typee* and the Perception of Culture," *Representations* 67 (1999): 27–43. I do not mean to suggest that Melville did not engage with Marquesan culture during his stay, but rather, that part of his process of revision might have involved a shift into meditating upon his current status and situation and adapting to the demands of authorship and American market culture.

36. In *Melville's Anatomies* (Berkeley: University of California Press, 1999), Samuel Otter explores the representational meanings of tattooing, arguing that Melville uses the tattoo to complicate racist distinctions between "civilized" and "primitive" (20–49).

37. See, for example, Willowdean Handy, *Tattooing in the Marquesas* (Honolulu: Bishop Museum, 1922), 5.

38. Mitchell Breitwieser, "False Sympathy in Melville's *Typee*," *American Quarterly* 34:4 (Fall 1982): 412.

39. Renker, *Strike through the Mask*, 19–23.

40. Georg Lukács, "Reification and the Consciousness of the Proletariat" (1922), in *History and Class Consciousness: Studies in Marxist Dialectics*, trans. Rodney Livingstone (Cambridge: MIT Press, 1971), 87.

41. Karl Marx, "Wage Labour and Capital" (1849), in *The Marx-Engels Reader*, ed. Robert C. Tucker (New York: Norton, 1972), 171.

42. Sean Wilentz, *Chants Democratic: New York City and the Rise of the American Working Class, 1788–1850* (New York: Oxford University Press, 1984), 112–15.

43. Blumin, *Emergence of the Middle Class*, 68–78.

44. C. Wright Mills, *White Collar: The American Middle Classes* (New York: Oxford University Press, 1953), 182.

45. Mills, *White Collar*, 182. It should be noted that my use of Mills could be subject to charges of anachronism: Mills is specifically addressing what he calls the "new middle class," dating its emergence to the last quarter of the nineteenth century and its predominance in the twentieth. It is hardly appropriate either to see the work of Melville's first book confirming his status as an "employee." On the other hand, there is no question that Melville's authorship in *Typee* is decisively constructed as a marketing of personality. Moreover, this process of constructing and marketing an identity is clearly a process at work among the entry-level, nonmanual labors in the urban economy of the antebellum era, a demand reflected by the proliferation of conduct manuals in the period, particularly those directed at young men, but more generally aimed at the urban middle class. See Halttunen, *Confidence Men and Painted Women*, 33–52. For a more recent discussion of the

construction of "character" as a marketable commodity among young men of the new middle class, see Thomas Augst, *The Clerk's Tale: Young Men and Moral Life in Nineteenth-Century America* (Chicago: University of Chicago Press, 2003).

46. Melville to John Murray, 15 July 1846, *Correspondence* (Chicago: Northwestern University Press–Newberry Library, 1993), 56.

47. Parker demonstrates *Typee's* presence in the culture in a variety of ways: from Margaret Fuller's recommendation of the book to "sewing societies of the country villages" to Thoreau's poring over it for hints on life at Walden Pond, and from poetic satires in newspapers to the earnest poetic retelling in "The Island Nukuheva" by Ellery Channing, nephew of the famous Unitarian minister William Ellery Channing. Parker, *Herman Melville*, 413 and 460.

48. N. P. Willis, "Change in Authorship," *Home Journal*, October 1849, cited in *The Melville Log*, 1:320.

49. Daniel Boorstin, *The Image: a Guide to Pseudo-Events in America* (1961; New York: Atheneum, 1981), 57.

50. On the antebellum origins of the culture of celebrity, see Thomas N. Baker, *Sentiment and Celebrity: Nathaniel Parker Willis and the Trials of Literary Fame* (New York: Oxford University Press, 1999), 3–12, and Michael Newbury, *Figuring Authorship in Antebellum America* (Palo Alto: Stanford University Press, 1997), 79–118, and Peter Buckley, "To the Opera House: Culture and Society in New York City, 1820–1860" (Ph.D. diss., SUNY-Stony Brook, 1984), 498–510.

51. Baker, *Sentiment and Celebrity*, 5.

52. Leo Braudy, *The Frenzy of Renown: Fame and Its History* (New York: Oxford University Press, 1986), 380.

53. Baker discusses the erotic nature of the "dream-work" of antebellum celebrity as part of his insightful study of the career of N. P. Willis, *Sentiment and Celebrity*, 10.

54. Caroline Kirkland, "An Apology for Authors," *Knickerbocker Magazine* 19 (February 1842): 97.

55. *Broadway Journal* 10 (March 8, 1845), 153.

56. Buckley, "To the Opera House," 501.

57. Emerson, "Aristocracy," *English Traits* (Cambridge: Harvard University Press, 1966), 125 (*my italics*). I must acknowledge my debt to Peter Buckley for his recognition of the significance of this passage in reference to antebellum notions of celebrity. See "To the Opera House," 502.

58. Emerson, "Aristocracy," 125.

59. For more on the cultural significance of Lind and Emerson as celebrities in antebellum America, see my discussion of them in relationship to middlebrow culture in Chapter 4.

60. Nathaniel Parker Willis, "The Propriety of Sketches of Fashionable Society," *Hurry-Graphs: or, Sketches of Scenery, Celebrities and Society, Taken from Life* (New York: Charles Scribner, 1851), 316.

61. See Mary Ryan, *The Cradle of the Middle Class: The Family in Oneida County, New York, 1790–1865* (New York: Cambridge University Press, 1981).

62. Blumin, *Emergence of the Middle Class*, 239.

63. Kirkland, "An Apology for Authors," 97–98.

64. Newbury, *Figuring Authorship*, 85.

65. On the religious and symbolic meaning of Cook's body, see Marshall Sahlins, *Islands of History* (Chicago: University of Chicago Press, 1985), 104–35.

66. Cited in Parker, *Herman Melville*, 445. On Byron's claim after the publication of *Childe Harold*, see Braudy, *The Frenzy of Renown*, 408.

67. Cited in Parker, *Herman Melville*, 464.

68. Cited in Parker, *Herman Melville*, 541.

69. Cited in Parker, *Herman Melville*, 541.

70. Cited in Parker, *Herman Melville*, 753.

71. Hershel Parker comments, "'The kindest way of looking at the Old Zack anecdotes is to see them as what Melville's New York friends gave him instead of a bachelor party," in *Herman Melville*, 537.

72. Melville, "Authentic Anecdotes of 'Old Zack,'" in *The Piazza Tales and Other Prose Pieces: 1839–1860* (Chicago: Northwestern University Press–Newberry Library, 1987), 212.

73. Melville, "Authentic Anecdotes," 213.

74. Melville, "Authentic Anecdotes," 213.

75. Melville, "Authentic Anecdotes," 218.

76. Melville, "Authentic Anecdotes," 225.

77. Melville, "Authentic Anecdotes," 225.

78. Melville, "Authentic Anecdotes," 225.

79. On the association of *Typee* and freakishness, see Leonard Cassuto, *The Inhuman Race* (New York: Columbia University Press, 1997), 170–85. See also my discussion of American tattoo freaks in an earlier version of this chapter, "Made in the Marquesas": *Typee*, Tattooing and Melville's Critique of the Literary Marketplace," *Arizona Quarterly* 48:4 (Winter 1992), 29–36.

CHAPTER TWO

1. Grace Greenwood (Sara Jane Lippincott), "Letter from the Author of *Typee*," *Saturday Evening Post* (October 9, 1847), cited in Jay Leyda, ed. *Melville Log: A Documentary Life of Herman Melville, 1819–1891* (New York: Harcourt, Brace, 1951), 1:262–63. Melissa Homestead engages with this parody as part of a series and the larger ramifications of antebellum women authors' discussion of copyright. See her *American Women Authors and Literary Property, 1822–1869* (New York: Cambridge University Press, 2006).

2. Herman Melville, *Correspondence* (Chicago: Northwestern University Press–Newberry Library, 1993), 100, 106.

3. William Charvat, *The Profession of Authorship in America, 1800–1870*, ed. Matthew J. Bruccoli (1968; New York: Columbia University Press, 1992).

4. On the rise of New York as national publishing center, see Ronald J. Zboray, *A Fictive People: Antebellum Economic Development and the American Reading Public* (New York: Oxford University Press, 1993), 55–68.

5. Perry Miller, *The Raven and the Whale: The War of Words and Wits in the Era of Poe and Melville* (New York: Harcourt, Brace, 1956). Examples of more recent work that have perpetuated Miller's vision of the New York City literary community as an opposition between "Knickerbocker" and "Young Americans" include Edward L. Widmer's *Young America: The Flowering of Democracy in New York City* (New York: Oxford University Press, 1999), and Peter Buckley's "To the Opera House: Culture and Society in New York City, 1820–1860," (Ph.D. diss., SUNY–Stony Brook, 1984), 268–93.

6. On Fuller's status as employee of *The Tribune*, see Lawrence Buell's observation in *New England Literary Culture from Revolution through Renaissance* (New York: Cambridge

University Press, 1986), 57, and Steven Fink's more sustained discussion in "Margaret Fuller, Woman of Letters," in *Reciprocal Influences: Literary Production, Distribution, and Consumption in America*, ed. Steven Fink and Susan S. Williams (Columbus: Ohio State University Press, 1999), 55–74.

7. On distinctions between residual and emergent cultural forms, see Raymond Williams, *Marxism and Literature* (Oxford: Oxford University Press, 1977), 121–27. For a typology of artists in relationship to the marketplace, see also his *Sociology of Culture* (1981; Chicago: University of Chicago Press, 1995), 44–52.

8. The most notable examples of the early criticism, to which this chapter is heavily indebted, are Luther S. Mansfield's "Herman Melville: Author and New Yorker" (Ph.D. diss., University of Chicago, 1936), and Merrell R. Davis's *Melville's Mardi: A Chartless Voyage* (New Haven: Yale University Press, 1952).

9. For "symbolic" readings, see Charles Feidelson's *Symbolism and American Literature* (Chicago: University of Chicago Press, 1953), 166–75, and Richard Brodhead's essay "Creating the Creative," in *New Perspectives on Melville*, ed. Faith Pullin (Kent, Ohio: Kent State University Press, 1978), 29–53. The "allegorical" school is best embodied by Wai Chee Dimock's *Empire for Liberty: Melville and the Poetics of Individualism* (Princeton: Princeton University Press, 1989), 140–75, and Cindy Weinstein's *The Literature of Labor and the Labors of Literature: Allegory in Nineteenth-Century American Fiction* (New York: Cambridge University Press, 1995), 89–99.

10. *Melville Log*, 1:253.

11. The most substantial meditation on Melville's debt to Irving can be found in John Bryant's *Melville and Repose: The Rhetoric and Humor in the American Renaissance* (New York: Oxford University Press, 1993). Bryant, however, deals primarily with *Typee* and *Moby-Dick*, mentioning *Mardi* only briefly (despite the fact that the rather astute Duyckinck made that observation while Melville was writing *Mardi*).

12. Melville, *Correspondence*, 100, 106.

13. Michael Davitt Bell makes a case for the importance of Irving in the development of an American tradition of romance, in which "reality" is eschewed for imagination. See Bell, *The Development of American Romance: The Sacrifice of Relation* (Chicago: University of Chicago Press, 1980), 63–85. The "romance" model has been central to the construction of a national literary tradition in America. For a formative statement, see Richard Chase, *The American Novel and Its Tradition* (Garden City, N.Y.: Doubleday, 1957).

14. John Paul Pritchard, *The Literary Wise Men of Gotham: Criticism in New York, 1815–1860* (Baton Rouge: Louisiana State University Press, 1963), 9.

15. Cited in Ann Douglas, *Feminization of American Culture* (New York: Knopf, 1977), 237.

16. Douglas, *Feminization of American Culture*, 237. Although Douglas includes these writers in her critique of sentimentalism generally, Sandra Tomc has argued, about Willis particularly, that this literary persona functioned to herald "the new entrepeneurial-style professionalism demanded by the expanding book industry," in "An Idle Industry: Nathaniel Parker Willis and the Workings of Literary Leisure," *American Quarterly* 49:4 (December 1997): 781. Tomc's argument demonstrates the contradictions at the heart of Willis's literary persona without necessarily proving Willis's importance in the articulation of new models of literary work. Irving, like his descendent Willis, was strongly aware of the commercial possibilities of his work and, also like Willis, actively constructed an anachronistic literary persona that appealed to a status-aspiring middle-class literary audience.

17. Herman Melville, *Mardi; and a Voyage Thither* (Chicago: Northwestern University Press–Newberry Library, 1970), 14. All future references will be to this edition and will be noted in parenthetical citation by chapter and page numbers.

18. For an important chronology of Melville's reading during this period, see Davis, *Melville's Mardi*, 60–78.

19. Ik Marvel, *Dream-Life: A Fable of the Seasons* (1851; New York: Scribner's, 1892), 10.

20. This feverish plotting seems to join Irving to the darker romanticism of Byron, Keats, Shelley, and Southey. On the possible influence of the Romantics on the Yillah romance, see Davis, *Melville's Mardi*, 125–41.

21. In *The Literature of Labor and the Labors of Literature*, Cindy Weinstein argues that "A Calm" explores tensions in the work ethic in antebellum American life, setting the tone for Melville's use of allegory in *Mardi* to defend a new kind of symbolic nonmanual labor (89–99). It should be noted, however, that Weinstein's reading is based on an assumption of a more unified model of *Mardi*'s project than mine. From "A Calm," *Mardi*'s allegories are still at least a hundred pages away.

22. Margaret Fuller, "The Rich Man—An Ideal Sketch," in *Margaret Fuller, Critic: Writings from the New-York Tribune, 1844–46*, ed. Judith Mattson Bean and Joel Myerson (New York: Columbia University Press, 2000), 359.

23. The earliest critical studies of *Mardi*, especially Luther Mansfield's 1936 dissertation, "Herman Melville: Author and New Yorker, 1844–1851" and Merrell Davis's *Mardi: A Chartless Voyage* of 1952, have enumerated the sources and critical thrust of Melville's allegories carefully.

24. Weinstein, *The Literature of Labor and the Labors of Literature*, 89–99.

25. The historical literature on antebellum reformism is extensive. An instructive exchange among historians Thomas L. Haskell, David Brion Davis, and John Ashworth on the logic of abolition was compiled by Thomas Bender in *The Antislavery Debate: Capitalism and Abolitionism as a Problem in Historical Interpretation* (Berkeley: University of California Press, 1992).

26. For a sample of the range of arguments for the correlation between antebellum reform movements and middle-class identity, see Paul Johnson, *The Shopkeeper's Millenium: Society and Revivals in Rochester, New York, 1815–1837* (New York: Hill and Wang, 1978), Stuart Blumin, *The Emergence of the Middle Class: Social Experience in the American City, 1760–1900* (New York: Cambridge University Press, 1989), and John Ashworth, *Slavery, Capitalism and Politics in the Antebellum Republic* (New York: Cambridge University Press, 1995).

27. The literature on women's roles in antebellum reform is enormous. An important early articulation of this as part of a class movement was gathered together in Carroll Smith-Rosenberg's *Disorderly Conduct: Visions of Gender in Victorian America* (New York: Knopf, 1985), 109–64.

28. Lydia Maria Child, *Letters from New-York*, ed. Bruce Mills (Athens: University of Georgia Press, 1998), 17.

29. On Fuller as America's first full-time book reviewer, see Thomas Bender, *New York Intellect: A History of Intellectual Life in New York City* (New York: Knopf, 1987), 158. Christina Zwarg develops Fuller's reformist notion of literature as "the great mutual system of interpretation between all kinds and classes of men" in her excellent essay, "Reading Before Marx: Margaret Fuller and the New-York Daily Tribune," in *Readers in History: Nineteenth-Century American Literature and the Contexts of Response*, ed. James Machor (Baltimore: John Hopkins University Press, 1993), 229–58.

30. Margaret Fuller, *Margaret Fuller's New York Journalism: A Biographical Essay and Key Writings* (Knoxville: University of Tennessee Press, 1995), 178–79.

31. William Starbuck Mayo, *Kaloolah, or Journeyings to the Djebel Kumri: An Autobiography of Jonathan Romer* (New York: George Putnam, 1849), 463.

32. Mayo, *Kaloolah*, 465–66.

33. See Elizabeth Blackmar, *Manhattan for Rent, 1785–1850* (Ithaca: Cornell University Press, 1989), and Kenneth A. Scherzer, *The Unbounded Community: Neighborhood Life and Social Structure in New York City, 1830–1875* (Durham: Duke University Press, 1992).

34. For examples of George Foster's city profiles, see the reprint edition of *New York by Gaslight and Other Urban Sketches*, ed. Stuart Blumin (Berkeley: University of California Press, 1990). In his *God in the Street: New York Writing from the Penny Press to Melville* (Philadelphia: Temple University Press, 1995), Hans Bergmann explores what he sees as Melville's engagement with, and transcendence of, New York sensational and sentimental writings about the poor in his next book *Redburn* (108–13).

35. On the emergence of the distinction between manual and nonmanual labor as key to middle-class identity in the period, see Blumin, *Emergence of the Middle Class*, 66–107. For a further discussion of Melville's engagement with the manual/nonmanual divide, see Chapter 5.

36. Blumin notes that writers commenting on New York's "shopkeeper aristocracy" ranged from Foster to John Jacob Astor's grandson, Charles Astor Bristed (*Emergence of the Middle Class*, 234).

37. On New York City's enthusiastic response to the revolutions, see Larry J. Reynolds, *European Revolutions and the American Literary Renaissance* (New Haven: Yale University Press, 1988), 10–12.

38. Georg Lukács, *The Historical Novel*, trans. Hannah and Stanley Mitchell (1962; Lincoln, Nebr.: 1983), 171.

39. Reynolds discusses the conservatism of Melville's critical response to the 1848 revolutions, in *European Revolutions*, 49.

40. Lukács, *Historical Novel*, 175.

41. On conservative anxieties within middle-class reform, see Burton J. Bledstein, *The Culture of Professionalism: The Middle Class and the Development of Higher Education in America* (New York: Norton, 1976), 182.

42. One of the few American writers who continued to support the 1848 uprisings was Margaret Fuller, whose postings to the *Tribune* from Europe were rated by many as the high point of her literary career. See the collection, *These Sad But Glorious Days: Dispatches from Europe, 1846–1850* (New Haven: Yale University Press, 1991). Fuller's history of the Italian revolution was lost when she drowned with her husband and child on their return to New York.

43. Michael Paul Rogin, *Subversive Genealogy: The Politics and Art of Herman Melville* (New York: Knopf, 1979), 21. The European retreat into aestheticism post-1848 is mapped out more precisely in T. J. Clark, *The Absolute Bourgeois: Artists and Politics in France, 1848–1851* (Greenwich, Conn.: New York Graphic Society, 1973).

44. The most influential reading emphasizing *Mardi*'s "symbolism" is Feidelson's famous *Symbolism and American Literature*, 166–75.

45. Brodhead, "*Mardi*: Creating the Creative," 39.

46. Dimock, *Empire for Liberty*, 44.

47. For dates on the founding of various American professional associations, see Bled-

stein, *Culture of Professionalism*, and Magali Sarfatti Larson, *The Rise of Professionalism: A Sociological Analysis* (Berkeley: University of California Press, 1977).

48. Larson, *Rise of Professionalism*, xvi.

49. Thomas Haskell, *The Emergence of Professional Social Science: The American Social Science Association and the Nineteenth-Century Crisis of Authority* (Urbana: University of Illinois Press, 1977), 67.

50. Magali S. Larson, "Expertise and Expert Power," in *The Authority of Experts: Studies in History and Theory*, ed. Thomas Haskell (Bloomington: Indiana University Press, 1984), 36. The term "cultural capital" is primarily associated with Pierre Bourdieu, whose work, *Distinction: A Social Critique of the Judgment of Taste*, trans. Richard Nice (Cambridge: Harvard University Press, 1984), elaborates it most substantially. A related discussion can be found in Alvin Gouldner, *The Future of Intellectuals and the Rise of the New Class* (New York: Seabury Press, 1979).

51. Bourdieu, *Distinction*, 291.

52. Melville was invited (but declined) to attend and speak at Cooper's memorial, initially scheduled for December 1851 but held in February 1852. See Leyda, *The Melville Log*, 1:440. By the time of the Fruit and Flower Festival, Melville was no longer a resident of New York nor a prominent enough member of the literary community to be invited. On the festival, see Susan Coultrop-McQuin, *Doing Literary Business: American Women Writers in the Nineteenth Century* (Chapel Hill: University of North Carolina Press, 1990), and Michael Newbury, *Figuring Authorship in Antebellum America* (Stanford: Stanford University Press, 1997), 79–80.

53. In *The Rules of Art: Genesis and Structure of the Literary Field*, trans. Susan Emanuel (Stanford: Stanford University Press, 1996), Pierre Bourdieu describes the Parisian salons as sites that display the "continuity" of "fields of power," demonstrating his argument about distinctive fields of cultural capital (50–53).

54. These clubs, including the "Bread and Cheese" of the 1820s and the "Sketch Club" of the 1830s and onward into the 1840s, demonstrated the continuity of New York City's artist community with that of the patrician elites in the period. See Bender, *New York Intellect*, 122–23.

55. John S. Hart, *Female Prose Writers of America* (Philadelphia: E. H. Butler, 1852).

56. George Foster, "The Literary Soirees," New York *Tribune*, September 27, 1848. Later published in *New York in Slices* (New York: William H. Graham, 1849).

57. Brodhead, "Creating the Creative," 39.

58. Feidelson, *Symbolism and American Literature*, 167.

59. Melville, October 8, 1849, *Correspondence*, 139.

60. On the association of romanticism with specialization, see Raymond Williams, "The Romantic Artist," *Culture and Society: 1785–1950* (New York: Columbia University Press, 1983), 30–48, and Buell, *New England Literary Culture*, 56–83. It should be noted that Williams distinguishes this specialization from professionalism, while Buell explicitly links the two (without tying it to class formation).

61. Pierre Bourdieu, *Outline of a Theory of Practice*, trans. Richard Nice (1972; New York: Cambridge University Press, 1977), 197. For Bourdieu, the world of art thus becomes a perfect object of sociological study, and for that reason, his work has turned frequently and profitably to cultural attitudes toward the consumption of art (*Distinction*) and its production (*The Rules of Art*).

62. Bourdieu, *Rules of Art*, 82.

63. Bourdieu, *Rules of Art*, 142.

64. Bourdieu, *Rules of Art*, 142.

65. Melville comments on Murray's disapproving "tenor" in his June 19, 1848, letter. See *Correspondence*, 109.

66. Pierre Bourdieu, "The Field of Cultural Production, or: The Economic World Reversed," in *The Field of Cultural Production: Essays on Art and Literature*, ed. Randal Johnson (New York: Columbia University Press, 1993), 36.

67. In *The Raven and the Whale*, Perry Miller charts *Mardi*'s critical failure against the literary feuds of literary nationalism vs. Knickerbocker Anglophilia. More recently, in *Correspondent Colorings: Melville in the Marketplace* (Amherst: University of Massachusetts Press, 1996), Sheila Post-Lauria has argued that *Mardi* failed due to the waning popularity of the philosophically oriented "mixed form" novel. Despite my disagreements with these two readings, both books have been invaluable in my attempt to understand the literary milieu of antebellum New York City.

68. New York *Tribune*, May 10, 1849, cited in *Melville: The Critical Heritage*, ed. Watson G. Branch (London: Routledge & Kegan Paul, 1974), 161.

69. *Saroni's Musical Times*, September 29, 1849, cited in Branch, *Melville: The Critical Heritage*, 184.

70. Cindy Weinstein argues that *Mardi*'s allegory "transgressed the ideology of the work ethic on a number of levels, [including] the author's relation to the work of writing" (*The Literature of Labor and the Labors of Literature*, 90). Though I do not find the concern with allegory consistent in critical response to the novel, Weinstein's insights on *Mardi* and labor have been highly influential to my reading.

71. *Literary World*, April 21, 1849, cited in Branch, *Melville: The Critical Heritage*, 153–54.

72. *Literary World*, April 21, 1849, cited in Branch, *Melville: The Critical Heritage*, 151.

73. *Albion*, April 21, 1849, 183, cited in Branch, *Melville: The Critical Heritage*, 158.

74. Branch, *Melville: The Critical Heritage*, 186.

75. *Examiner*, March 31, 1849, cited in Branch, *Melville: The Critical Heritage*, 144.

76. Cited in Branch, *Melville: The Critical Heritage*, 177.

77. Cited in Branch, *Melville: The Critical Heritage*, 177.

78. Cited in Branch, *Melville: The Critical Heritage*, 177–78.

79. Cited in Branch, *Melville: The Critical Heritage*, 178.

CHAPTER THREE

1. Lawrence W. Levine, *Highbrow/Lowbrow: The Emergence of Cultural Hierarchy in America* (Cambridge: Harvard University Press, 1988). Levine is not so much the originator of this claim as its popularizer. For earlier statements of this claim, see David Grimsted, *Melodrama Unveiled: American Theater and Culture, 1800–1850* (Chicago: University of Chicago Press, 1968); Paul Dimaggio, "Cultural Entrepreneurship in Nineteenth-Century Boston: The Creation of an Organizational Base for High Culture in America," in *Media, Culture and Society* 4 (1982): 33–50, 303–22; Peter Buckley, "To the Opera House: Culture and Society in Antebellum New York, 1820–1860" (Ph.D. diss., SUNY–Stony Brook, 1984).

2. See Bluford Adams, *E Pluribus Barnum: The Great Showman and the Making of U.S. Popular Culture* (Minneapolis: University of Minnesota Press, 1997), and Donald M. Scott, "The Popular Lecture and the Creation of a Public in Mid-Nineteenth-Century America," *Journal of American History* 66:4 (March 1980): 791–809.

3. In *Highbrow/Lowbrow*, Lawrence Levine uses Shakespeare as the central example of his archaeology of social distinctions of "culture" in American life, with the endpoint in Shakespeare's "high"-culture association, 13–81.

4. This has become almost a truism of American cultural studies. The Riots assumed a place of importance in David Grimsted's 1968 social history of nineteenth-century American theater, *Melodrama Unveiled*. More recently, Peter Buckley has situated the Riots as the central event in his cultural history of nineteenth-century New York City in "To the Opera House." The Riots also assume weighty social and cultural significance in Lawrence Levine's narrative of the rise of cultural hierarchy in American life, *Highbrow/Lowbrow*. In addition to those already mentioned, urban and cultural historians who have developed readings of the development of class distinctions in American culture through the Astor Place Riots include Sean Wilentz, *Chants Democratic: New York City and the Rise of the Working Class, 1788–1850* (New York: Oxford University Press, 1984); Richard C. Allen, *Horrible Prettiness: Burlesque and the American Culture* (Chapel Hill: University of North Carolina Press, 1991); and Eric Lott, *Love and Theft: Blackface Minstrelsy and the American Working Class* (New York: Oxford University Press, 1993).

5. The events of the Astor Place riots have been narrated a number of times, in many instances with different emphases and interpretive frames. My narrative of the sequence of events is a synthesis of descriptions by Richard Moody, *The Astor Place Riot* (Bloomington: Indiana University Press, 1958), and Levine, *Highbrow/Lowbrow*, Buckley, "To the Opera House," and Allen, *Horrible Prettiness*.

6. On the history of theater riots, see Bruce McConachie, *Melodramatic Formations: American Theater and Society, 1820–1870* (Iowa City: University of Iowa Press, 1992).

7. Cited in Moody, *Astor Place Riot*, 117. For a social and occupational survey of signers of the petition, see Buckley, "To the Opera House," 198–220. He notes that eight of the signatories qualify as members of the "wealthiest one thousand New Yorkers" (207).

8. *Philadelphia Public Ledger*, May 16, 1849, cited in Buckley, "To the Opera House," 20.

9. McConachie, *Melodramatic Formations*, 69–72. Throughout much of his career, Forrest was identified as the preeminent American actor and his audience was not limited to the working class. However, Buckley argues in "To the Opera House" that the Astor Place Riots were an index of social distinctions being made through theatrical preferences, and he claims that Forrest's identification with the downtown, working-class audience was a part of the development of class-oriented uptown and downtown cultures in antebellum New York (157).

10. McConachie, *Melodramatic Formations*, 92.

11. Evert Duyckinck, "Mr. Forrest in *Lear*," *The Literary World* 95 (November 25, 1848): 854.

12. Levine discusses the Tate version and its American popularity in *Highbrow/Lowbrow*, 44–45.

13. Bruce McConachie identifies the "American Committee" as "a group of nativist politicians and their gangs," in *Melodramatic Formations*, 147.

14. E. P. Thompson, "The Moral Economy of the English Crowd in the Eighteenth Century," in *Customs in Common* (New York: The New Press, 1991), 185–258. On the tradition of rioting in New York City, see Paul Gilje, *The Road to Mobocracy: Popular Disorder in New York City, 1763–1834* (Chapel Hill: University of North Carolina Press, 1987).

15. Mary Ryan traces the progressive disenfranchisement of embodied collectivities in American political and social life over the course of the nineteenth century in *Civic*

Wars: Democracy and Public Life in the American City During the Nineteenth Century (Berkeley: University of California Press, 1997). Ryan's thesis extends the work of Michael Warner on late-eighteenth century American politics and print culture, with the print-oriented Constitution functioning to counter the threatening embodiment of the American revolutionary public. See his *Letters of the Republic: Publication and the Public Sphere in Eighteenth-Century America* (Cambridge: Harvard University Press, 1990), 97–114. On the role of the theater to threaten or throw into doubt this construction, see my article "*The Contrast:* The Problem of Theatricality and Political and Social Crisis in Postrevolutionary America," *Early American Literature* 31 (1996): 74–97. On the persistence of the popular rioting crowd, see McConachie, *Melodramatic Formations*, 65–155.

16. *Literary World* 1:4 (February 27, 1847), 88.

17. "Municipal Government," *United States Magazine and Democratic Review* 24 (June 1849): 485, 486, 487. For a similar statement of the populist American tradition of audience sovereignty in the context of the Astor Place Riots, see the pamphlet written by the pseudonymous "American Citizen," *A Rejoinder to "The Replies from England, etc. to certain statements circulated in this country respecting the lamentable occurences at the Astor Place Opera House, on the 10th of May, 1849"* (New York: Stringer & Townsend, 1849), 100–101.

18. Cited in Lott, *Love and Theft*, 65.

19. Cited in Lott, *Love and Theft*, 67.

20. Henry N. Hudson, *Lectures on Shakespeare* (New York: Baker & Scribner, 1848), 1:131. For a discussion of Hudson, see John Stafford, "Henry Norman Hudson and the Whig Use of Shakespeare" *PMLA* 66:5 (1951): 649–61.

21. Cited in Evert Duyckinck, "Miscellany," *Literary World* 5:121 (May 26, 1849), 459. Bellows' involvement with the Melvilles has become a source of some controversy. Letters to Bellows in 1867 from Melville's wife, Elizabeth, and his brother-in-law speak of removing her from the Melville household owing to Herman's "insanity" and "ill treat[ment]" of her. Since their discovery in 1975, Melville scholars have meditated on the significance of this exchange, considering the possibility of Melville's "wife-beating." See the collection of essays in response to this discovery in *The Endless, Winding Way in Melville: New Charts by Kring and Carey*, ed. Donald Yannella and Hershel Parker (Glassboro, N.J.: Melville Society, 1981). More recently, Elizabeth Renker has accused Melville scholars of willfully ignoring the evidence of Melville's "wife-beating" in *Strike through the Mask: Herman Melville and the Scene of Writing* (Baltimore: Johns Hopkins University Press, 1996), 49–68.

22. An American Citizen, *A Rejoinder to "The Replies from England,"* 117.

23. Thomas Augst, *The Clerk's Tale: Young Men and Moral Life in Nineteenth-Century America* (Chicago: University of Chicago Press, 2003), 181–83.

24. Cited in Rachel N. Klein, "Art and Authority in Antebellum New York City: The Rise and Fall of the American Art-Union," *Journal of American History* 81:4 (March 1995): 1534. Continuing, Headley asserted: "Some one has said, give me the writing of the *songs* of a country, and you may make its laws. I had almost said, give me the control of the *art* of a country, and you may have the management of its administrations." Cited in Patricia Hills, "The American Art-Union as Patron for Expansionist Ideology in the 1840s," in *Art in Bourgeois Society, 1790–1850*, ed. Andrew Hemingway and William Vaughan (New York: Cambridge University Press, 1998), 326.

25. Emanuel Leutze's *George Washington Crossing the Delaware* was displayed in the Art-Union's Hall, while prints of George Caleb Bingham's happy "common men" were frequently offered as prizes. Patricia Hills analyzes the ideological content of American Art-Union selections in "The American Art-Union as Patron."

26. Klein, "Art and Authority," 1548–59.

27. On changes in newspaper culture in the period, see Michael Schudson, *Discovering the News: A Social History of American Newspapers* (New York: Basic Books, 1978), and Dan Schiller, *Objectivity and the News: The Public and the Rise of Commercial Journalism* (Philadelphia: University of Pennsylvania Press, 1981). On Bennett's career, see James L. Crouthamel, *Bennett's New York Herald and the Rise of the Popular Press* (Syracuse: Syracuse University Press, 1989).

28. In making this claim, I disagree with Peter Buckley, who argues in "To the Opera House," that "[a]n *absence* of bourgeois 'hegemony' over theatre culture . . . led to this external application of power" (195). While I must acknowledge a deep debt to Buckley's reading of the Riots, I still see not simply a divide between "bourgeois" and "proletarian," but also the presence of the middle class, whose members would take up varying positions on the Riot and actively participate on both sides, but the meaning of whose participation cannot be subsumed simply into the associations of either of the other groups.

29. Buckley surveys the wealth, vocation, and public and private involvements of the petition signers (in "To the Opera House" 206–21). The petition included members, trustees, and managers of the New-York Historical Society, the American Art-Union, Columbia University, and the new Astor Library.

30. Buckley, "To the Opera House," 209.

31. Buckley, "To the Opera House," 211.

32. Buckley, "To the Opera House," 211.

33. An American Citizen, *A Rejoinder*, 100–101.

34. Cited in *The Melville Log: A Documentary Life of Herman Melville, 1819–1891*, ed. Jay Leyda (New York: Harcourt, Brace & Company, 1951), 1: 303.

35. On the republican print culture of the late eighteenth century, see Michael Warner, *The Letters of the Republic*, 34–72.

36. In *Intellect and Public Life: Essays on the Social History of Academic Intellectuals in the United States* (Baltimore: Johns Hopkins University Press, 1993), Thomas Bender discusses the new dependence in antebellum America upon public "personality" as a means of "establish[ing] the trust and authority essential for the conduct of intellectual life in a milieu of strangers" (38–39).

37. The concept of symbolic capital finds its fullest articulation in the work of Pierre Bourdieu. In *Outline of a Theory of Practice*, trans. Richard Nice (New York Cambridge University Press, 1977), Bourdieu argues that symbolic capital is "always *credit*, in the widest sense of the word, i.e., a sort of advance which the group alone can grant to those who give it the best material and symbolic *guarantees*"(181). It is no mere coincidence that Bourdieu finds the nearest equivalent to precapitalist society, an archaic social structure primarily dependent upon symbolic capital, in the modern "domain of art and culture" (197). In his later work, *The Rules of Art: Genesis and Structure of the Literary Field*, trans. Susan Emanuel (Stanford: Stanford University Press, 1996), Bourdieu rigorously reconstructs the field of literary production in late-nineteenth-century France to understand the work of Flaubert. Although I make no such claims to "science," the social, political, and cultural intersections of the Astor Place Riots can help us to see articulations and exchanges of symbolic capital and the modern forms of social and cultural reproduction emerging in antebellum America.

38. Evert Duyckinck, "Miscellany," *The Literary World* 5:120 (May 19, 1849), 438.

39. On Melville's discussion of Macready in London, see Joel Porte, *In Respect to Egotism: Studies in American Romantic Writing* (New York: Cambridge University Press,

1991), 207–8, and Dennis Berthold, "Class Acts: The Astor Place Riots and Melville's 'The Two Temples,'" *American Literature* 71:3 (September 1999): 429–61. Strikingly, the two offer distinctly different readings of the tale's reaction to Macready, with Porte finding criticism of Macready's gentility and Berthold finding approval.

40. In addition to readings by Porte and Berthold cited above, see also Alan Ackerman Jr., *The Portable Theater: American Literature and the Nineteenth-Century Stage* (Baltimore: Johns Hopkins University Press, 1999), and Barbara Foley's "From Wall Street to Astor Place: Historicizing Melville's 'Bartleby,'" *American Literature* 72:1 (March 2000): 87–116.

41. Hershel Parker, *Herman Melville: A Biography, 1819–1851* (Baltimore: John Hopkins University Press, 1996), 1:632. To the extent that scholars have addressed Melville's participation in the Riots as an act with any political or social motivation, they have tended to assume that he acted on the basis of antipopulist feeling. Both Dennis Berthold in "Class Acts," and Laurie Robertson-Lorant in *Melville: A Biography* (Amherst: University of Massachusetts Press, 1996), identify the source of Melville's participation with his abhorrence of "mob violence." Porte's *In Respect to Egotism* presents Melville's stance as ambivalent, torn between loyalty to Duyckinck and his admiration for Forrest and the protesting crowd's "democratic" vision of Shakespeare (205).

42. February 24, 1849, Herman Melville, *Correspondence* (Chicago: Northwestern University Press–Newberry Library, 1993), 119. Melville's famous difficulties with spelling are notably evident in the various ways he spelled Shakespeare's name. In fact, Shakespeare's name was often spelled variously in the antebellum era, but the variety of Melville's attempts is extreme. Rather than clutter the quotations with further emendations, I will leave his spellings as they stand in the original documents.

43. *Correspondence*, 119.

44. *Correspondence*, 122.

45. *Correspondence*, 122.

46. On the correspondence between literary and political Young America, see Edward Widmer, *Young America: The Flowering of Democracy in New York City* (New York: Oxford University Press, 1999).

47. Oxford English Dictionary, 1991, s.v. "snob."

48. David Scobey, "Anatomy of the Promenade: The Politics of Bourgeois Sociability in Nineteenth-Century New York," *Social History* 17:2 (May 1992): 205.

49. Edward Spann, *The New Metropolis: New York City, 1840–1857* (New York: Columbia University Press, 1981), 96.

50. Scobey, "Anatomy of the Promenade," 204.

51. Cited in Scobey, "Anatomy of the Promenade," 203.

52. On Bowery culture rituals, accoutrements, and entertainments, see Sean Wilentz, *Chants Democratic*, Christine Stansell, *The City of Women: Sex and Class in New York City, 1789–1860* (New York: Knopf, 1986), Richard Stott, *Workers in the Metropolis: Class, Ethnicity, and Youth in Antebellum New York City* (Ithaca: Cornell University Press, 1990), and Eric Lott, *Love and Theft*.

53. Herman Melville, "Hawthorne and His Mosses," *The Piazza Tales and Other Prose Pieces* (Chicago: Northwestern University Press–Newberry Library, 1981), 244. All subsequent references will be to this edition, cited parenthetically in the text.

54. On Cibber's interpolated line, frequently used in popular productions of the play, see Harrison Hayford, "Notes on 'Mosses,'" in *Piazza Tales and Other Prose Pieces*, 667.

55. Without acknowledging the context of the Astor Place Riots, Perry Miller iden-

tifies this passage as a commentary on Forrest's acting in *The Raven and the Whale: The War of Words and Wits in the Era of Poe and Melville* (New York: Harcourt, Brace, 1956), 283.

56. Hudson, "Whipple's Essays and Reviews," *Whig Review* 9 (February 1849), cited in Stafford, "Henry Norman Hudson and the Whig Use of Shakespeare," 654–55.

57. Spann, *New Metropolis*, 430.

58. The conflicted nature of Melville's attitudes in "Hawthorne and His Mosses" has been explored by Dennis Berthold in "Class Acts." In his "Mathews's Mosses? Fair Papers and Foul," *New England Quarterly* 67:4 (December 1994), P. Marc Bousquet speculates that the ambivalences of Melville's views reflect joint authorship with Cornelius Mathews. Although evidence of Melville's additions and deletions hint at his waning support for "Young American" nationalism, these conflicted terms emerge later in his work (including *Moby-Dick*), suggesting, in my opinion, not multiple authorship, but conflicted views.

59. In 1940, Leon Howard delineated Melville's debt to Coleridge's vision of Shakespeare in "Hawthorne and His Mosses." This influential reading, like Matthiessen's, helped to establish Melville as an important romantic author. While Coleridge's vision of Shakespeare's method clearly shaped Melville's thinking, especially in the formation of the character of Ahab, this does not negate the social context for Melville's working through the politics of Shakespeare in the period. See Leon Howard, "Melville's Struggle with the Angel," in *The Recognition of Herman Melville: Selected Criticism since 1846*, ed. Hershel Parker (Ann Arbor: University of Michigan Press, 1967), 223–37.

60. "Hawthorne and His Mosses," 244.

61. "Hawthorne and His Mosses," 244.

62. "Hawthorne and His Mosses," 244.

63. Melville, *Correspondence*, 191.

64. Melville, *Correspondence*, 190.

65. Magali Sarfatti Larson, *The Rise of Professionalism: A Sociological Analysis* (Berkeley: University of California Press, 1977), 134.

66. Melville, *Correspondence*, 191.

67. On the canonizing role of Matthiessen's work, see Giles Gunn, *F. O. Matthiessen: The Critical Achievement* (Seattle: University of Washington Press, 1975), 69, and Jonathan Arac, "F. O. Matthiessen: Authorizing an American Renaissance," in *The American Renaissance Reconsidered*, ed. Walter Benn Michaels and Donald E. Pease (Baltimore: Johns Hopkins University Press, 1985), 90–112.

68. F. O. Matthiessen, *American Renaissance: Art and Expression in the Age of Emerson and Whitman* (New York: Oxford University Press, 1941), xiii. On the importance of *Moby-Dick* to Matthiessen's critical task, see William E. Cain, *F. O. Matthiessen and the Politics of Criticism* (Madison: University of Wisconsin Press, 1988), 176–79.

69. Matthiessen, *American Renaissance*, xiii.

70. The critical association of *Moby-Dick* with Shakespeare began with Charles Olson's 1937 essay "*Lear* and *Moby Dick*," which was later expanded into his book, *Call Me Ishmael* (1947; London: Jonathan Cape, 1967), which came out of his discovery of Melville's annotations in his copy of Shakespeare. Matthiessen's reading has been expanded upon by a variety of scholars over the years. See William E. Sedgwick, *Herman Melville: The Tragedy of the Mind* (Cambridge: Harvard University Press, 1944), Edward Rosenberry, *Melville and the Comic Spirit* (Cambridge: Harvard University Press, 1955); Sharon Cameron, *The Corporeal Self: Allegories of the Body in Melville and Hawthorne*

212 ➣ notes to pages 100–102

(1981; New York: Columbia University Press, 1991), Larzer Ziff, *Literary Democracy: The Declaration of Cultural Independence in America* (New York: Knopf, 1982); and Julian Markels, *Melville and the Politics of Identity: From King Lear to Moby-Dick* (Urbana: University of Illinois Press, 1993).

71. Matthiessen, *American Renaissance*, 426.

72. Herman Melville, *Moby-Dick*, ed. Harrison Hayford and Hershel Parker (New York: Norton, 1967), 36:141. All further references will be to this edition, cited parenthetically in the text by chapter and page number.

73. Levine, *Highbrow/Lowbrow*, 36.

74. McConachie, *Melodramatic Formations*, 115–16.

75. Cited in Berthold, "Class Acts," 434.

76. Disagreeing with Matthiessen's praise of Melville, Joel Porte's *In Respect to Egotism* points out the melodramatic qualities of Ahab's Shakespeareanized speeches (196). In a similar gesture, John Bryant suggests that Melville does not so much emulate as "deconstruct" Shakespeare in *Moby-Dick*, turning to a mode of "parodic Shakespeareanism" in a refutation of Shakespeare's meaning for populist demagogues in the period after the Astor Place Riots. See his "*Moby-Dick* as Revolution," in *The Cambridge Companion to Herman Melville*, ed. Robert S. Levine (New York: Cambridge University Press, 1998), 80–85. Clearly meant as a curative to the hagiographic tone taken by most Melvilleans, Porte and Bryant's readings are limited by their failure to account for the positive version of Shakespeare that Melville poses in "Hawthorne and His Mosses" and displays through Ahab later in the novel.

77. The debate between Ahab and Starbuck has been read as an allegory of a number of antebellum political and social divides in historicist analyses of *Moby-Dick*. The most influential, Alan Heimert's "*Moby-Dick* and American Political Symbolism," in *American Quarterly* 16 (April 1963): 498–534, situates the debate as a conflict between Democrats (Ahab) and Whigs (Starbuck).

78. In *Critical Theory and the Novel: Mass Society and Cultural Criticism in Dickens, Melville, and Kafka* (Madison: University of Wisconsin Press, 1994), David Suchoff eschews a precise historical allegory, but I believe captures the conflict when he likens Ahab's scene of persuasion to "repressive populism," with Starbuck's response as that of the embattled cultural elites (102).

79. Heimert's reading in "*Moby Dick* and American Political Symbolism," has generated others, most notably Michael P. Rogin in *Subversive Genealogy: The Politics and Art of Herman Melville* (1983; Berkeley: University of California Press, 1985), 102–51. Clearly, my reading is influenced by this historicist tradition, but I find its unwillingness to come to terms with the Shakespearean form of the encounter striking. For example, in her influential reading in *Empire for Liberty: Melville and the Poetics of Individualism* (Princeton: Princeton University Press, 1989), Wai Chee Dimock sees Ahab's Shakespearean eloquence as "archaic (like the eloquence so often ascribed to Indians) . . . and therefore only . . . another sign of his doom" (118). The most substantial reading of the Quarterdeck chapter and the politics of its "scene of persuasion" is that of Donald Pease, *Visionary Compacts: American Renaissance Writings in Cultural Context* (Madison: University of Wisconsin Press, 1987). But Pease's excellent reading ultimately says more about the Cold War politics of canonizing readings of *Moby-Dick* than the meaning for Melville of his use of Shakespeare in this scene: Melville's Shakespeare is presented as exerting "'unapproachable' power . . . over the mob" (240). Given that Melville seemed to be complaining about the tendency to present the works of Shakespeare as an "unapproachable"

aesthetic accomplishment, it seems to me that Pease misreads the complexity of Melville's stance on Shakespeare and the multiple forms of "cultural persuasion" in antebellum America.

80. McConachie, *Melodramatic Formations*, 143–55.

81. This is essentially what John Bryant does in his essay "*Moby-Dick* as Revolution," 80–85.

82. Olson, *Call Me Ishmael*, 47–62.

83. *Correspondence*, 127.

84. The relationship of Ahab to Pip is a crucial element in a number of readings of antiracist impulses in *Moby-Dick*. For the most important example, see Carolyn Karcher, *Shadow Over the Promised Land: Slavery, Race, and Violence in Melville's America* (Baton Rouge: Louisiana State University Press, 1980), 87.

85. In *By the Sweat of the Brow: Literature and Labor in Antebellum America* (Chicago: University of Chicago Press, 1993), Nicholas Bromell casts the Carpenter as an embodiment of the "enigma, or paradox" of manual labor, a mark of Melville's investment in hierarchical distinctions (37).

86. Paul Royster has commented on how labor in *Moby-Dick* is repeatedly shifted into nature, with the result of naturalizing and de-alienating the experience of work. See his "Melville's Economy of Language," in *Ideology and Classic American Literature*, ed. Sacvan Bercovitch and Myra Jehlen (New York: Cambridge University Press, 1986), 313–36. Melville's depiction of the Carpenter, however, is not naturalized, but rather denaturalized and functions to question whether or not the mechanical manual laborer remains human or becomes a machine. Nicholas Bromell notes that the apparent omnipresence of work in the novel gives way to an invisibility, making manual labor "a process composed of unlocated actions," *By the Sweat of the Brow*, 37.

87. On the evident Shakespearean parallel, see Matthiessen, *American Renaissance*, 424.

88. Cameron, *Corporeal Self*, 60.

89. The Carpenter has also been read as a symbol of Melville as author, bound to produce whatever is demanded by his readership. Responding to the resonance between Melville's bitter complaint that *Redburn* and *White-Jacket* were "two *jobs*" that he was "forced" to do, "as other men are to sawing wood," Harrison Hayford and Michael T. Gilmore have linked the Carpenter to Melville himself. Although this reading is suggestive of Melville's experience of producing for the marketplace, it does not, however, engage with the limitations of the Carpenter's own understanding of his labor. See Hayford, "Unnecessary Duplicates," in *New Perspectives on Melville*, ed. Faith Pullin (Kent State, Ohio: Kent State University Press, 1978), 160, and Gilmore, *American Romanticism and the Marketplace* (Chicago: University of Chicago Press, 1985), 124–25.

90. Lowell's comments were first given as a speech in 1887, but were published in the *Atlantic Monthly* 68 (December 1891), cited in Levine, *Highbrow/Lowbrow*, 72.

91. "Uses of Shakespeare off the Stage," *Harper's New Monthly Magazine* 65 (August 1882), cited in Levine, *Highbrow/Lowbrow*, 73.

92. Matthiessen, *American Renaissance*, 427.

93. Cited in Matthiessen, *American Renaissance*, 427.

94. Janice Radway, *A Feeling for Books: The Book-of-the-Month Club, Literary Taste, and Middle-Class Desire* (Chapel Hill: University of North Carolina Press, 1997), 141.

95. As Henry Hudson, the Whig Shakespearean explicator, in *Lectures on Shakespeare*, would assert of Shakespeare: "The lectures, as will be obvious to the slightest inspection of

them, are not so properly on Shakspeare as on human nature, Shakspeare being the text.... The constituent, then, of genius, is spontaneous sympathy and harmony with the natural order of things, as original innocence was with the moral order of things. It is from this very harmony, indeed, that genius derives its power over us" (1:vi, 131).

96. William Charvat, "Melville," in *The Profession of Authorship in America, 1800–1870*, ed. Matthew J. Bruccoli (1968; New York: Columbia University Press, 1992), 247–48.

97. Cited in *Moby-Dick*, 619.

98. From the London *New Monthly Review*, 1853, cited in *Moby-Dick*, 620.

99. From the Washington *National Intelligencer*, 1851, cited in *Moby-Dick*, 618.

100. From the New York *Literary World* 9 (November 22, 1851), cited in *Moby-Dick*, 614.

101. See Miller, *Raven and the Whale*, 297–304. Sheila Post-Lauria's more recent and substantial survey of the values of antebellum reviewers of Melville in *Correspondent Colorings: Melville in the Marketplace* (Amherst: University of Massachusetts Press, 1996), identifies *Moby-Dick*'s failure with the waning popularity of the "mixed-form" novel, a forgotten genre of the antebellum literary marketplace (123–27).

CHAPTER FOUR

1. Donald M. Scott, "The Popular Lecture and the Creation of a Public in Mid-Nineteenth-Century America," *Journal of American History* 66:4 (March 1980): 791, and "The Profession That Vanished: Public Lecturing in Mid-Nineteenth-Century America," in *Professions and Professional Ideologies in America*, ed. Gerald L. Geison (Chapel Hill: University of North Carolina Press, 1983), 13.

2. William Charvat, "Melville," *The Profession of Authorship, 1800–1870*, ed. Matthew J. Bruccoli (1968; New York: Columbia University Press, 1992), 246.

3. Max Horkheimer and Theodor Adorno, "The Culture Industry: Enlightenment as Mass Deception," in *Dialectic of Enlightenment*, trans. John Cumming (1944; New York: Herder and Herder, 1972), 121.

4. For example, see Dwight McDonald, "Masscult and Midcult, I and II," *Partisan Review* 27 (Spring and Fall 1960): 203–33 and 589–631.

5. In his *The Genuine Article: Race, Mass Culture, and American Literary Manhood* (Durham: Duke University Press, 2001), Paul Gilmore explores the institutions of antebellum mass culture and the distinctive way in which this mass culture deployed race to trace the construction of what he calls "American literary manhood."

6. Horkheimer and Adorno, *Dialectic of Enlightenment*, 131.

7. For extended discussions of middlebrow taste and institutions, see Joan Shelley Rubin, *The Making of Middlebrow Culture* (Chapel Hill: University of North Carolina Press, 1992), and Janice Radway, *A Feeling for Books: The Book-of-the-Month Club, Literary Taste, and Middle-Class Desire* (Chapel Hill: University of North Carolina Press, 1997).

8. Jonathan Freedman, *The Temple of Culture: Assimilation and Anti-Semitism in Literary Anglo-America* (New York: Oxford University Press, 2000), 93.

9. See Bluford Adams, *E Pluribus Barnum: The Great Showman and the Making of U.S. Popular Culture* (Minneapolis: University of Minnesota Press, 1997), and Bruce McConachie, "Museum Theatre and the Problem of Respectability for Mid-Century Urban Americans," in *The American Stage: Social and Economic Issues from the Colonial Period to the Present*, ed. Ron Engle and Tice L. Miller (New York: Cambridge University Press, 1993), 65–80.

10. Pierre Bourdieu, *Distinction: A Social Critique of the Judgment of Taste*, trans. Richard Nice (Cambridge: Harvard University Press, 1984), 323.

11. Bourdieu, *Distinction*, 330–31. It should be noted that I do not adhere to the rigidity of Bourdieu's social classifications, drawn from sociological research in France of the 1970s. In *The Temple of Culture*, Jonathan Freedman suggests that twentieth-century American cultural experience would never fit as clearly into Bourdieu's social classification (237, n.11). I would argue that this point must be further extended or amplified in the context of antebellum America, where modern class identities and cultural distinctions were in the process of formation.

12. Bourdieu, *Distinction*, 323.

13. Herman Melville to Evert Duyckinck, March 3, 1849, *Correspondence* (Chicago: Northwestern University Press–Newberry Library, 1993), 121 (*my italics*).

14. On definitions of "self-culture," see Mary Kupiec Cayton, "The Making of an American Prophet: Emerson, His Audiences, and the Rise of the Culture Industry in Nineteenth-Century America," *American Historical Review* 92 (1987): 605. See also Joan Shelley Rubin, *The Making of Middlebrow Culture*, 2–22.

15. On the antebellum world of self-culture, see John Cawelti, *Apostles of the Self-Made Man* (Chicago: University of Chicago Press, 1965), 39–98. On young middle-class men entering the cities as the focus of this self-culture, see Allan Horlick, *Country Boys and Merchant Princes: The Social Control of Young Men in New York* (Lewisburg, Pa.: Bucknell University Press, 1975), and Karen Halttunen, *Confidence Men and Painted Women: A Study of Middle-Class Culture in America, 1830–1870* (New Haven: Yale University Press, 1982), 1–55. More recently, Thomas Augst in *The Clerk's Tale: Young Men and Moral Life in Nineteenth-Century America* (Chicago: University of Chicago Press, 2003), has sought to revalidate the moral and intellectual project of antebellum self-culture, honoring the experiences of young men entering into a changing economy and way of life. Although my project offers a far more skeptical vision of antebellum self-culture, one that reflects Melville's anxious professional biases, I want to acknowledge Augst's sympathetic insights into the experiences of men whom Melville might have closely resembled, if his life had gone another way.

16. Horlick, *Country Boys and Merchant Princes*, 179–209.

17. Noted lecturer Carl Schurz, cited in Burton J. Bledstein, *The Culture of Professionalism: The Middle Class and the Development of Higher Education in America* (New York: Norton, 1976), 26.

18. J. G. Holland, "The Popular Lecture," *Atlantic Monthly* (March 1865), cited in Scott, "Profession," 25–26.

19. Carl Bode, *The American Lyceum: Town Meeting of the Mind* (New York: Oxford University Press, 1956), 145.

20. Scott, "The Popular Lecture and the Creation of a Public," 806.

21. Emerson's early difficulties with vocation have long been an important subject of critical discussion. See Henry Nash Smith, "Emerson's Problem of Vocation," *New England Quarterly* 12 (1939): 52–67, and Mary Kupiec Cayton, *Emerson's Emergence: Self and Society in the Transformation of New England, 1800–1845* (Chapel Hill: University of North Carolina Press, 1989).

22. In "The Profession that Vanished," 12, Scott notes that a variety of claims for the new professional status of the lecturer were made during the 1850s in *Harper's*, *Putnam's* and the *New-York Tribune*.

23. On the typology of antebellum lecturers, see Scott, "Profession That Vanished," 15–18.

24. William Charvat, "A Chronological List of Emerson's American Lecture Engagements," *Bulletin of the New York Public Library* 64 (Sept. 1960): 492.

25. Thomas Augst presents a more sympathetic reading of Emerson's involvement with the lyceum in "Popular Philosophy and Democratic Voice: Emerson in the Lecture Hall," in *The Clerk's Tale*, 114–57. He suggests that the twentieth-century critical validation of the experience of reading Emerson over those who "merely" listened to him in the lyceum fails to capture "the complex range of intellectual and emotional engagement on the part of the audience" (119).

26. Mary Kupiec Cayton, "The Making of an American Prophet," 614.

27. Cayton, "Making of an American Prophet," 609.

28. Cayton, "Making of an American Prophet," 614.

29. Augst, in *The Clerk's Tale*, sees Emerson's engagement with these terms as "a set of strategies for responding to the problems of knowledge and decision-making that arise in a market culture" (122), adapting the themes of self-culture to the question of "what it means to practice philosophy in a democracy" (121).

30. Bode, *American Lyceum*, 218.

31. Cited in Bode, *American Lyceum*, 218–19.

32. On the history of the museum in America, see Paul DiMaggio, "Cultural Entrepreneurship in Nineteenth-Century Boston: The Creation of an Organizational Base for High Culture in America," *Media, Culture and Society* 4 (1982), 33–50, 303–22; Bruce McConachie, "Museum Theatre and the Problem of Respectability"; and Neil Harris, "Museums, Merchandising, and Popular Taste," in *Material Culture and the Study of American Life*, ed. Ian M. G. Quinby (New York: Norton, 1978), 140–74.

33. Peter Buckley, "To the Opera House: Culture and Society in Antebellum New York, 1820–1860" (Ph.D. diss., SUNY–Stony Brook, 1984), 490.

34. Adams, *E Pluribus Barnum*, 116–63, and McConachie, "Museum Theatre and the Problem of Respectability," 65–80.

35. Where Stowe's novel asked its readers to choose between a Christian law and the nation's laws upholding slavery, the American Museum's version let its white middle-class Northern audience "have it both ways." On H. J. Conway's adaptation of *Uncle Tom's Cabin* at Barnum's Museum, see Adams, *E Pluribus Barnum*, 130–39.

36. On the social dynamics of Lind's donations, see Adams, *E Pluribus Barnum*, 46–47.

37. Cited in Buckley, "To the Opera House," 535. Willis followed Lind's tour closely, using it as a perfect example for his new version of a middle-class dominated American cultural life.

38. Adams, *E Pluribus Barnum*, 68.

39. New York *Herald*, 25 October 1850, cited in Adams, *E Pluribus Barnum*, 68.

40. This was not without a certain degree of willful blindness, as working-class crowds often massed outside the building, hoping to hear Lind's performances from open windows. These crowds occasionally turned violent as well. See Adams, *E Pluribus Barnum*, 64–68.

41. Historians of each of these separate institutions or events has made that exact claim for what they were individually studying. On Barnum's construction of a public through the museum, see Buckley, "To the Opera House," 472. For Lind's embodiment of that public, see Adams, *E Pluribus Barnum*, 68. For the lyceum's construction of a public, see Scott, "Popular Lecture," 808–9.

42. Melville, letter to the Albany *Microscope*, March 31, 1838, cited in Hershel Parker, *Herman Melville: A Biography, 1819–1851* (Baltimore: Johns Hopkins University Press, 1996), 1:97.

43. See Parker, *Herman Melville*, 97–98.

44. Louis Althusser discusses the interpellative effects of educational and cultural institutions like the lyceum, establishing ideological visions of normative behavior and identity in its constitution of an audience in his "Ideology and Ideological State Apparatuses (Notes Towards an Investigation)," in *Lenin and Philosophy and Other Essays*, trans. Ben Brewster (New York: Monthly Review Press, 1971), 127–86.

45. In *Country Boys and Merchant Princes*, Allan Horlick describes the ways local merchant leaders sought to address the problem of their young male workers, newly independent in the cities, through institutions such as mercantile libraries and lyceum halls.

46. William Ellery Channing, *Self-Culture* (1838; New York: Arno Press, 1969), 27.

47. Channing, *Self-Culture*, 28. It should be noted, however, that Channing's overarching logic is idealistic, not purely oriented toward material success and upward mobility.

48. Cited in Bode, *American Lyceum*, 208.

49. Cited in Bode, *American Lyceum* 213.

50. Henry Ward Beecher, *Addresses to Young Men* (1846; Philadelphia: Henry Altemus, 1892), 210.

51. Beecher, *Addresses to Young Men*, 9–10.

52. Beecher, *Addresses to Young Men*, 18.

53. *First Annual Report of the New York Young Men's Christian Association, presented May 16, 1853*, cited in Horlick, *Country Boys and Merchant Prince's*, 236.

54. Cited in John Cawelti, *Apostles of the Self-Made Man*, 60–61.

55. Carolyn Porter argues that "in Ishmael, Melville created a narrator who speaks with the full authority of the culture whose authority he is out to subvert." See her "Call Me Ishmael, or How to Make Double-Talk Speak," in *New Essays on Moby-Dick*, ed. Richard Brodhead (New York: Cambridge University Press, 1986), 93.

56. Scott, "Popular Lecture," 806.

57. Bode, *American Lyceum*, 212.

58. Cited in Bode, *American Lyceum*, 212.

59. William T. Porter, in *Spirit of the Times* (December 6, 1851), 494, cited in *Melville: The Critical Heritage*, ed. Watson G. Branch (Boston: Routledge and Kegan Paul, 1972), 278. Carolyn Porter also notes Porter's persuasion by "The Affadavit," in "Call Me Ishmael," 99.

60. Howard P. Vincent argues that 45 chapters comprise the "cetological" center of the book, while James Barbour argues for a narrower definition, seeing only 20 chapters as cetological. See Howard P. Vincent, *The Trying-Out of "Moby-Dick"* (Boston: Houghton Mifflin, 1949), and James Barbour, "The Composition of Moby-Dick," *American Literature* 47 (1975): 343–60. The critical debate seems to hinge on whether to include not only the attempts to analyze the whale's body through scientific discourses, but also discussions of whaling processes and whaling's significance to the world, using such discourses as history and law.

61. J. G. Holland, "The Popular Lecture," *Atlantic Monthly* (March 1865), cited in Scott, "Profession That Vanished," 25–26.

62. In "Call Me Ishmael," Carolyn Porter highlights the mocking voice in this project of categorization (100). Reading the cetology sections as a critique of empiricism has been an essential part of the novel's modern critical tradition. See J. A. Ward, "The Function of the Cetological Chapters in *Moby-Dick*," *American Literature* 28 (1956): 164–83; Richard Moore, *That Stunning Alphabet: Melville's Aesthetics of Nature* (Amsterdam: Rodolphi, 1982), 59–176; William V. Spanos, *The Errant Art of Moby-Dick: The Canon, the*

Cold War, and the Struggle for American Studies (Durham: Duke University Press, 1995), 190–203.

63. For a history of the introduction and spread of phrenology in the U.S., see Charles Colbert, *A Measure of Perfection: Phrenology and the Fine Arts in America* (Chapel Hill: University of North Carolina Press, 1997).

64. Whitman, who was strongly influenced by phrenology, was introduced to the subject through a lecture by Orson Fowler in 1846. He would later use the brothers' publishing house, Fowlers and Wells, to distribute his first edition of *Leaves of Grass* (1855) and publish his second. See David S. Reynolds, *Walt Whitman's America: A Cultural Biography* (New York: Knopf, 1995), 207–10.

65. In *The Cultural Meaning of Popular Science: Phrenology and the Organization of Consent in Nineteenth-Century Britain* (New York: Cambridge University Press, 1984), Roger Cooter argues that phrenology's validation of intellect as atop the physiological hierarchy of mental faculties combined with its easy applicability ("democratically open to the observations and common sense of all") spoke directly to middle-class social concerns (72).

66. See Halttunen, *Confidence Men and Painted Women*, 33–55.

67. Bode, *American Lyceum*, 144.

68. Cited in Samuel Otter, *Melville's Anatomies* (Berkeley: University of California Press, 1999), 121.

69. Horlick, *Country Boys and Merchant Princes*, 215.

70. Horlick in *Country Boys and Merchant Princes*, argues that the Fowlers and their partner, Samuel Wells, "saw phrenology as a tool adding precision to social arrangements that already functioned adequately. Phrenology was seen as a contributor to existing social stability, not as a way of undermining it" (222). Cooter argues in *The Cultural Meaning of Popular Science*, that phrenology's social project was twofold, "rationalizing [new middle-class] ambitions in the face of the collapsing old social hierarchy and . . . instilling in workers bourgeois normative values" (138). Although Cooter sees the beginnings of phrenology's spread in Great Britain as tied to the rise of a new professional middle class in the 1820s, he suggests that by the 1840s it found its "popular niche among the literate and self-improving stratum" (136), the group that I associate with middlebrow self-culture.

71. Cited in Colbert, *Measure of Perfection*, 7.

72. In *Melville's Anatomies*, the most substantial exploration of Melville's use of these "sciences," Samuel Otter connects Melville's use of phrenology to the racialist science of craniology, arguing that Melville engages sincerely with the possibilities of phrenology, in an earnest attempt to use the interpretative discourses of the period to investigate the meaning of the body and to challenge the racist assumptions of the period (132–59).

73. Edward Everett, "Hieroglyphics," *The North American Review* 32 (1831), cited in John T. Irwin, *American Hieroglyphics: The Symbol of the Egyptian Hieroglyphics in the American Renaissance* (Baltimore: Johns Hopkins University Press, 1983), 5.

74. Oxford English Dictionary, 1991, s.v. "subtilize."

75. Oxford English Dictionary, 1991, s.v. "subtlety."

76. Agassiz traveled widely in the late 1840s, lecturing on such subjects as "Glaciers" and "Natural Relations Between Animals." In 1845, Silliman conducted a twelve-lecture course on geology, "the last ones being devoted to the history of fossil animals." Bode, *American Lyceum*, 85.

77. On Agassiz's role in the AAAS, see Thomas L. Haskell, *The Emergence of Profes-*

sional Social Science: The American Social Science Association and the Nineteenth-Century Crisis of Authority (Urbana: University of Illinois Press, 1977), 69–74.

78. Edward Lurie, *Louis Agassiz: A Life in Science* (Chicago: University of Chicago Press, 1960), 127.

79. Lurie, *Louis Agassiz*, 127.

80. Neil Harris, *Humbug: The Art of P. T. Barnum* (Boston: Little, Brown, 1973), 74.

81. Louis Agassiz, *Methods of Study in Natural History* (Boston: Ticknor & Fields, 1863), 42.

82. Samuel Otter, *Melville's Anatomies*, 157.

83. Vincent, *Trying-Out of Moby-Dick*, 361.

84. Cited in McConachie, "Museum Theatre and the Problem of Respectability," 66.

85. Buckley, "To the Opera House," 494.

86. Horkheimer and Adorno, *Dialectic of Enlightenment*, 158.

87. On the quote from Holmes, see Merton Sealts, *Melville as Lecturer* (Cambridge: Harvard University Press, 1957), 5–6.

88. Herman Melville, *Pierre; or, The Ambiguities* (Chicago: Northwestern University Press–Newberry Library, 1971), 252.

89. On Melville's experience on the lecture circuit, see Sealts, *Melville as Lecturer*.

90. Scott, "Profession That Vanished," 26–27

91. Scott, "Profession That Vanished," 26–27.

92. Scott, "Profession That Vanished," 27.

93. Cited in Levine's *Highbrow/Lowbrow*, 184.

94. In a reading indebted to C. L. R. James, Donald Pease elaborates the Cold War context of readings of the Ahab–Ishmael divide. See *Visionary Compacts: American Renaissance Writings in Cultural Context* (Madison: University of Wisconsin Press, 1987). With Pease and James, I see both Ahab and Ishmael as complicit in the establishment of a hierarchy, one that I would identify not so much with geopolitical discourse, but of cultural distinctions. James's reading is a powerful one that reflects the personal effects of his own persecution during the Cold War era, but his vision of Melville's "democratic" alternative to Ishmael and Ahab in the experience of the polyglot crew is one that I find inspiring, but not wholly justified by the text. See his *Mariners, Renegades, and Castaways: The Story of Herman Melville and the World We Live In* (New York: C.L.R. James Books, 1953).

95. Janice Radway opens her study of the Book-of-the-Month Club, *A Feeling for Books*, 2, with memories of her adolescent purchases from the club, including such an edition of *Moby-Dick*.

CHAPTER FIVE

1. Herman Melville, *Pierre, or, The Ambiguities* (1852; Chicago: Northwestern University Press–Newberry Library, 1971), 244. All further references to the book are to this edition and are cited parenthetically within the chapter.

2. Readings that place Pierre as a stand-in for Melville range from Henry Murray's psychoanalytic introduction to the 1949 edition of *Pierre* (New York: Hendricks House/Farrar, Straus, 1949) to Wai Chee Dimock's new historicist interpretation in *Empire for Liberty: Melville and the Poetics of Individualism* (Princeton: Princeton University Press, 1989), in which the novel emerges as "the fictionalization of a literary credo, the narrative enactment of an authorial fantasy" (141).

3. Influential readings that have emphasized the coherence of *Pierre*'s critical project include Sacvan Bercovitch's *"Pierre, or the Ambiguities of American Literary History,"* in *The Rites of Assent: Transformations in the Symbolic Construction of America* (New York: Routledge, 1993), 246–306, and John Carlos Rowe's "A Critique of Ideology: Herman Melville's *Pierre,"* in *At Emerson's Tomb: The Politics of Classic American Literature* (New York: Columbia University Press, 1997), 63–95.

4. Brian Higgins and Hershel Parker describe this turn to the literary as "a drastic change in Melville's authorial purpose" that destroys the unity of the novel, turning it into a deeply "flawed" work of art. See "The Flawed Grandeur of Melville's *Pierre,"* in *New Perspectives on Melville*, ed. Faith Pullin (Kent, Ohio: Kent State University Press, 1978): 162–96. The supposed damaging effects of this shift in *Pierre* has been a topic Parker has pursued in articles since the 1970s. See his "Why *Pierre* Went Wrong," in *Studies in the Novel* 8 (Spring 1976): 7–23. This critical project culminated in the 1995 "Kraken" edition of *Pierre*, a textual editing experiment that excises all references to Pierre's authorship. While Parker's Kraken edition of *Pierre* (New York: HarperCollins, 1995) is a fascinating demonstration of his critical principles, this reading differs from his understanding of Melville's intent on nearly every claim.

5. On the literary interests of Young America, see Perry Miller, *The Raven and the Whale: The War of Words and Wits in the Era of Poe and Melville* (New York: Harcourt, Brace & World, 1956). More recently, Edward Widmer has sought to restore some luster to "Young America" and particularly its political voice, John O'Sullivan, but also to Duyckinck and his circle in *Young America: The Flowering of Democracy in New York City* (New York: Oxford University Press, 1999). Widmer's project, however, is limited by a desire to separate out critical elements that he endorses from the later jingoism of the "Young America" movement.

6. Thomas Bender, *New York Intellect: A History of Intellectual Life in New York City* (New York: Knopf, 1987), 121–22.

7. The common practice of anonymous publication in newspapers and magazine made "puffery" a relatively simple task. The critical chicanery of puffing was, in fact, performed by some of the period's most famous writers. Melville himself drafted a review of *Typee*, which was never sent off, but for his review of Hawthorne in "Hawthorne and His Mosses," he took up the pose of a "Virginian" visiting New England and claimed no prior knowledge of Hawthorne, even though they had recently met. Whitman himself also wrote some of the early reviews of *Leaves of Grass*.

8. Charles Briggs, "Topics of the Month," in *Holden's Dollar Magazine* 2:1 (July 1848): 446.

9. Cornelius Mathews, "City Characters, No. 1, 'The Puff Critic,'" *Yankee Doodle* 2 (October 17, 1846): 21.

10. William A. Jones, "Amateur Authors and Small Critics," in *The United States Magazine and Democratic Review* 17 (July 1845): 65.

11. Jones, "Amateur Authors and Small Critics," 66.

12. On the significance of Fuller's appointment, see Bender, *New York Intellect*, 158. Bender also identifies Poe's arrival in New York City in 1844 as a watershed, with Fuller and Poe embodying politicized and formalist visions of the role of literature and criticism.

13. Miller, *The Raven and the Whale*, 83–85.

14. Miller, *The Raven and the Whale*, 307.

15. Herman Melville, February 12, 1851, *Correspondence* (Chicago: Northwestern University Press–Newberry Library, 1993), 180.

16. In his most successful novel, *The Career of Puffer Hopkins* (New York: D. Appleton & Co, 1842), Cornelius Mathews satirized the "pirate" magazine in the fictional example of the "Mammoth Mug" whose editor proclaims, "We shall pirate all foreign tales regularly; and where we can purloin proof sheets shall publish in advance of the author himself; shall in all cases employ third-rate native writers at journeyman–cobbler's wages, and swear to their genius as a matter of business; shall reprint old annuals and almanacs, systematically, as select extracts and facetiae, and shall reproduce their cuts and illustrations, as new designs from the burin of Mr. Tinto, the celebrated Engraver" (138). In fact, Mathews' satire is hardly too broad: many editors embraced and even flaunted their "piracy." For example, one of N. P. Willis's early editorial ventures was entitled "The Corsair." In *American Literature and the Culture of Reprinting, 1834–1853* (Philadelphia: University of Pennsylvania Press, 2003), Meredith McGill has sought to reconsider the significance of this practice of piracy, finding it not the lamentable hindrance to American literature as it has long been read, but a tool that many authors used to develop a new model of authorship.

17. See my more extended discussion of Jones's "Amateur Authors and Small Critics" in the Introduction for a demonstration of this point.

18. Hershel Parker, "Introduction" to the "Kraken" edition of *Pierre; or, The Ambiguities* (New York: HarperCollins, 1995), xlii.

19. It must be noted that the novel itself seems uncertain about Charlie's professional status. At first, Charlie seems nothing more than a copyist who conducts his business from a "small dusty law-office . . . among empty pigeon-holes, and directly under the eye of an unopened bottle of ink" (279–80). Later, however, he proclaims that, while Pierre struggled with his writing, he had "argued five cases before the court" among other tasks. This inconsistency might be another flaw in the novel's construction, or it could symbolize the particular porousness of professional identity in the period. Melville's 1853 short story, "Bartleby, The Scrivener," also features a copyist who is apparently arguing cases in court. It is precisely this uncertainty about what defined the profession of law that would lead to the formalization of educational standards, a crucial project of modern professionalization begun in the antebellum era. See Burton J. Bledstein, *The Culture of Professionalism: The Middle Class and the Development of Higher Education in America* (New York: Norton, 1976), 184–91.

20. Mrs. Glendinning holds up Falsgrave's plebian origins and his current comportment to Pierre as "a splendid example of the polishing and gentlemanizing influences of Christianity upon the mind" (98).

21. Cited in Bledstein, *Culture of Professionalism*, 177.

22. For the famous discussion of the Protestant "calling" and the rise of capitalism, see Max Weber, *The Protestant Ethic and the Spirit of Capitalism*, trans. Talcott Parsons (New York: Scribner's, 1958).

23. In *The Early Lectures of Ralph Waldo Emerson*, ed. Stephen Whicher, Robert Spiller, and Wallace Williams (Cambridge: Harvard University Press, 1964), 2:124.

24. Emerson, "Trades and Professions," 114.

25. Emerson, "Trades and Professions," 124.

26. Emerson himself was hardly consistent in his attitude toward labor. In a May 1843 journal entry he wrote: "The life of labor does not make men, but drudges." Cited in David Leverenz, *Manhood and the American Renaissance* (Ithaca: Cornell University Press, 1989), 58.

27. Histories of the de-skilling of working-class labor and its reaction are numerous. See Edward Pessen, *Most Uncommon Jacksonians: The Radical Leaders of the Early Labor*

Movement (Albany: State University of New York Press, 1967), Sean Wilentz, *Chants Democratic: New York City and the Rise of the American Working Class, 1788–1850*, (New York: Oxford University Press, 1984), and Bruce Laurie, *Artisans into Workers: Labor in Nineteenth-Century America* (New York: Hill and Wang, 1989).

28. Wilentz, *Chants Democratic*, 157.

29. Pessen, *Most Uncommon Jacksonians*, 175.

30. Cited in Pessen, *Most Uncommon Jacksonians*, 175.

31. Stuart Blumin, *The Emergence of the Middle Class: Social Experience in the American City, 1760–1900* (New York: Cambridge University Press, 1989), 66–137.

32. Cited in Nicholas Bromell, *By the Sweat of the Brow: Literature and Labor in Antebellum America* (Chicago: University of Chicago Press, 1993), 7.

33. Bromell, *By the Sweat of the Brow*, 23–27.

34. Cited in Bromell, *By the Sweat of the Brow*, 25.

35. Bromell's study *By the Sweat of the Brow* brilliantly charts the difficulties of antebellum authors' attempts to characterize manual labor, illustrating its resistance to meaningful representation in the literature of the period.

36. As Frederick Douglass demonstrated conclusively in his 1845 *Narrative*, when slaves contracted out their own labor, slave owners absented themselves completely from any form of labor, either "mind" or "body," becoming nothing more than "pirates." John Carlos Rowe reads this passage from *Pierre*, in the context of Douglass's *Narrative*, as a commentary on "artistic idealism" in "A Critique of Ideology," 89–90. My understanding of the novel has been greatly influenced by Rowe's reading, though my interest in "ideology" in the text is more specifically grounded in the class discourse of the period.

37. Cited in Bromell, *By the Sweat of the Brow*, 26.

38. *The Plantation* 1 (1860), 267, cited in John Ashworth, *Slavery, Capitalism and Politics in the Antebellum Republic* (New York: Cambridge University Press, 1995), 97. Ashworth points out several important issues regarding white Southern attitudes on this subject that reveal the contradiction within the racist hierarchy of labor. First, they distinguished between the "mechanic" arts available to the white working-class and field labor. Second, they argued against bringing slaves into mechanical or factory settings, not only because they weren't suited to it, but also because it would encourage them to resist their enslavement.

39. This comment from the Southern physician Samuel Cartwright is cited in Eugene D. Genovese, *The Political Economy of Slavery: Studies in the Economy and Society of the Slave South* (1961; Middletown, Conn.: Wesleyan University Press, 1989), 47.

40. Cited in Ashworth, *Slavery, Capitalism and Politics*, 159.

41. Cited in Ashworth, *Slavery, Capitalism and Politics*, 94.

42. William Lloyd Garrison, the fiery radical abolitionist, asserted, "In a republican government, especially where hereditary distinctions are obsolete, and the people have unlimited power; where the avenue to wealth, distinction and supremacy are open to all; it must be in the nature of things, be full of unequals." Cited in Ashworth, *Slavery, Capitalism and Politics*, 161. Ashworth demonstrates more generally the Abolitionists' rejection of radical views of wage labor (157–69).

43. See Myra Jehlen, *American Incarnation: The Individual, the Nation, and the Continent* (Cambridge: Harvard University Press, 1986), 185–226; as well as Dimock, *Empire for Liberty*, 140–75, and Rowe, "A Critique of Ideology."

44. Bledstein, *Culture of Professionalism*, 87–88.

45. John and Barbara Ehrenreich, "The Professional Managerial Class," *Between Labor and Capital*, ed. Pat Walker (Montreal: Black Rose Press, 1976), 22. As discussed in my Introduction, it should be noted that the Ehrenreichs date the rise of the PMC to a later date than I do.

46. Eliot Friedson, "Are Professions Necessary?" *The Authority of Experts: Studies in History and Theory*, ed. Thomas Haskell (Bloomington: Indiana University Press, 1984), 22.

47. Bledstein, *Culture of Professionalism*, 92.

48. On the antebellum crisis of masculinity and its reflection in classic nineteenth-century American literature, see Leverenz, *Manhood and the American Renaissance*.

49. Amy Dru Stanley, "Home Life and the Morality of the Market," in *The Market Revolution in America: Social, Political and Religious Expressions, c. 1800–1880* (Charlottesville: University of Virginia Press, 1996), 85.

50. Cited in Bromell, *By the Sweat of the Brow*, 17.

51. Bledstein, *Culture of Professionalsim*, 92.

52. Bledstein, *Culture of Professionalsim*, 92.

53. Bledstein, *Culture of Professionalsim*, 87 (*my italics*).

54. Bledstein, *Culture of Professionalsim*, 116.

55. Ralph Waldo Emerson, in *Complete Works*, vols. (Boston: Houghton, Mifflin, 1904), 10: 326, 329.

56. Rowe, "Critique of Ideology," 90.

57. The ambiguous nature of the text has led to varied critical responses, from being read as pure sophistry by some to a reflection of Melville's "true" religious beliefs by others. On Plinlimmon as a reflection of Melville's religious beliefs, see, for example, William Braswell, *Melville's Religious Thought: An Essay in Interpretation* (Durham: Duke University Press, 1943), 81–85, and James E. Miller, *A Reader's Guide to Herman Melville* (New York: Farrar, Straus, 1962), 132–38. For the contrary view, see Brian Higgins, "Chronometricals and Horologicals," in *Critical Essays on Melville's "Pierre; or, The Ambiguities,"* ed. Brian Higgins and Hershel Parker (Boston: G. K. Hall, 1983), 221–25. Given the intentional ambiguity of the novel, it seems impossible to derive Melville's attitude toward Plinlimmon's ideas. After all, Pierre may have ostensibly followed those ideas in "marrying" Isabel, yet if he acted merely to satisfy unacknowledged desires, how can the act be judged "moral"? If anything, the ambiguities of *Pierre* should encourage a deep skepticism about firm answers to any of the problems that plague the characters. The question of *Pierre*'s ambiguities will occupy the next section.

58. Dimock, *Empire for Liberty*, 172.

59. Critical work on the role of discipline within the reproduction of middle-class social standing in mid-nineteenth-century American life, particularly within "domestic" or "sentimental" literature, is extensive. See Richard Brodhead, "Sparing the Rod: Discipline and Fiction in Antebellum Fiction," *Representations* 21 (Winter 1988), 67–96; G. M. Goshgarian, *To Kiss the Chastening Rod: Domestic Fiction and the Sexual Ideology in the American Renaissance* (Ithaca: Cornell University Press, 1992); Mary Ryan, *The Empire of Mother: American Writing About Domesticity, 1830–1860* (New York: Institute for Research in History and Haworth Press, 1982); Lora Romero, *Home Fronts: Domesticity and Its Critics in the Antebellum United States* (Durham: Duke University Press, 1997), and Karen Sanchez-Eppler, *Touching Liberty: Abolition, Feminism, and the Politics of the Body* (Berkeley: University of California Press, 1993).

60. Henry David Thoreau, *Walden* (New York: Everyman, 1995), 6.

61. Herman Melville, *White-Jacket, or The World in a Man-of-War* (1850; Chicago: Northwestern University Press–Newberry Library, 1970), 191. Further references will be to this edition, cited parenthetically.

62. On this public–people divide in Romanticism, see Raymond Williams, *Culture and Society: 1780–1950* (1958: New York: Harper & Row, 1966), 31–36.

63. William Charvat, *The Profession of Authorship in America, 1800–1870*, ed. Matthew J. Bruccoli (New York: Columbia University Press, 1992), 255.

64. The Oxford English Dictionary identifies the "subjective" experience of "ambiguity" as its earliest usage in the English language. *Oxford English Dictionary*, 1991, s.v. "Ambiguity."

65. "Ambiguity," *Oxford English Dictionary*.

66. New York *Herald*, September 18, 1852, in *Herman Melville: The Contemporary Reviews*, ed. Brian Higgins and Hershal Packer (New York: Cambridge University Press, 1999), 437.

67. It is difficult to do proper justice to the range of response to *Pierre* in this vein. Critics such as Henry Murray and Hershel Parker have defended Melville's exploration of psychology, associated with the *bildungsroman*. David S. Reynolds, Charlene Avallone, and Sheila Post-Lauria have all explored Melville's debt to the popular narrative forms of sentimental and sensational novels. In *Beneath the American Renaissance* (New York: Knopf, 1988), for example, David Reynolds ironically proclaims "*Pierre* was too broadly representative of antebellum popular culture—with all its crippling moral paradoxes—to have wide appeal" (159). See also Charlene Avallone, "Calculations for Popularity: Melville's *Pierre* and *Holden's Dollar Magazine*," *Nineteenth-Century Literature* 43 (1988): 82–110, and Sheila Post-Lauria, *Correspondent Colorings: Meville in the Marketplace* (Amherst: University of Massachusetts Press, 1996), 127–47. On *Pierre* as an expression of an individualist ethos, see Myra Jehlen, *American Incarnation*, Wai Chee Dimock, *Empire for Liberty*, and Gillian Brown, *Domestic Individualism: Imagining Self in Nineteenth-Century America* (Berkeley: University of California Press, 1990), 135–69.

68. Examples of this mode include Rowe, "Critique of Ideology," Bercovitch, "*Pierre*, or the Ambiguities," and Priscilla Wald, "Hearing Narrative Voices in Melville's *Pierre*," *Boundary 2* 17:1 (1990): 100–32.

69. Melville, April 16, 1852. *Correspondence*, 228.

70. On Melville's fantasy of literary orphanhood and anonymity as a source of freedom, see Brown, *Domestic Individualism*, 135–42.

71. McGill discusses how Poe and Hawthorne used anonymous publication to broaden their market. See her *American Literature and the Culture of Reprinting*, 141–44 and 219–20.

72. *Oxford English Dictionary*, 1991, s.v. "subtilizing."

73. *Oxford English Dictionary*, 1991, s.v. "subtlety."

74. As Priscilla Wald suggests, *Pierre* "is a compilation of unraveling that frustrates narrative expectations as it explores the impulse to narrativize," in "Hearing Narrative Voices in Melville's *Pierre*," 100.

75. Edgar A. Dryden, "The Entangled Text: Melville's *Pierre* and the Problem of Reading," *Boundary 2* 7:3 (1979): 163.

76. Dryden, "The Entangled Text," 166.

77. William Empson, *Seven Types of Ambiguity* (1930; 3d ed.; New York: New Directions, 1947), 1. This is a revision of his initial claim, which was that ambiguity "adds some nuance to a direct statement of prose"—deemed to "beg a philosophical question."

78. David Shumway, *Creating American Civilization: A Genealogy of American Literature as an Academic Discipline* (Minneapolis: University of Minnesota Press, 1994), 232.

79. Ransome, "Criticism, Inc.," in *The World's Body* (New York: Charles Scribner's Sons, 1938), cited in Gerald Graff, *Professing Literature: An Institutional History* (Chicago: University of Chicago Press, 1987), 148.

80. Cleanth Brooks's *The Well Wrought Urn* (New York: Reynal & Hitchcock, 1947), based on New Critical readings of poems taught in a college English class at the University of Michigan in 1942, became a paradigmatic text of applied literary analysis.

81. As Gerald Graff explains, "The theorists of American literature conceived the organic structure of a literary work as a microcosm of collective psychology or myth and thus made New Criticism into a method of cultural analysis" (*Professing Literature*, 217).

82. While devoting most of his critical energy to close readings of the texts, F. O. Matthiessen, in *American Renaissance: Art and Expression in the Age of Emerson and Whitman* (New York: Oxford University Press, 1941), would also proclaim the "common denominator" of his writers as "their devotion to the possibilities of democracy" (ix) and speak of their vision of "an organic union between labor and culture" (xv).

EPILOGUE

1. A notable example of this prominence can be seen in the fact that the story was the subject of two book collections by 1979. The first was the published proceedings of the 1965 Melville Society Symposium, *"Bartleby the Scrivener": A Symposium*, ed. Howard P. Vincent (Kent, Ohio: Kent State University Press, 1966) and the second was Thomas Inge's *Bartleby the Inscrutable: A Collection of Commentary on Herman Melville's Tale, "Bartleby the Scrivener"* (Hamden, Conn.: Archon Books, 1979). Each testified to the importance of "Bartleby" by including bibliographic checklists of the critical readings of the story.

2. Herman Melville, "Bartleby, the Scrivener," *The Piazza Tales and Other Prose Pieces, 1839–1860* (Chicago: Northwestern University Press–Newberry Library, 1987), 19. All further references will be to this edition and cited parenthetically in the text. The tradition of biographical readings of "Bartleby, the Scrivener" lies at the heart of Melville studies, encompassing many of the earliest and most important critical studies. For examples, see Lewis Mumford, *Herman Melville: A Study of His Life and Works* (New York: Harcourt, Brace, 1929), 236–39; Newton Arvin, *Herman Melville* (1950; New York: Compass Books, 1957), 242–44; Richard Chase, *Herman Melville: A Critical Study* (New York: Macmillan, 1949); Leo Marx, "Melville's Parable of the Walls," *Sewanee Review* 61 (Autumn 1953), 602–27.

3. In a recent reading of "Bartleby" that shows certain affinities with mine, Thomas Augst's *The Clerk's Tale: Young Men and Moral Life in Nineteenth-Century America* (Chicago: University of Chicago Press, 2003) poses professionalized literary critical response to Melville's story against the ethical dilemmas of the story. Presenting the lawyer–narrator as an author-manqué, Augst asks, rather rhetorically, "How do literary tastes serve the practice of moral authority in the social world of the white-collar office?" (240). Augst sees Melville's story as a criticism of the privatization of the "professional ethos," a criticism also transferred to professionalized literary scholarship, which makes "critical reading" the primary means of enacting ethical practice. Augst's deeply sympathetic reading of the moral and ethical discourses directed at and produced by antebellum clerks, nonmanual laborers at the bottom rung of middle-class status, is an interesting counterpoint to my study of Melville's professional literary career.

4. For examples, see H. Bruce Franklin, *The Wake of the Gods: Melville's Mythology* (Stanford: Stanford University Press, 1963), 127–36; John Gardner, "*Bartleby*: Art and Social Commitment," *Philological Quarterly* 43 (1964): 87–98; John Seelye, *Melville: The Ironic Diagram* (Evanston, Ill.: Northwestern University Press, 1970); and William Shurr, "Melville and Christianity," *Essays in Arts and Sciences* 5 (1976): 138.

5. H. Bruce Franklin, *The Victim as Criminal and Artist: Literature from the American Prison* (New York: Oxford University Press, 1978), 58–59.

6. William Bysshe Stein, "Bartleby: The Christian Conscience," *'Bartleby, the Scrivener': A Symposium*, ed. Howard P. Vincent (Kent, Ohio: Kent State University Press, 1966), 104–12.

7. See, for example, Joyce Carol Oates, "Melville and the Tragedy of Nihilism," *Texas Studies in Literature and Language* 4 (1962): 11–29; Kingsley Widmer, "Melville's Radical Resistance: The Method and Meaning of 'Bartleby,'" *Studies in the Novel* 1 (1969): 444–58; David B. Zink, "Bartleby and the Contemporary Search for Meaning," *Forum* 8 (1970): 46–50; Stanley Brodwin, "To the Frontiers of Eternity: Melville's Crossing in 'Bartleby the Scrivener,'" *Bartleby the Inscrutable: A Collection of Commentary on Herman Melville's Tale, "Bartleby the Scrivener"* (Hamden, Conn.: Archon Books, 1979), 174–96; Ethel F. Cornwell, "Bartleby the Absurd," *International Fiction Review* 9 (1982): 93–99.

8. Kingsley Widmer, "The Negative Affirmation: Melville's 'Bartleby,'" *Modern Fiction Studies* 8 (1962): 286.

9. For examples of this critical reading, see Scott Donaldson, "The Dark Truth of *The Piazza Tales*," *PMLA* 85 (1970): 1082–86; Louise K. Barnett, "Bartleby as Alienated Worker," *Studies in Short Fiction* 11 (1974), 379–85; Franklin, *Victim as Criminal and Artist*, 56–59; Marvin Fisher, *Going Under: Melville's Short Fiction and the American 1850's* (Baton Rouge: Louisiana State University Press, 1977); James C. Wilson, "'Bartleby': The Walls of Wall Street," *Arizona Quarterly* 37 (1981): 335–46; Stephen Zelnick, "Melville's 'Bartleby the Scrivener': A Study in History, Ideology and Literature," *Marxist Perspectives* 2 (Winter 1979–80): 74–92; Michael Paul Rogin, *Subversive Genealogy: The Politics and Art of Herman Melville* (New York: Knopf, 1983), 198–201; Michael T. Gilmore, "'Bartleby the Scrivener' and the Transformation of the Economy," *American Romanticism and the Marketplace* (Chicago: University of Chicago Press, 1985), 132–45; David Kuebrich, "Melville's Doctrine of Assumptions: The Hidden Ideology of Capitalist Production in 'Bartleby,'" *New England Quarterly* 69:3 (1996), 381–405.

10. Cornelia Vismann, "Cancels: On the Making of Law in Chanceries," *Law and Critique* 7:2 (1996), 142.

11. Wayne Booth, "Arts and Scandals, 1982," *PMLA* 98 (May 1983), 315, cited in Evan Watkins, *Work Time: English Departments and the Circulation of Cultural Value* (Stanford: Stanford University Press, 1989), 209.

12. Pierre Bourdieu, "The Intellectual Field: A World Apart," *In Other Words: Essays Towards a Reflexive Sociology*, trans. Matthew Adamson (Cambridge: Polity Press, 1990), 145.

13. The literature of the "Culture Wars" is extensive, from the critical attacks on the "politicized" academy in Roger Kimball, *Tenured Radicals: How Politics Has Corrupted Our Higher Education* (New York: Harper and Row, 1990); Allan Bloom's *The Closing of the American Mind: How Higher Education Has Failed Democracy and Impoverished the Souls of Today's Students* (New York: Simon & Schuster, 1987), and Dinesh D'Souza's *Illiberal Education: The Politics of Race and Sex on Campus* (New York: Free Press, 1991), to academic defenses in collections such as *Higher Education Under Fire: Politics, Economics and the*

Crisis of the Humanities, ed. Cary Nelson and Michael Berubé (New York: Routledge, 1995), and *After Political Correctness: The Humanities and Society in the 1990s*, ed. Christopher Newfield and Ronald Strickland (Boulder, Colo.: Westview Press, 1995).

14. John Guillory, "Literary Critics as Intellectuals: Class Analysis and the Crisis of the Humanities" in *Rethinking Class: Literary Studies and Social Formations*, ed. Wai Chee Dimock and Michael T. Gilmore (New York: Columbia University Press, 1994), 134. This comment is an extension of Guillory's broad claim on humanities scholarship in *Cultural Capital: The Problem of Literary Canon Formation* (Chicago: University of Chicago Press, 1993). For a rebuttal of this vision of the humanities and cultural capital in the contemporary academy, see Michael Berubé, *The Employment of English: Theory, Jobs, and the Future of Literary Studies* (New York: New York University Press, 1998), 19–35.

15. Throughout his work, Pierre Bourdieu describes intellectuals as "the dominated fraction of the dominant class." In a variety of ways, this speaks to the simultaneously privileged and embattled mindset that could be said to characterize academics, particularly those in the humanities. See *Distinction: A Social Critique of the Judgment of Taste*, trans. Richard Nice (Cambridge: Harvard University Press, 1984), 176; and his "The Intellectual Field: A World Apart," 145.

16. See the essays in *Will Teach for Food: Academic Labor in Crisis*, ed. Cary Nelson (Minneapolis: University of Minnesota Press, 1997).

17. See Ann Douglas, *The Feminization of American Culture* (New York: Knopf, 1977), 315–17, and Hershel Parker, "The Sequel in 'Bartleby,'" in *Bartleby the Inscrutable: A Collection of Commentary on Herman Melville's Tale, "Bartleby, the Scrimener"* (Hamden, Conn.: Archor Books, 1979), 159–73. For other like-minded critiques, see William Dillingham, "Unconscious Duplicity" in *Melville's Short Fiction, 1853–1856* (Athens: University of Georgia Press, 1977): 178–84; Robert Weisbuch, "Melville's 'Bartleby' and the Dead Letter of Charles Dickens," in *Atlantic Double-Cross: American Literature and British Influence in the Age of Emerson* (Chicago: University of Chicago Press, 1986), 36–54.

18. Dan McCall, *The Silence of Bartleby* (Ithaca: Cornell University Press, 1989), 99–154. For an example of the "bad faith" claim against the lawyer, see Michael Rogin, *Subversive Genealogy*, 198.

19. Watkins, *Work Time*, 143–246.

20. Robert Scholes, *Textual Power: Literary Theory and the Teaching of English* (New Haven: Yale University Press, 1985), 5.

21. Watkins, *Work Time*, 160.

22. Parker, "The 'Sequel' in 'Bartleby,'" 164.

23. See Guillory's comment on lawyers and their relation to humanities scholars in "Literary Critics as Intellectuals," 132.

24. These assessments of the lawyer's narration come, respectively, from David Kuebrich, "Melville's Doctrine of Assumptions," and Ann Douglas, *Feminization of American Culture*, 316.

25. Paul Lauter, "Melville Climbs the Canon," *American Literature* 66:1 (March 1994), 1–24.

INDEX